# INQUIRY INTO THE ORIGIN OF HUMANITY

D1548513

# KURODA INSTITUTE
## Classics in East Asian Buddhism

The Kuroda Institute for the study of Buddhism and Human Values is a non-profit, educational corporation, founded in 1976. One of its primary objectives is to promote scholarship on Buddhism in its historical, philosophical, and cultural ramifications. The Institute thus attempts to serve the scholarly community by providing a forum in which scholars can gather at conferences and colloquia. To date, the Institute has sponsored six conferences in the areas of Buddhist Studies, and volumes resulting from these conferences are published in the Institute's Studies in East Asian Buddhism series. To complement these scholarly studies, the Institute will also make available reliable translations of some of the major classics of East Asian Buddhism in the present series.

# INQUIRY INTO THE ORIGIN OF HUMANITY

An Annotated Translation of
Tsung-mi's *Yüan jen lun*
with a Modern Commentary

Peter N. Gregory

A KURODA INSTITUTE BOOK
University of Hawai'i Press • Honolulu

**Library of Congress Cataloging-in-Publication Data**

Gregory, Peter N., 1945–
Inquiry into the origin of humanity: An annotated
translation of Tsung-mi's Yüan jen lun with a modern
commentary / edited and translated by Peter N. Gregory.
p. cm.
"A Kuroda Institute book."
Includes bibliographical references and index.
ISBN 0–8248–1728–1 (alk. paper). — ISBN 0–8248–1764–8
(pbk.: alk. paper)
1. Tsung-mi, 780–841. Yüan jen lun. 2. Hua-yen Buddhism—
Doctrines. 3. Man (Buddhism) I. Tsung-mi, 780–841.
Yüan jen lun. 1995. II. Title.
BQ8249. T784Y8336 1995
294.3'422—dc20 95–15874
CIP

Publication of this book has been assisted
by a grant from the Chiang Ching-kuo Foundation
for International Scholarly Exchange

Designed and Typeset by Gigantic Computing

This book is dedicated to the memory of
Hakuyu Taizan Maezumi Roshi (1931-1995),
who founded the Kuroda Institute in 1976,
with deep appreciation for all of his support.
May his vows be completely realized.

羯諦羯諦

波羅羯諦

波羅僧羯諦

菩提薩婆訶

# Contents

# Figures

# Preface

This book is written in the hope of proving useful in middle- and upper-level undergraduate and lower-level graduate courses on Buddhism—college and university courses, that is, that can presume some background in Buddhism or Chinese thought. I also hope that it will help make Chinese Buddhist thought accessible to scholars in other fields of study—that scholars of Indian, Tibetan, or Theravāda Buddhism, for example, might find it valuable in providing a point of comparison and contrast, that it might encourage scholars of Chinese history to overcome their allergy to Buddhist materials, or that other colleagues in religious studies might find it interesting for the comparative questions it implicitly raises in regard to hermeneutics, soteriology, or cosmogony.

As yet, there is no reliable general introduction to Chinese Buddhist thought available in English.[1] Having now had several years of often frustrating experience trying to teach Chinese Buddhism to undergraduates, as well as trying to talk intelligibly about it with my colleagues in other fields of study, have become acutely aware of the need for such a book and have gradually come to convince myself that, properly presented, Tsung-mi's *Inquiry into the Origin of Humanity* (*Yüan jen lun*) could well be used to fill the bill. Indeed, I believe that Tsung-mi's essay is well suited for this task because (1) it presents a systematic analysis of the range of Buddhist teachings important for the Chinese, (2) it illustrates one of the most important genres of Chinese Buddhist dogmatics (*p'an-chiao*), (3) it reflects the thought of two of the major traditions of Chinese

1. Kenneth Ch'en's *Buddhism in China: A Historical Survey* is far too simplistic in its accounts of Buddhist doctrine; Takakusu Junjirō's *The Essentials of Buddhist Philosophy* is too uncritical; and David Chappell's *T'ien-t'ai Buddhism: An Outline of the Fourfold Teachings,* although an admirable work of scholarship in its own right, is too technical and restricted in its coverage

Buddhism (Hua-yen and Ch'an), and (4) it sheds light on the interaction of Buddhism with the indigenous intellectual and religious
traditions of Confucianism and Taoism.

Tsung-mi's *Inquiry* has often been used in East Asia as a primer
of Buddhist thought. In the pages that follow, I have tried my best
to provide the kind of explanatory material necessary to make this
text useful as an introduction to Chinese Buddhist thought for the
nonspecialist. But explanation must stop somewhere, and I fear that
a Western student with no background in either Buddhism or Chinese thought is apt to find the book taxing in places. The implicit
background that an East Asian reader would bring to the text cannot
be simply taken for granted or completely filled in.

This book complements my study of Tsung-mi's life and thought
published in 1991 as *Tsung-mi and the Sinification of Buddhism*.
The present book incorporates and adapts some sections of my
earlier study, and I would accordingly like to thank Princeton University Press for its permission to use this material. Despite the
inevitable areas of overlap, the two books have different focuses
and were written for different purposes with different audiences in
mind. There is also much more that is new in this book, and the
two works should thus be able to stand on their own as independent
publications. My earlier study tries to place Tsung-mi's thought within the context of T'ang-dynasty Buddhism and Chinese intellectual
history, and its focus is on Tsung-mi and his historical significance.
By contrast, the present book is not so much concerned with the
figure Tsung-mi as it is with using a work by him to illustrate some
of the major ideas and methods of medieval Chinese Buddhist scholastic thought as a whole.

After pondering various ways to present the translation, I finally
decided to adopt a commentary format in order to separate material
that I thought would be of interest to the general reader and to the
specialist. Whereas many students will probably want to skip over
most of the footnotes, their presence at the bottom of the page will
make matters of more technical interest readily available to advanced
students and scholars. I have also included an unannotated, running
translation of the text, which is short enough to be read in a single
sitting, so that it will be possible to get an overall sense of the text
as a complete work. I have placed it before the annotated commentary to allow readers to form their own impression of the work
independent of my interpretations. I would thus recommend reading
the running translation first. In the case of classroom use, I would

suggest that students be urged to record their initial impressions of the text before reading the commentary or consulting the annotation. I would further suggest that they be urged to read the running translation once again after having read through the annotated commentary, comparing their reactions the second time around to those of their first reading.

I have provided a glossary of names, terms, and texts, as well as suggestions for further reading, so as to maximize the book's usefulness as a reference. Students should be cautioned, however, that the material in the glossary tends to be defined in terms of its relevance to the text and not necessarily in terms of its intrinsic importance. Hence a term that in a more general context would warrant an extended definition might be treated cursorily here because of its tangential importance to Tsung-mi's *Inquiry*, whereas another term that has received a lengthy explanation here might not even be included in a more general context. Depending on how the book is used, the materials presented in the supplementary readings could be used to assemble a course reader for students to go along with the text, by the instructor as sources for lectures or class discussions, for paper topics, or simply for follow-up reading on topics of interest. Full bibliographic references are given in the bibliography.

The incorporation of the Chinese text within the commentary should be useful for more advanced students and scholars. Tsung-mi's text is a good model of Chinese Buddhist scholastic writing, and the inclusion of Chinese characters should provide students an opportunity to absorb some vocabulary useful for reading Chinese Buddhist texts. Needless to say, the Chinese text should be the feature that makes the book most attractive to scholars. They should be aware, however, that, although I have generally followed the Taishō text, I have made several minor emendations, and that I have repunctuated the text to accord with my translation.

I first read the *Yüan jen lun* in 1976 as a graduate student at Harvard under the guidance of Professors Masatoshi Nagatomi and Francis Cleaves, and I would like to thank them both here for the time and knowledge that they so generously shared with me. The text eventually became the focus of my dissertation, completed in 1981. Since then, I have reworked the translation several times, and I am indebted to many friends, students, and colleagues for their comments and suggestions. Although I cannot mention them all by name here, I would like to single out Carl Gibson for special thanks.

A National Endowment for the Humanities Summer Stipend and a Hewlitt Summer International Research Grant, both for 1986, provided an impetus to revise my earlier translation in its entirety, and I hereby gratefully acknowledge their support. I would also like to express my special appreciation to Maezumi Rōshi for the calligraphy that graces the cover.

In the preparation of the present book, I would like to thank two trusted colleagues and friends at the University of Illinois, Gary Porton and Patricia Buckley Ebrey, both of whom had much valuable advice to offer. Two students served as willing guinea pigs, Steve Smith (a graduate student at the University of Illinois) and David Borgeson (an undergraduate at Macalester College), and I would like to express my appreciation of their travails and helpful feedback. Finally, I would like to extend my special thanks to the two reviewers of the manuscript for the Kuroda series, Professor Jan Nattier of Indiana University and Professor Hal Roth of Brown University. Their thoughtful and painstaking comments did much to improve the final product and spare me embarrassment.

# Abbreviations and Conventions

The following abbreviations have been used in the notes and bibliography:

B = Broughton, Jeffrey, "Kuei-feng Tsung-mi: The Convergence of Ch'an and the Teachings"

K = Kamata, Shigeo, *Zengen shosenshū tojo,* Zen no goroku, vol. 9

HTC = *Hsü tsang ching,* Hong Kong reprint of *Dainippon zokuzōkyō*

LS = *Yüan-chüeh ching lüeh-shu,* by Tsung-mi, T no. 1759

LSC = *Yüan-chüeh ching lüeh-shu ch'ao,* by Tsung-mi, HTC vol. 15

T = *Taishō shinshū daizōkyō*

TS = *Yüan-chüeh ching ta-shu,* by Tsung-mi, HTC vol. 14

TSC = *Yüan-chüeh ching ta-shu ch'ao,* by Tsung-mi, HTC vols. 14-15

I have divided the translation of Tsung-mi's text into paragraphs, or, in the case of the annotated translation and commentary, sometimes even smaller units. I have also provided headings and subheadings for Tsung-mi's text in order to give structure and coherence to the discussion of it in the commentary. For easy reference, page, column, and line numbers for the Taishō edition of the *Yüan jen lun* are given at the beginning of each paragraph or unit of Tsung-mi's text in both the running translation and the annotated translation with commentary.

For the convenience of advanced students and scholars, I have included the Chinese text of the *Yüan jen lun* in the annotated translation and commentary. I have also included Chinese for terms discussed in the commentary or annotation. So as not to make the book appear too intimidating to students unfamiliar with Chinese, however, I have restricted the use of Chinese for names and texts to the Glossary and the Bibliography. I have tried to include Sanskrit for basic Buddhist doctrinal terminology, as it is in this form that students are most likely to encounter these terms in different contexts.

Because this book is geared to students and nonspecialists, I have tried to give references to sources in English whenever possible, even in cases where those sources are of questionable reliability (such as Leo Pruden's English translation of La Vallée Poussin's French translation of the *Abhidharmakośabhāṣya*). Where possible, I have tried to give references to bilingual editions. Hence I have used James Legge's translations in *The Chinese Classics* for all references to the Confucian Classics (I have, however, changed Legge's romanization to Wade-Giles). I have accordingly used Z. D. Sung's rearrangement of Legge's translation of the *Classic of Change* (*I ching*) because it incorporates the Chinese text. For other texts where a bilingual edition was not available (such as the *Chuang-tzu or Hsiao ching*), I have cited the Harvard-Yenching Sinological Index Series text or, when that was not available, some other standard version.

Citations from the Taishō Canon are given according to the following conventions. Entire works are cited by author (where appropriate), title, and Taishō serial number (e.g., *She ta-sheng lun,* T no. 1593). Specific passages are cited by author (where appropriate), title, Taishō volume number, page number(s), column(s) (a, b, or c), and, if appropriate, line number(s) (e.g., *Ch'eng wei-shih lun,* T 31.10a17). In the case of texts contained in the *Hsü tsang ching,* entire works are cited by author (where appropriate), title, and HTC volume number. Specific passages are cited by author (where appropriate), title, HTC volume number, page number(s), column(s) (a, b, or c), and, if appropriate, line number(s).

Transliteration of Chinese names and terms are given according to the Wade-Giles system; Japanese, revised Hepburn. As a rule, Sanskrit is used when a Chinese term is itself a transcription of Sanskrit or when the Chinese renders a Buddhist technical term that has now come into common English usage (e.g., dharma, karma). Buddhist Sanskrit terminology that appears in *Webster's Third New International Dictionary* or that is used commonly throughout this book is not italicized.

The titles of Buddhist sūtras and exegetical works are rendered in various ways. For texts that are well known to Western readers, I have generally tried to adopt the most commonly used English, Sanskrit, or Chinese equivalent (e.g., *Abhidharmakośabhāṣya, Lotus*

*Sūtra, Awakening of Faith, Ch'eng wei-shih lun*). In the case of the *Avataṃsaka Sūtra,* I have retained the Chinese title, and accordingly refer to it as the *Hua-yen Sūtra,* so as to make explicit its connection with the Hua-yen tradition. The titles of texts that are mentioned frequently throughout this book or that appear in a significant context in the *Yüan jen lun* are often translated. But I have not tried to be entirely consistent. Other texts (such as the *Ch'eng wei-shih lun*), for which I could not come up with a felicitous translation, are simply referred to by their Chinese titles.

# INTRODUCTION

# A Window on Chinese
# Buddhist Thought

This book was written to introduce Chinese Buddhist thought to the nonspecialist with some general background in Buddhism or Chinese philosophy. It uses an early-ninth-century essay, the *Inquiry into the Origin of Humanity* (*Yüan jen lun*) by the Hua-yen and Ch'an master Kuei-feng Tsung-mi (780-841), as a window through which to survey the landscape of medieval Chinese Buddhist thought. The focus of this book is predicated on the conviction that one of the best ways to understand another tradition is through the careful reading and study of an exemplary primary text in translation. I believe that such a method of presenting Chinese Buddhism is particularly useful because the framework and orientation of an illustrative text exemplify the methodology, assumptions, and questions of medieval Chinese Buddhists just as the content of the text reveals what they thought about. Of course, not only will the content of such a text be unfamiliar to a contemporary reader, but the way of thinking embodied in it is also likely to seem equally as foreign. My own commentary thus tries to bridge the historical and cultural distance that separates us from the world of medieval Chinese Buddhism by using Tsung-mi's *Inquiry* to show not only *what* medieval Chinese Buddhists thought about but also *how* they thought about it.

Indeed, Tsung-mi's essay is well suited for this task. It presents a systematic overview of the major teachings within Chinese Buddhism, yet it is brief and accessible, having been written for a general audience not necessarily versed in the arcana of Buddhist scholasticism. It thus does not presuppose the kind of detailed knowledge of Buddhist doctrine that other more technical expositions of Buddhist teachings do, and it can well serve as a primer, as it has often done in East Asia. It also has a thematic focus that gives it coherence as a unified work. Even though Tsung-mi's systematic presentation of Buddhism is carried out from a specific doctrinal point of view, its perspective reflects some of the major orientations of Chinese Buddhist thought as a whole. The framework within which Tsung-mi organizes the various Buddhist teachings he discusses, moreover, represents one of the primary methods that Chinese Buddhists devised to organize and make sense out of the diverse body of teachings they received from India. Finally, Tsung-mi's essay is especially noteworthy in that it includes Confucianism and Taoism within its purview. It thus reflects some of the ways in which Buddhism interacted with the indigenous intellectual and religious traditions of China and how the process of cultural accommodation shaped Buddhism into distinctively Chinese forms.

Although a window is necessary to view a world otherwise closed off to us by historical and cultural barriers, it also delimits our field of vision. The shape and size of a window frames the view that can be seen through it. An oval, round, square, rectangular, diamond, or other shaped window organizes the same view into a different compositional structure. The size of the window opening likewise determines how much of that view can be seen, whether it is grand and encompassing or whether it is intimate and confined. The point of view from which one looks through the window, moreover, affects how the view is seen. The view will appear differently depending on if one stands to one side or the other, if one looks up or down, or if one gazes straight out.

Like any window, Tsung-mi's essay has its own frame, and it looks out from its own particular perspective. Far from delimiting the applicability of Tsung-mi's essay, however, its framework and point of view tell us as much about medieval Chinese Buddhist thought as do the content of the various teachings that it surveys, and this book will thus be as much about the window and its perspective as the view that it enables us to see.

### THE FRAME: DOCTRINAL CLASSIFICATION

The framework through which Tsung-mi surveys the landscape of medieval Chinese Buddhist thought in his *Inquiry* is provided by the genre of Chinese Buddhist scholastic literature known as doctrinal classification (*p'an-chiao* 判教). Doctrinal classification is a hallmark of Chinese Buddhist scholasticism, and we cannot understand how medieval Chinese Buddhist scholars thought without understanding how it works. Tsung-mi's systematic classification of Buddhist teachings thus exemplifies one of the most characteristic modes of Chinese Buddhist scholastic writing, and understanding how this genre developed gives us an insight into the process by which Buddhism became acculturated into the medieval Chinese world.[1]

Doctrinal classification provided a broad and flexible methodology for dealing with a range of interrelated issues and was used by Chinese Buddhists to serve several different purposes. First of all, it provided them with a hermeneutical method for organizing into a coherent and internally consistent doctrinal framework the diverse corpus of sacred scriptures to which they were heir.[2] From the beginning of the fifth century on, as an increasing number of texts became available in Chinese translations from Sanskrit and other Indic languages, one of the most vexing problems Chinese Buddhists faced was hermeneutical: how to account for the discrepancies, and sometimes even outright contradictions, found within the sacred body of scriptures believed to have been taught by the Buddha. As the Buddha's word, these teachings could not be false. Some framework thus had to be found to explain how the conflict among different teachings contained within the sacred canon was merely apparent, and not real, and how their differences therefore did not undermine the truth or integrity of the tradition as a whole.

Chinese Buddhists turned to the doctrine of expedient means (*upāya; fang-pien* 方便) to help deal with the hermeneutical problem of reconciling the disparities among the different teachings attributed to the Buddha. In simplest terms, this doctrine held that the differences in the teachings that the Buddha delivered in the course of his forty-nine-year ministry were the result of the different audiences that he addressed. Expedient means was thus a context based hermeneutic—that is, it held that a teaching could only be properly understood by understanding its context and intent.[3] The

---

1. I have explored this topic in greater depth in my *Tsung-mi and the Sinification of Buddhism,* see especially chapter 3.

2. As I use the term here and throughout, hermeneutics has to do with the methodological principles on which the interpretation of a text, or body of texts, is based. See the introduction and papers collected in *Buddhist Hermeneutics,* edited by Donald Lopez.

3. Expedient means played a particularly important role in the development of Mahāyāna Buddhism, which claimed that the earlier "Hīnayāna" teachings were merely expedients used by the Buddha to prepare the way for a higher revelation. The use of expedient means to justify the new Mahāyāna teachings is especially prominent in the *Lotus Sūtra.* See Michael Pye, *Skilful Means.*

doctrine of expedient means enabled Chinese Buddhists to arrange the teachings in such a way that each teaching served as an expedient measure to overcome the particular shortcoming of the teaching that preceded it while, at the same time, pointing to the teaching that was to supersede it. In this fashion a hierarchical progression of teachings could be constructed, starting with the most elementary and leading to the most profound.

But doctrinal classification was not a neutral methodology. Nor did the rubric of expedient means offer any basis on which to decide the order in which the various teachings were to be classified. The order in which the teachings were ranked was a matter of interpretation that called for value judgments in regard to which scripture or scriptural corpus was to be taken as authoritative. Hence the point of view from which the teachings were ranked was determined by the doctrinal orientation of the different traditions of Chinese Buddhism. Thus, in addition to providing a hermeneutical method by which the diverse teachings put forward in different scriptures could be harmonized, doctrinal classification also furnished the means by which the different traditions of Chinese Buddhism advanced their own sectarian claims for being recognized as the true, ultimate, or most relevant teaching of Buddhism. Different traditions defined themselves vis-à-vis one another in terms of their classification of doctrines, and doctrinal classification was thus an integral part of the polemical discourse engaged in by Chinese Buddhists.

The hermeneutical and sectarian functions of doctrinal classification reflect its dual character: it provided a framework that tended to fix sectarian differences at the same time that it claimed to harmonize doctrinal differences. On the one hand, it served as a critical tool by which different teachings could be evaluated and put in their place, thereby establishing a hierarchical grading of teachings that could be used for polemical purposes to justify the sectarian claims of different traditions. On the other hand, the very means that it used to subordinate some teachings to others at the same time created a framework in which those teachings could be subsumed, and thereby validated, within a broader vision of Buddhism. Doctrinal classification thus also had a synthetic function built into its critical framework. The logic by which these two functions worked together was dialectical and is most accurately denoted by the term "sublation" (*aufheben*). For Tsung-mi, the value of such a dialectical logic was that it provided an approach to conflicting points of view that avoided absolute judgments of right and wrong.

Different teachings are not so much wrong as they are limited or partial. There is thus a gradient of truth along which all teachings can be arranged. And the way in which one supersedes the other is dialectical, each teaching overcoming in turn the particular limitation or partiality of the one that preceded it. The supreme teaching, of course, is the one that succeeds in offering the most comprehensive point of view in which all other teachings can be harmoniously sublated. The highest teaching was therefore often referred to as *yüan* 圓 (literally, "round," i.e., having no sides or partiality, not leaning in any direction), the perfect teaching in which all the others were consummated.

Whereas doctrinal classification was a method that Chinese Buddhists developed to provide a comprehensive framework for understanding the teachings believed to have been taught by the Buddha, Tsung-mi's *Inquiry* is especially interesting in that it implicitly extends the framework of doctrinal classification to Confucianism and Taoism. Chinese Buddhists were not only confronted with the problem of making systematic sense of Buddhism, they also had to square Buddhism with their Chinese cultural heritage. Even though Tsung-mi subordinates Confucianism and Taoism to the most elementary Buddhist teaching, his low ranking of them must be regarded in the larger context of his inclusion of them within the same world of discourse as the teachings of the Buddha. His treatment of the two teachings well illustrates the dual character of doctrinal classification: it enables Tsung-mi to incorporate, and thereby validate, Confucianism and Taoism by subordinating them within a more comprehensive Buddhist framework.

Doctrinal classification also served a third function, one that plays an especially prominent role in Tsung-mi's *Inquiry:* it provided a map of the Buddhist path, and in this sense it could be said to have a soteriological function in addition to its hermeneutical and sectarian functions.[4] The arrangement of Buddhist teachings as a graded progress moving from the most elementary to the most profound mirrored the deepening stages of understanding through which Buddhist adepts moved in their advancement along the path. The ordered progression of teachings can thus be thought of as forming a curriculum of study. Ultimately, the soteriological progress

4. Soteriology has to do with the theory and methods of salvation. See the excellent introduction by Robert Gimello and Robert Buswell to their jointly edited volume, *Paths to Liberation.*

described by the sequence of teachings in the *Inquiry* is based on Tsung-mi's cosmogonic vision[5]—that is, the order of the teachings reverses the process by which the world of delusion and suffering comes into being and is perpetuated to arrive at the ultimate origin of humanity, which is the intrinsically pure and enlightened mind.

### THE POINT OF VIEW: INTRINSIC ENLIGHTENMENT

The point of view from which Tsung-mi's classification of Buddhist teachings is organized in his *Inquiry* is provided by the doctrine of intrinsic enlightenment (*pen-chüeh* 本覺), a Chinese elaboration of the Indian Buddhist idea of the potentiality for enlightenment inherent in all sentient beings. This doctrine was developed in the *Awakening of Faith in Mahāyāna (Ta-sheng ch'i-hsin lun)* into a monistic ontology based on the mind as the ultimate ground of all experience. Although this text purports to be a Chinese translation of a treatise by the venerable Indian master Aśvaghoṣa, modern scholars are generally agreed that it was an apocryphal work most likely composed in China during the third quarter of the sixth century. Whatever its provenance, the *Awakening of Faith* was surely one of the most influential texts for the development of the distinctly Chinese forms of Buddhism that became the matrix for the subsequent development of Korean and Japanese forms of Buddhism as well. As we shall see, this text provided the foundation on which Tsung-mi elaborated his classification of teachings and is thus the key to understanding the structure of his *Inquiry*.

Although there is no Sanskrit term corresponding to intrinsic enlightenment, the idea is based on the teaching of the *tathāgata-garbha (ju-lai-tsang* 如來藏) found in a number of Indian Mahāyāna texts translated into Chinese. Since this term is a cornerstone of Tsung-mi's understanding of Buddhism, and it will be used fre-

5. I am here using "cosmogony" in the sense of the original Greek terms from which the word is derived, namely an account of the genesis of the cosmos. As Charles Long notes: "Cosmogony thus has to do with myths, stories, or theories regarding the birth or creation of the universe as an order or the description of the original order of the universe" (*Encylopedia of Religion* 4.94). I would accordingly distinguish a "cosmogony" from a "cosmology" in the following way: whereas the former has to do with an account of the origin of the universe, the latter has to do with a description of the structure of the universe. The three realms and five (or six) modes of existence, discussed in the chapter, the Teaching of Humans and Gods, would thus fall under the heading of cosmology.

quently throughout the following pages, a brief explanation might be helpful at this point. It is composed of two elements, *tathāgata* and *garbha*. "Tathāgata" (*ju-lai* 如來) is an epithet for the Buddha meaning "thus come",[6] and it accordingly designates someone who has succeeded in arriving at the other shore of liberation through a penetrating insight into the way things really are. "Tathāgata" is thus related to tathatā (*chen-ju* 眞如), "suchness" or "thusness," a term used to refer to reality, the ways things really are, or, in the context of *Awakening of Faith,* the absolute. Because the true nature of reality is beyond conceptualization, it cannot be designated by any term. It is therefore said to be "such" or "thus." The *Awakening of Faith* accordingly claims that the term "suchness" does not designate anything at all but is merely a device used to put an end to discursive discourse.[7] The second part of the compound, "garbha" (*tsang* 藏), denotes both a womb and its contents. Hence "tathāgatagarbha" can mean both the womb of the Tathāgata and the embryo of the Tathāgata,[8] and it consequently has two implications. On the one hand, it can refer to the Buddhahood that exists "embryonically" as an inherent potential within all sentient beings; on the other hand, it can also refer to the Tathāgata that is "enwombed" within the sentient condition. In either case, the defilements (*kleśa; fan-nao* 煩惱)[9] that hide the Tathāgata from view are said to be adventitious—that is, their existence is accidental and not innate. The Chinese translation of "garbha" as *tsang* (store, repository, treasury)[10] emphasizes the

6. The Sanskrit term "Tathāgata" is ambiguous and can be analyzed as being composed of either *tathā-gata* (thus gone) or *tathā-āgata* (thus come). In translating the term as *de-bzhin gshegs-pa,* the Tibetan tradition, like the Sanskrit, is ambiguous; the Chinese tradition follows the second line of analysis in translating it as *ju-lai* 如來 (thus come).

7. T 32. 576a8-15.

8. "Tathāgatagarbha" is here interpreted as a genitive (*tatpuruṣa*) compound. Nevertheless there is some discussion among Buddhologists whether it should be analyzed as a determinative (*bahuvrīhi*) compound. In his definitive study of Sanskrit and Tibetan tathāgatagarbha literature, Ruegg concludes that the term is far more frequently used as a genitive compound (see his *La Théorie du Tathāgatagarbha et du Gotra,* pp. 507-513).

9. The term translated here as "defilements" is sometimes also rendered as "afflictions," "perturbations," or "passions." Tsung-mi identifies the defilements with the three poisons of greed, anger, and delusion.

10. The use of *tsang* 藏 to translate "garbha" made it easier for Chinese Buddhists to identify the tathāgatagarbha with the ālayavijñāna, which was often rendered as *tsang-shih* 藏識 or 'store consciousness'.

second sense of the term; when used as a verb, *ts'ang,* the same Chinese character means "to hide" or "to conceal." In the context of Tsung-mi's essay, the tathāgatagarbha connotes the absolute that is immanent within phenomenal appearances.

This doctrine never had the prominence in Indian Buddhism that it came to assume in China, where it became the foundation on which new and uniquely Chinese doctrinal systems and practices were built, and these doctrines and practices in turn became the matrix for the development of East Asian Buddhism as a whole. Indeed, the Chinese appropriation of this doctrine reveals some of the central concerns within Chinese thought that affected the ways in which Buddhism developed in China. In order for Buddhism to speak to the Chinese in a meaningful way that was relevant to their perception of the human condition, it had to address a set of questions different from those asked by Indian Buddhism, and these questions reflected different presuppositions about the nature of the world and human beings that informed Indian and Chinese views of the purpose of human existence. Buddhism, for example, began as a religion of radical world renunciation, and salvation (nirvāṇa) was defined as an escape from the world of birth-and-death (saṃsāra). Confucianism, by contrast, was a religion in which "salvation" was achieved by locating oneself within the human community. The tathāgatagarbha assumed paramount significance in Chinese Buddhism because it resonated with some of the primary issues in traditional Chinese thought, and it thus provided a basis for developing forms of belief and practice that could be justified by Buddhist canonical authority and yet had deep Chinese resonances as well.

The relevance of this doctrine for such longstanding Chinese concerns as defining human nature, elucidating the ontological foundation of moral values, and discerning the underlying ground from which the phenomenal world evolves is reflected in the use of the term "Buddha-nature" (*fo-hsing* 佛性) as a synonym for the tathāgatagarbha. "Nature" (*hsing* 性) was a central term in Chinese philosophical discourse before the introduction of Buddhism, and Buddha-nature consequently has connotations that go beyond the meaning of the Sanskrit terms it was used to translate.[11] The Chinese

---

11. Such as *buddhadhātu* and *buddhagotra*. "Buddhadhātu" refers to the element of Buddhahood inherent within sentient beings that acts as the cause of their attaining enlightenment. "Buddhagotra" means "clan" or

word *hsing* 性 overlaps with the English word "nature" in the sense in which we speak of the nature of something.[12] Etymologically the Chinese word derives from the word *sheng* 生, "to give birth to," "to be born." As it was used in early Chinese texts, the "nature" of something referred to its inherent potential, which, given the proper conditions, it would realize in the natural course of events. The word had both a descriptive and prescriptive meaning—that is, it referred to that which something would become if its natural development were unthwarted as well as that which it should become in order for it to be what it ought to be. It was this sense of moral imperative implicit within the idea of nature that led to its incorporation into Confucian discourse in the fourth century B.C. by Mencius, who located the source of morality within human nature. He argued that the incipient potentialities (*ssu-tuan* 四端) for Confucian moral values could be found within the heart/mind (*hsin* 心) of all human beings. For people to become moral was for them to fulfill what it meant to be truly human. What prevented people from realizing their inherently moral nature was due to external, environmental factors.[13] Mencius thus emphasized the importance of recovering one's original, childlike mind as the pre-condition for moral cultivation.[14]

The idea of nature was important for Confucian theorists because it grounded morality in the natural order of things (the ways things ought to be in the moral order was also the way things were in the natural order), thereby laying an ontological basis for moral values and thus countering the charge that they were merely the fabrication of human society and therefore arbitrary—or even that they went against the natural order. For Chinese Buddhists, "Buddha-

---

"lineage of the Buddha," hence it designates the "genetic" potentiality for Buddhahood possessed by members of this "clan." The tathāgatagarbha theory's assertion of the univeral accessibility of Buddhahood was opposed to the theory of five gotra, espoused in Fa-hsiang, according to which the spiritual potentialities of sentient beings were classified into five categories, three of which precluded the realization of Buddhahood.

12. The Chinese uses different words for "naturally" (*tzu-jan* 自然) and "nature" (as in "the order of nature" or "the laws of nature") (such as *t'ien* 天 or *tao* 道).

13. Or misguided effort, as in the case of the farmer from Sung who killed his crops by trying to help them grow, or Kao-tzu who deformed human nature by trying to make it conform to an externalized moral ideal.

14. See A. C. Graham's excellent article, "The Background of the Mencian Theory of Human Nature."

nature" gave the tathāgatagarbha doctrine a much heavier ontological weight than had been borne by the original Sanskrit term. Like the Confucian use of the term "nature," which was adapted to counter the "proto-Taoist" claim that human nature lacked any inherent moral direction, "Buddha-nature" was important for Chinese Buddhists like Tsung-mi as a counterbalance to the Buddhist doctrine of emptiness (śūnyatā; k'ung 空), which, taken out of context, could be construed to undercut all moral values as being mere convention and therefore as being ultimately false.

"Nature" is an axial term for Tsung-mi's *Inquiry*, as witnessed by his designation of the ultimate teaching as that which Reveals the Nature. Tsung-mi uses "nature" to mean Buddha-nature, in which case it is synonymous with the tathāgatagarbha; more broadly he uses it to designate the underlying ground of all phenomenal appearances, in which case it stands for a series of terms roughly equivalent to the absolute. Two of the most important of these terms are *dharmakāya* (*fa-shen* 法身) and *dharmadhātu* (*fa-chieh* 法界), both of which the *Awakening of Faith* had identified with the one mind (*i-hsin* 一心). "Dharma" (*fa* 法), which figures in both of these terms, has wide range of meanings in Buddhism. Primary among these is the meaning of the dharma as the truth realized by the Buddha, as well as the teachings that he left behind. Even though the Buddha was a real historical person who was born and died, Buddhists believed that the truth he realized was eternal and imperishable and so transcended its temporal manifestation. After all, it was his insight into the dharma that made the Buddha the "enlightened" or "awakened" one. The dharmakāya thus came to refer to the eternal and imperishable body on which Buddhahood was based (as distinguished from the perishable human body in which it was manifested historically).[15] The multiple connotations of the term "dharmadhātu" cannot adequately be conveyed by any single English translation.[16] "Dhātu" (*chieh* 界) has a range of meaning almost as broad as "dharma."[17] Among other

15. See Nagao, "On the Theory of Buddha-body," in *Mādhyamika and Yogācāra*.

16. See Kang Nam Oh, "*Dharmadhātu*: An Introduction to Hua-yen Buddhism," which summarizes his more detailed survey of the wide range of meanings that "dharmadhātu" has throughout Buddhist thought in his dissertation, "A Study of Chinese Hua-yen Buddhism with Special Reference to the Dharmadhātu (*fa-chieh*) Doctrine."

17. Fa-tsang indicates some of the ways in which dharmadhātu could be interpreted in his discussion at the beginning of his commentary on the

things, it can mean "element," "cause," "essence," and "realm"; hence the compound "dharmadhātu" can refer to the "dharma-element" that inheres in all beings as the "cause" of their enlightenment as well as the "essence of all dharmas" or the "realm of dharma" that is realized in enlightenment.

The identification of Buddha-nature with the tathāgatagarbha also suggested the idea of returning back to a natural, unsullied state of mind, before it had become clouded over by external factors (*kleśa; fan-nao* 煩惱)—an implication even more explicit in the connection of nature with the idea of intrinsic enlightenment (*pen-chüeh* 本覺) elaborated in the *Awakening of Faith*. Intrinsic enlightenment was the true nature of human beings. Literally meaning "root," *pen* 本 (intrinsic) carried substantial import in Chinese philosophical discourse. Ontologically it connotes the underlying ground on which phenomenal appearances (its branches, *mo* 末) are based. In temporal terms, it refers to that which exists *ab aeterno* (as opposed to something whose existence has an inception in time); hence it is *a priori* (as opposed to contingent). In cosmogonic terms, it designates the primordial, that which existed before the creation of the manifold world of differentiated phenomena. All of these different frames of reference emphasize that what is *pen* is most fundamental, most real, or most important.

For Tsung-mi, nature refers to the Buddhahood that exists inherently within all sentient beings as their intrinsically enlightened

---

"Ju fa-chieh p'in" ("Entering the Dharmadhātu Chapter") of the *Hua-yen Sūtra* in his *T'an-hsüan chi* (T 35.440b11ff.—cf. T 44.63b18-21). He points out that in the compound "dharmadhātu" (*fa-chieh* 法界), "dharma" (*fa* 法) can have three meanings: (1) that which upholds (*ch'ih* 持), (2) that which serves as a norm (*kuei-tse* 軌則), and (3) mental object (*tui-i* 對意). "Dhātu" (*chieh* 界) likewise has three meanings: (1) the cause (*yin* 因) (upon which noble path is realized), (2) the nature (*hsing* 性) (upon which all dharmas are based), and (3) the differentiated (*fen-ch'i* 分齊) (since all conditionally originated phenomena are distinct from one another). According to the first and second senses of dhātu, "dharmadhātu" refers to either the cause for the realization of the noble path or the underlying nature of phenomenal reality. In either case, its meaning is closely related to the tathāgatagarbha, and, indeed, in tathāgatagarbha texts such as the *Ratnagotravibhāga* the two terms are used synonymously. In the third sense of dhātu, however, Fa-tsang points out that dharma is equivalent to dhātu; "dharmadhātu" can thus also be understood to refer to differentiated phenomena. Tsung-mi, of course, understands the dharmadhātu in terms of the tathāgatagarbha.

mind, which is identical with the one mind that underlies all phenomenal reality and is the ground of all experience. It is the ultimate
origin of humanity, and it is thus the culmination of his investigation
in part 3 of the *Inquiry*. As the ultimate ground from which the
world of birth-and-death evolves,[18] it is also the basis of the cosmogony that Tsung-mi outlines in the fourth and concluding part
of his essay. Even though Tsung-mi phrases his cosmogony in terms
of the consequences of the bifurcation of consciousness into subject
and object and his language is thoroughly epistemological, there is
a mythic paradigm underlying his explanation of phenomenal evolution, one that has a greater resemblance to Chinese cosmogonies
than to Indian ones.[19] His cosmogony is essentially a myth of the
fall, and like all such myths its import is soteriological, as the need
for salvation presupposes a prior fall. And the way in which the fall
is conceived defines the religious problem that confronts human
beings.

To rephrase Tsung-mi's scheme in more explicitly mythical
terms, we could say that *in the beginning* there is the intrinsically
enlightened mind, which is pure and eternal. This mind exists before
the process of differentiation, according to which perceiving subject
and perceived object emerge, and it is referred to as the one mind.
The *fall* is accordingly described as the process by which consciousness beomes increasingly differentiated. As we shall see in more
detail later, the first subtle movement of thought leads to a separation
of subject (perceiver) and object (perceived), which leads to attachment to self and things as real and independent entities, which leads
to the generation of karma, which leads to further entanglement in
the process of birth-and-death, which leads to bondage in the unremitting round of rebirth. Human beings, of course, find themselves
in a fallen state in which they are ignorant of or have lost access to
this mind, which is covered over by defilements (*kleśa*). Buddhism
is therefore necessary to point the way to salvation, which thus
entails a *return to the original state* of the intrinsically enlightened
mind, before the fall into differentiation, and the process leading to

18. Although I use "evolve" to translate *pien* 變 (*pariṇāma*), the term
does not carry the connotation of progress conveyed by the English word;
as we shall see shortly, Tsung-mi conceives of phenomenal evolution as
a fall.

19. Or at least to Indian Buddhist ones; Carl Bielefeldt (personal com-
munication) has pointed out suggestive parallels with Sāṃkhya theories
of the evolution of the world out of *prakṛti*.

liberation accordingly involves tracing the mind back to its original state of undifferentiateness. Soteriology is thus inextricably related to cosmogony.

Even though Tsung-mi criticizes Taoist cosmogony in the first part of his essay, he bears an unacknowledged debt to its underlying mythic paradigm: a primordial beginning in a state of undifferentiated oneness, the creation of the world of multiplicity seen as a fall into a condition of duality, and the consequent necessity to return back to the original source. The tripartite structure of this paradigm bears a striking parallel to the cosmogony described by Girardot in his study of the myth of "chaos" (*hun-tun* 混沌) in early Taoism.[20] The focus and language of the two cosmogonies, however, are different. The Taoist cosmogony is at once a myth of the creation of the physical world and the living beings within it, of the emergence of human civilization as a function of social differentiation and moral distinctions, and of the process of socialization that takes place as individuals assume the identity of their socially defined roles. Tsung-mi's cosmogony deals with the structure and dynamics of consciousness, and it is therefore much more explicitly epistemological in its terminology and focus—and herein lies its specifically Buddhist dimension.

To appreciate the Buddhist dimension of Tsung-mi's cosmogony and to understand better how it departs from inherited Indian models, we could do no better than to compare it with conditioned origination (*pratītyasamutpāda; yüan-ch'i* 緣起). It would be difficult to exaggerate the importance of this doctrine within Buddhism. It was used, as Tsung-mi does in his discussion of the Teaching of the Lesser Vehicle, to show that the concept of "self" that sentient beings cling to depended on a concatenation of conditionally arisen factors and so had no independent reality of its own. It also explained how there could be continuity within personal experience without presupposing a perduring self. This doctrine was typically encapsulated in terms of the twelve-link chain of conditioned origination, which, as Frank Reynolds has noted, represents a "samsāric cosmogony."[21] The cos-

---

20. See his *Myth and Meaning in Early Taoism,* especially chapters 2 and 3. This book has not been greeted with universal acceptance by Sinologists; see, for example, Hal Roth's review in the *Journal of the Royal Asiatic Society* (1985).

21. See his "Multiple Cosmogonies: The Case of Theravada Buddhism" in Robin Lovin and Frank Reynolds, eds., *Cosmogony and the Ethical Order,* pp. 203-224.

mos in question, of course, is not the "objective" universe that exists independent of beings' perception of it. Nor is the creation a single act that takes place in the beginning of time. Rather the "cosmos" is one that is continually generated through beings' construction of it. As it functions in early Buddhist psychology, the twelve-link chain of conditioned origination presents a coherent theory of the process of world construction by which beings ensnare themselves in self-reinforcing patterns of thought and behavior that keep them bound to the relentless wheel of birth-and-death.[22] The twelve-link chain might thus be better characterized as a "psychocosmogony."

It is because the process by which beings become bound in the round of rebirth (saṃsāra) is based on a complex pattern of conditioning that liberation (nirvāṇa) is possible. That is, because the process by which this whole mass of suffering comes about is predicated on a series of conditions, it is possible to reverse the process by successively eliminating the conditions on which each link in the chain is predicated. Thus the Buddha's enlightenment is often described in terms of his successive reversal of each link in the twelvefold chain of conditioned origination.[23]

It is in these terms, for instance, that Aśvaghoṣa describes the Buddha's enlightenment in the *Buddhacarita*.[24] Having seen the coming into existence and passing away of all beings and realized the full scale of the suffering entailed by the unremitting cycle of

22. For an interesting psychological interpretation of the twelve-link chain, see Rune Johansson, *The Dynamic Psychology of Early Buddhism.*

23. For a discussion of early accounts of the Buddha's enlightenment, see L. Schmithausen, "On Some Aspects of Descriptions or Theories of 'Liberating Insight' and 'Enlightenment' in Early Buddhism."

24. In the following account, I have drawn on the translation by E. B. Cowell reprinted in *Buddhist Mahāyāna Texts.* Cowell's translation was based on a corrupt and relatively late Nepalese text. A subsequent translation, based on an earlier and more reliable text, was made by E. H. Johnston in *The Buddhacarita, or Acts of the Buddha.* Although Johnston's translation is to be preferred, I have followed Cowell's translation for the purely expedient reason that its account corresponds more closely to the twelve-link chain. I am here concerned with the general pattern illustrated in the account of the Buddha's enlightenment and not with textual questions concerning the *Buddhacarita.* For one of many examples of the Buddha's enlightenment described in terms of the twelve-link chain of conditioned origination in the Pāli Canon, see *Saṃyutta-nikāya* 2.103, translated by Mrs. Rhys Davids in *The Book of the Kindred Sayings* 2.72-73.

birth and death in which all beings are trapped, the Buddha reflects on the necessary condition on which old age and death depend. Realizing that old age and death depend on birth, the Buddha then reflects on the necessary condition on which birth depends. Realizing that birth depends on becoming, the Buddha then reflects on the necessary condition on which becoming depends. The Buddha continues in this fashion, moving backwards from becoming to grasping, craving, sensation, contact, the six sense modalities, name and form, consciousness, impulses, all the way back to ignorance as the final condition on which this whole mass of suffering depends.[25] Having thus derived the twelvefold chain of conditioned origination, the Buddha then formulates the chain in its forward direction, beginning with ignorance and ending with old age and death. "When it is thus scorched by death's anguish great pain arises; such verily is the origin of this great trunk of pain."[26]

Having thus discerned the process by which this whole mass of suffering originates, the Buddha then realizes that the entire process can be brought to an end if each of the links of which it is constituted is successively stopped. Thus reflecting that old age and death may be brought to an end if birth is stopped, and that birth may be brought to an end if becoming is stopped, and so on, the Buddha moves back through the chain until he realizes that once ignorance has been brought to an end, impulses will no longer have any power. Thus ignorance is declared to be the root of this great mass of suffering; therefore it is to be stopped by those who seek liberation.[27]

The twelve-link chain could thus be taken as a map for Buddhist practice, and the process of conditioned origination accordingly was bidirectional: it could either move with the flow of samsāra (*anuloma; shun* 順) or move against the flow of samsāra (*pratiloma; ni* 逆), either further enmeshing one in bondage or advancing one toward liberation (nirvāṇa). The important point to note is the reciprocality that obtains between the two directions. It is because

---

25. In Johnston's translation, the Buddha originally traces the chain back to consciousness (*vijñāna*), leaving out impulses (*saṃskāra*) and ignorance (*avidyā*) (see p. 211 in the reprint edition). The Chinese translation by Dharmakṣema also omits these two terms (see *Fo-so-hsing tsan ching,* T 4.27c26-29).

26. Cowell, pp. 153-514; this verse is missing from both Johnston's and Dharmakṣema's text.

27. See Cowell, pp. 151-154; cf. Johnston, pp. 209-213; T 4.27c-28a.

*pratiloma* reverses *anuloma* that the twelve-link chain of conditioned origination provides a map for liberation.

Tsung-mi's cosmogony stands on the same premise as the twelve-link chain of conditioned origination: that it is only through insight into the complex process of conditioning by which beings become ever more deeply bound in self-reinforcing patterns of thought and behavior that they can begin to reverse the process, thereby freeing themselves from bondage. Again, it is the reciprocality of the two directions in the process that enables the various stages in the process of phenomenal evolution to provide a map for Tsung-mi's explanation of the nature and course of Buddhist practice. Tsung-mi's arrangement of the teachings in the first three parts of his *Inquiry* traces back this linkage and so mirrors the description of the Buddha's enlightenment in tracing back the twelve-link chain of conditioned origination (*pratiloma*). The cosmogony that he outlines in the fourth and concluding part of his *Inquiry* traces forward this linkage and so mirrors the Buddha's discovery of the twelve-link chain as the explanation for sentient beings' bondage in saṃsāra (*anuloma*).

Although Tsung-mi's cosmogony has the same soteriological function in his thought that the twelve-link chain of conditioned origination had in early Buddhism, there are also important differences in content. The most important difference is that conditioned origination posits no ultimate ontological basis; ignorance (the link on which all the others are based) is simply said to be beginningless. Tathāgatagarbha theory, however, could not escape the problem of the origin of ignorance. This problem became far more acute with the development of the tathāgatagarbha into a monistic ontology in the *Awakening of Faith,* where it was identified as the true nature. In texts other than the *Inquiry,* Tsung-mi explains that the process of phenomenal evolution is based on what is referred to as "nature origination" (*hsing-ch'i* 性起), a term that indicates that all phenomenal appearances are nothing but manifestations of the nature. Nature origination thus goes beyond conditioned origination in locating an ultimate ontological basis for the phenomenal world.

The doctrine of intrinsic enlightenment brought to the fore a set of problems that did not arise (or remained comfortably in the background) in Indian Buddhism. In baldest terms, the underlying philosophical problem was: if all of phenomenal reality is based on a single monistic principle that is intrinsically enlightened, how can the ignorance that causes beings to suffer in delusion be accounted for?

This problem is essentially a rephrasing of the problem of theodicy in Buddhist terms.[28] In its traditional formulation within Christian theology, a theodicy is the vindication of the justice of God given the reality of evil (especially the suffering of innocents). The problem arises because God is believed to have certain attributes that are essential to His nature. If God is good, then He should not want there to be evil. If God is also all powerful, then He should be able to eliminate evil. If, moreover, God is all knowing, then He should be able to foresee the possibility of evil before it even occurs and so prevent it from ever arising in the first place. The reality of evil thus seems to contradict the very attributes deemed most essential to God's nature. By extension, Tsung-mi's cosmogony is a theodicy in the sense that it attempts to vindicate the intrinsic enlightenment of the mind given the reality of delusion. The reality of suffering and delusion seem to call into question the very attributes deemed most essential to the nature of the mind as conceived of in the *Awakening of Faith*. If ignorance originates from the mind, then how can the mind be said to be intrinsically enlightened? If, on the other hand, ignorance originates outside of the mind, then how can the mind be said to be the single ground on which all of phenomenal reality is based? As we shall see, Tsung-mi ultimately had no more success in resolving this problem than did his Christian counterparts, and we are left with a mystery that, short of enlightenment, can only be grasped as a paradox.

## THE LANDSCAPE: THE TEACHINGS

Doctrinal classification and intrinsic enlightenment provide the basic framework and doctrinal orientation through which Tsung-mi's *Inquiry* allows us view the world of medieval Chinese Buddhism. The teachings that Tsung-mi surveys also include Confucianism and Taoism. The "teachings" (*chiao* 教) for Tsung-mi are those embodied in the canonical texts—that is, the scriptures or classics (alike referred to as *ching* 經 in Chinese)—of Confucianism, Taoism, and Buddhism.

For Tsung-mi, Confucianism was represented by the teachings embodied in the Five Classics—i.e., the *Classic of Change* (*I ching* or *Chou i*), the *Classic of History* (*Shu ching* or *Shang shu*), the *Spring and Autumn Annals* (*Ch'un-ch'iu*) with the *Tso Commentary* (*Tso chuan*), the *Classic of Poetry* (*Shih ching* or *Mao shih*), and the *Book of Rites* (*Li chi*)—plus the *Classic of Filiality* (*Hsiao ching*) and

28. See my "The Problem of Theodicy in the *Awakening of Faith*."

the *Analects of Confucius* (*Lun-yü*). According to the accepted traditon during the T'ang, the Five Classics were all closely associated
with Confucius, who was believed to have played a prominent role
in assembling and editing them. They were given canonical status
by the T'ang state, which made them the main curriculum for the
imperial examinations. Examination candidates were expected to
have mastered the *Classic of Filiality* and *Analects of Confucius* as
well. The centrality of the Confucian classics for the examination
system reflects Confucianism's historical association with the Chinese state, which sought ideological legitimation in its teachings. It
also reflects the state's power to legislate orthodoxy.

Taoism, for Tsung-mi, was represented by the teachings found in
the *Lao-tzu* (otherwise known as the *Tao te ching*), the *Chuang-tzu*,
and, to a lesser extent, the *Lieh-tzu*. Tsung-mi's focus on these texts,
and not those of the Taoist Canon (*Tao tsang*), reflects the ability of
the state to determine orthodoxy by defining the curriculum for the
examinations. Taoism enjoyed a privileged and semiofficial status under
the T'ang court. The T'ang imperial house claimed descent from Lao-
tzu, the fabled sixth-century B.C. "founder" of Taoism,[29] and the patronage of the religion was used as a means of bolstering dynastic
prestige. In the seventh century the *Lao-tzu* was made a compulsory
text for the civil service examinations. Taoism received its greatest imperial sponsorship during the reign of Hsüan-tsung (r. 713-756), who,
among other measures, had an imperial edition and commentary to
the *Lao-tzu* issued under his name,[30] raised the importance of the *Lao-
tzu* and other Taoist texts (including the *Chuang-tzu* and the *Lieh-tzu*)
within the examination system by instituting a separate Taoist exam,
promoted a nationwide system of schools for the study of Taoism, and
established the worship of Lao-tzu as an imperial ancestor.

Buddhism is represented by the teachings found in the Buddhist
sūtras, the scriptures collected in the Buddhist Canon that purported
to be a record of the teachings expounded by the Buddha.[31] The

29. Most Western scholars agree that Lao-tzu was not a historical per-
sonage and that the text that bears his name was most likely a compilation
of the third century B.C.

30. It is this version of the *Lao-tzu* that Tsung-mi cites.

31. As Kyoko Tokuno has shown in her excellent study of medieval
Chinese Buddhist catalogues of the canon, the state, in collaboration with
the Buddhist establishment, played a major role in determining Buddhist
orthodoxy as well. See her "The Evaluation of Indigenous Scriptures in
Chinese Buddhist Bibliographical Catalogues."

"teachings" thus do not necessarily correspond to particular doctrinal or sectarian traditions within Chinese Buddhism, although, as noted earlier, Chinese Buddhist traditions legitimated themselves in terms of their different classifications of the teachings. The teaching of the tathāgatagarbha, for example, was crucial for a number of different Chinese traditions, although they may have appealed to a different scripture as authority for that teaching. It is also interesting to note the importance of apocryphal texts—texts, that is, that purported to be translations of Indic originals but that were really written in Chinese—as the basis for some of the teachings that Tsung-mi enumerates.[32]

Since the content of the teachings will be discussed in detail below, a brief overview of the *Inquiry* should suffice to illustrate how the sequence by which the different teachings succeed one another reflects Tsung-mi's soteriological vision, and how that vision is grounded on his cosmogony. Such an overview also illustrates the dialectical logic by which each teaching supersedes the one that precedes it.

The whole structure of Tsung-mi's *Inquiry into the Origin of Humanity,* as the title suggests, is organized around what is an essentially cosmogonic question phrased in terms of the ultimate origin of humanity. As Tsung-mi glosses the title, his inquiry is not limited to probing the origin of human existence but encompasses all six modes of sentient existence[33] as conceived by Buddhist cosmology. In other words, his investigation takes in the whole of saṃsāra, the world of suffering and delusion in which beings are born and die without cease.

Tsung-mi's inquiry is twofold. In the first three sections of this work, he uses the doctrine of expedient means to organize the various teachings into a hierarchical structure according to the superficiality or profundity with which they address the question of the origin of human existence. The highest teaching reveals that the ultimate origin is the intrinsically enlightened mind possessed by all sentient beings.

---

32. Such as the *T'i-wei Po-li ching* for the Teaching of Humans and Gods, and the *Awakening of Faith* and *Scripture of Perfect Enlightenment* for the Teaching That Reveals the Nature. Although not an apocryphal text, the *Ch'eng wei-shih lun* is a product of eighth-century Chinese Buddhism and so gives a cast to Fa-hsiang teachings that differs from the Indian Yogācāra tradition.

33. Or sometimes five, depending on whether titans (*asura; a-hsiu-lo* 阿修羅) are included.

Enlightenment is based on and consists in insight into this mind. The order of the teachings in the first three parts of the *Inquiry* thus outlines a sequence of soteriological progress that traces the process of cosmogony from its farthest effects back to its ultimate origin.

The concluding section of the essay moves in the opposite direction, showing how the cosmogonic process begins from a unitary principle, whose division ultimately leads to the continual round of rebirth in which beings are bound. The various teachings that Tsung-mi so clearly differentiated from one another in his first three sections are here brought back together into an all-encompassing explanation of the process of phenomenal evolution. Since each teaching accounts for different stages in the process, they can all be harmonized together within a unified cosmogonic framework. The superficial teachings only deal with the most outward developments of the process of phenomenal evolution—its "branches" (*mo* 末). As the teachings become more profound, they come closer to the ultimate source—or "root" (*pen* 本)—until the highest teaching finally reveals it. The order of the teachings in Tsung-mi's classification scheme thus reverses the stages in the cosmogony he describes in the concluding section. Their arrangement is itself a description of the course of the spiritual path (*mārga*) leading from the suffering of delusion to the liberation of enlightenment.

The most elementary category of teaching in Tsung-mi's scheme is that of Humans and Gods (*jen-t'ien chiao* 人天教). It consists in the simple moral teaching of karmic retribution, which enables beings to gain a favorable rebirth as either a human being or a god. It goes beyond the teachings of Confucianism and Taoism, which are unaware of the process of rebirth by which good and bad deeds are requited in future lives. The Teaching of Humans and Gods thus explains how the apparent injustices of this world make sense within the broader moral framework supplied by the teaching of karma. In terms of Tsung-mi's cosmogonic scheme, this teaching overturns the last two stages in the process of phenomenal evolution, those of generating karma and experiencing the consequences.

Since the basic import of the Teaching of Humans and Gods hinges on the doctrine of rebirth, it naively assumes that there is, in fact, something that is reborn. It is thus superseded by the Teaching of the Lesser Vehicle (*hsiao-sheng chiao* 小乘教), whose doctrine of no-self (*anātman; wu-wo* 無我) refutes the belief in an unchanging self. This teaching develops a sophisticated psychological vocabulary of dharmas (here designating the basic categories into which all experience can be analyzed) in order to break down the conceit of self into an ever-changing concatenation of impersonal constituents, none of which can be grasped as a substantial entity. It thus overturns the next two stages in Tsung-mi's cosmogonic scheme, those of defilements and attachment to self.

In its psychological analysis, however, the Teaching of the Lesser Vehicle talks as if these dharmas were real. It is accordingly superseded by the third category of teaching, which deconstructs the reality of the dharmas by showing that they, like the conceit of self, are nothing but mental constructions. This category, referred to as the Teaching of the Phenomenal Appearances of the Dharmas (*fa-hsiang chiao* 法相教), is represented by the brand of Yogācāra introduced into China by Hsüan-tsang (600-664). It demonstrates that since both the conceptions of self and the dharmas are merely the projections of an underlying consciousness (the ālayavijñāna), they are therefore equally unreal. This teaching thus overturns the next stage in the process of phenomenal evolution, that of attachment to dharmas. It also points back to the underlying constructive process on which both attachment to self and dharmas is predicated. This constructive process is detailed in the next three phases of phenomenal evolution—those of the manifestation of perceived objects, the arising of the perceiving subject, and the arising of thought.

Yet this teaching is not final. Even though it clarifies how deluded thought arises, it still does not reveal its ultimate basis. Tsung-mi argues that the Teaching of the Phenomenal Appearances of the Dharmas fails to discern that the projecting consciousness and the projected objects are interdependent and hence equally unreal. This teaching is thus superseded by that which Tsung-mi refers to as the Teaching That Refutes Phenomenal Appearances (*p'o-hsiang chiao* 破相教), which demonstrates the emptiness of both the projecting consciousness and the projected objects. This teaching is represented by the Perfection of Wisdom scriptures and Madhyamaka treatises. Although this teaching offers a clear rationale for the supersedure of the third teaching, it does not have any obvious cosmogonic content. Nevertheless, the thrust of Tsung-mi's scheme impels him to correlate it with the second stage in the process of phenomenal evolution, that of unenlightenment.

While this fourth level of teaching succeeds in determining what ultimate reality is not, it still does not reveal what it is and is therefore superseded by the next and final teaching, that which Reveals the Nature (*hsien-hsing chiao* 顯性教). By clarifying that the underlying projecting consciousness, the ālayavijñāna, is based on the intrinsically enlightened pure mind, the tathāgatagarbha, this teaching reveals the ultimate source on which both delusion and enlightenment are based. It thus corresponds to the first stage in Tsung-mi's cosmogonic scheme, intrinsic enlightenment.

CORRELATATION BETWEEN TEACHINGS AND COSMOGONIC STAGES

| TEACHING | COSMOGONIC STAGE |
|---|---|

1. Humans and Gods 人天教
          10. Experiencing the Consequences 受報
         9. Generating Karma 起業

2. Lesser Vehicle 小乘教
         8. Defilements 煩惱
         7. Attachment to Self 我執

3. Phenomenal Appearances 法相教
         6. Attachment to Dharmas 法執
         5. Manifestation of Perceived Objects 境現
         4. Arising of Perceiving Subject 見起
         3. Arising of Thoughts 念起

4. Refutation of Phenomenal Appearances 破相教
         2. Unenlightenment 不覚

5. Revelation of the Nature 顯性教
         1. Intrinsic Enlightenment 本覺

# Historical Context

Tsung-mi was traditionally honored as the fifth patriarch in the Hua-yen scholastic tradition and the Ho-tse line of Southern Ch'an, and his *Inquiry into the Origin of Humanity* reflects a set of concerns that are closely connected with his involvement with both traditions. Hua-yen and Ch'an represent two of the major forms of Buddhism that took shape during the T'ang dynasty (618-907). It was during this period that the fully acculturated forms of Chinese Buddhism assumed their mature state, one that was at once authentically Buddhist and uniquely Chinese. The ideas formulated by these traditions served as the fundamental axioms on which subsequent developments in Chinese Buddhism were based, and the forms of Buddhism evolved during the T'ang are thus a natural focus for a general introduction to Chinese Buddhist thought. It was also during this time that Chinese Buddhist philosophical thought reached its apogee and that the main modes of Chinese Buddhist practice developed into some of their characteristic forms. While the Hua-yen tradition exemplifies the philosophical dimension of T'ang Buddhism, Ch'an exemplifies its more practice-oriented dimension. The two traditions that Tsung-mi was associated with therefore not only represent two of the major expressions of Chinese Buddhism but also its two poles as well. Tsung-mi's own place within these traditions is indicated by the fact that both saw fit to accord him the status of "patriarch."[1]

To appreciate the sense in which Buddhism can be said to have reached its mature state of development in the T'ang, we might do well to consider Buddhism's more than half a millenium of history

1. This chapter briefly touches on various points and themes that are elaborated more extensively in my *Tsung-mi and the Sinification of Buddhism,* chapter 2 of which contains a detailed biography of Tsung-mi.

in China before Li Yüan founded the T'ang dynasty in 618. This process of cultural accommodation, whereby an alien tradition gradually became "sinified," can be broken done into three major stages. The first, occupying the third and fourth centuries, was characterized by early Chinese attempts to understand Buddhism through the lens of their own intellectual and religious traditions, especially so-called Neo-Taoism (*hsüan-hsüeh* 玄學). Thus a difficult Buddhist idea like emptiness, for which the Chinese had no equivalent, was interpreted in terms of the Neo-Taoist notion of nonbeing (*wu* 無).[2] By the end of the fourth century, however, it had become evident to the more perceptive of the clerical elite that such an approach had only yielded a distorted image of the foreign religion. The second stage, whose beginning may be conveniently symbolized by Kumārajīva's arrival in Ch'ang-an in 401, was characterized by the attempt of Chinese Buddhists to understand Buddhism on its own terms, shorn of the cultural filters that had typified their earlier efforts. Chinese Buddhists accordingly looked to foreign authorities like Kumārajīva for a definitive exposition of the faith. This stage, occupying the fifth and sixth centuries, witnessed the translation of a large body of Buddhist texts and is marked by an increasingly scholastic turn as Chinese monks slowly mastered the doctrinal intricacies of their Indian heritage, especially the complex theories of mind found in Yogācāra tomes. The third stage, beginning with the Sui (581-617) reunification of China in 589 and extending through the three centuries of the T'ang, represents the period in which Chinese Buddhism finally came of age with the emergence of the fully sinified traditons of T'ien-t'ai, Hua-yen, Ch'an, and Pure Land.[3]

Hua-yen and Ch'an, like the other new traditions that emerged during the Sui and T'ang, can be seen in part as a reaction against the mounting weight of Chinese Buddhist scholasticism. The sheer bulk and daunting complexity of the scholastic enterprise contrib-

---

2. This stage of Chinese Buddhist history is covered in brilliant detail by Eric Zürcher's classic study, *The Buddhist Conquest of China*.

3. For the differences between the exegetical Buddhism of the fifth and sixth centuries and the new Buddhism of the Sui and T'ang, see Stanley Weinstein's classic article, "Imperial Patronage in the Formation of T'ang Buddhism"; Robert Gimello, "Chih-yen (602-668) and the Foundations of Hua-yen Buddhism"; and the first chapter of my *Tsung-mi and the Sinification of Buddhism*. Gimello's work remains the best study of Chinese Buddhism during the sixth and seventh centuries.

uted to a sense of crisis among some of the learned Buddhists during the Sui and early T'ang. The texts that they strove to comprehend were often at odds with one another, and it was not always clear what doctrines should be accepted as orthodox. Nor did they address what many felt to be the more urgent religious issues of the day. In times when the very existence of the religion was threatened, as many felt it had been by the Northern Chou persecution (574-577), Chinese Buddhists' anxiety was not allayed by the dismaying prospect of the bodhisattva career that the Indian treatises portrayed as requiring three incalculable eons. In an evil and corrupt age of the decline of the dharma (*mo-fa* 末法), new practices and a new theology to justify them were called for. The new traditions thus drew on the promise of universal salvation guaranteed by the tathāgata-garbha to emphasize the possibility of the attainment of enlightenment in this lifetime and fashioned a religious approach that affirmed the importance of activity in this world.

In an effort to make Buddhism speak to more immediate spiritual needs, the Sui-T'ang innovators discarded foreign models of the path, rejecting the authority of the Indian scholastic tradition in favor of a return back to those texts believed to contain the word of the Buddha, the sūtras. The prior centuries of scholastic apprenticeship had gradually earned Chinese Buddhists a hard-won confidence in their own authority to interpret the tradition in accord with their own experience. This turn back to the fount of the tradition in scriptural word also opened up a new dimension of interpretative possibilities. The parables and metaphors so abundant in the sūtras, as opposed to the argument and syllogism more representative of the scholastic literature, offered a range of interpretive possibilities that could be made to speak more directly to Chinese experience and needs. Accordingly the new traditions of Chinese Buddhism preferred to designate themselves in terms of the scripture on which they based their authority rather than on a body of scholastic literature, as was more typically the case with the exegetical traditions of the fifth and sixth centuries. This rejection of Indian authority can also be seen in their gradual construction of a Chinese patriarchate. No longer were the "patriarchs" hallowed Indian exegetes or foreign translators but the charismatic Chinese masters who were retrospectively judged as "founders" of the new traditions.

Hua-yen and Ch'an both represented themselves as lineages (*tsung* 宗), although they claimed to be based on different kinds of authority. The Hua-yen tradition took its name and spiritual warrant from the *Hua-yen (Avataṃsaka) Sūtra*, which it claimed to be the first and most profound teaching of the Buddha. The Ch'an tradition, on the other hand, claimed to represent a historical transmission of the Buddha's enlightened understanding down through an unbroken succession of Indian and Chinese patriarchs. Although Ch'an apologists appealed to extra-canonical authority, they too rejected the scholastic tradition and looked back to the ultimate authority of the Buddha.

## THE AUTHOR

The *Inquiry* reflects some of the major concerns that recur throughout Tsung-mi's writings. These concerns, in turn, reflect Tsung-mi's own experience, which was shaped by the conditions of Chinese Buddhism in the late eighth and early ninth centuries. A brief look at his life and the historical conditions in which his thought developed should thus shed some light on the context within which to understand his *Inquiry*. There are three layers to Tsung-mi's thought (i.e., Confucian, Ch'an, and Hua-yen), each of which can be seen as corresponding to a particular stage in his intellectual and religious development. The first stage covers roughly the first twenty-four years of his life, during which he devoted his primary energy to Confucian studies, presumably in preparation for the civil service examination that would open the door to an official career in the imperial bureaucracy. The next stage begins with his meeting of the Ch'an master Tao-yüan in 804, and it includes his initial enlightenment experience and his subsequent Ch'an training in Szechwan. The third stage begins in 810 with his discovery of Ch'eng-kuan's commentary and subcommentary to the *Hua-yen Sūtra* and encompasses his two years of intense study under Ch'eng-kuan's tutelage (812-813).

Tsung-mi was born in 780 into a family of local prominence in a town in the southwestern province of Szechwan. He received a solid classical education in the Confucian and Taoist texts that were the basis of the national civil service examinations, which provided one of the major channels of social and economic advancement during the second half of the T'ang dynasty. He lost his father in his teens, and during the three years of mourning prescribed by Confucian ritual, he became interested in Buddhism. He spent the next two years enrolled in a local Confucian academy in preparation for the civil service examinations. Tsung-mi's classical background shaped some of his major values, especially his sensitivity to the moral implications of different teachings, and later was a major factor in his acceptance by a number of prominent scholar officials of his day.

In 804 Tsung-mi met the Ch'an master Tao-yüan and was so impressed that he abandoned his ambitions for an official career and decided to become a Buddhist monk. Tao-yüan claimed to be a member of the Southern Ch'an lineage of Ho-tse Shen-hui (684-758), the famous champion of the cause of Hui-neng (638-713) as the true sixth Ch'an patriarch.[4] Shortly after receiving the tonsure, Tsung-mi had an enlightenment experience when he chanced to read a few pages from the *Scripture of Perfect Enlightenment* (*Yüan-chüeh ching*). The study of the text that catalyzed this experience dominated Tsung-mi's life for the next two decades, culminating in a series of commentaries to it that have remained influential to this day.

Tsung-mi received full ordination in 807. In the following year he left for the provincial capital of Ch'eng-tu to study with his teacher's master, who, impressed with his intelligence and ability, urged him to proceed to the imperial capital of Ch'ang-an (present-day Xian) to spread the dharma. On his way there, in 810, Tsung-mi met a dying monk, who introduced him to the commentary and subcommentary to the *Hua-yen Sūtra* by the preeminent Hua-yen master of the time, Ch'eng-kuan (738-839). This encounter proved to be so powerful that Tsung-mi began a correspondence with Ch'eng-kuan, with whom he then studied Hua-yen thought intensively for two years (812-813) in Ch'ang-an. Tsung-mi subsequently embarked on an extensive reading of the Buddhist Canon. In 816, after availing himself of the monastic libraries in Ch'ang-an, he left the capital to continue his research at various temples on Mount Chung-nan, where he spent much of the remainder of his life. This period of prolonged study bore fruit in a series of authoritative commentaries and subcommentaries to the *Scripture of Perfect Enlightenment* completed during 823 and 824, the fulfillment of a vow he had made after his first encounter with the text nearly two decades before in Szechwan.

In 828 he left Mount Chung-nan in response to an imperial edict inviting him to court. Tsung-mi congratulated the emperor on the occasion of his birthday and was subsequently honored with a pur-

4. For the story of the Sixth Patriarch, see Philip Yampolsky's introduction to his *The Platform Sutra of the Sixth Patriarch;* for Shen-hui, see John McRae's "Shen-hui and the Teaching of Sudden Enlightenment in Early Ch'an Buddhism."

ple robe and the title of "Great Worthy." His imperial acclaim and presence at court brought him into contact with a number of the leading intellectual and political figures of his day, and the character of his writing shifted as a result. From this point on Tsung-mi largely abandoned the scholastic focus of his earlier commentaries to address broader intellectual concerns of his new literati audience, as seen in his *Inquiry*.

Tsung-mi returned to Mount Chung-nan sometime in 829 or 830, where he carried on an active correspondence with a number of scholar-officials. He also wrote two major works on Ch'an, which are some of our major sources for understanding T'ang-dynasty Ch'an. The first of these, *Preface to the Collected Writings on the Source of Ch'an* (or *Ch'an Preface* for short), was a preface to a collection of writings of the various Ch'an schools of the late T'ang that Tsung-mi gathered together as a special supplement to the Buddhist Canon. The second, *Chart of the Master Disciple Succession within the Ch'an School That Transmits the Mind Ground in China* (or *Ch'an Chart* for short), documents the lineal filiations and teachings of four of the major Ch'an traditions current in the late T'ang.[5]

Tsung-mi was unfortunately implicated in the Sweet Dew Incident of 835, an abortive attempt to oust the eunuchs from power at court, when one of the conspirators with whom he was acquainted sought asylum in his temple on Mount Chung-nan.[6] As a result, Tsung-mi fell into public eclipse, and nothing is known about his activities from 835 until his death in 841.

This brief sketch suffices to reveal the three formative influences that shaped Tsung-mi's life and thought: his classical background and Confucian education, his Ch'an training in Szechwan, and his study of Hua-yen doctrine under Ch'eng-kuan, and each of these influences is reflected in different ways in his *Inquiry*.

Looked at in the context of the Hua-yen tradition, Tsung-mi's systematic presentation of Buddhist teachings in his *Inquiry* marks a significant revision of the tradition from its classical formulation by Fa-tsang (643-712). If we compare Tsung-mi's fivefold classification of Buddhist teachings with the corresponding fivefold classification of Fa-tsang, there are a number of striking differences between the two schemes. Tsung-mi, for example, includes the

5. For a full discussion of Tsung-mi's writings, see Appendix I to my *Tsung-mi and the Sinification of Buddhism.*

6. For an account of this incident, see Jennifer Jay, "The Li Hsün Faction and the Sweet Dew Incident of 835."

Teaching of Humans and Gods as the most elementary teaching and omits the Sudden Teaching, the fourth teaching in Fa-tsang's system.[7]

COMPARISON OF FA-TSANG'S AND TSUNG-MI'S CLASSIFICATION SCHEMES

| FA-TSANG | TSUNG-MI |
|---|---|
| | (1) Humans and Gods |
| (1) Hīnayāna ————▷ | (2) Lesser Vehicle |
| (2) Elementary Mahāyāna | |
|   (a) Fa-hsiang/Yogācāra ——▷ | (3) Phenomenal Appearances of Dharmas |
|   (b) Madhyamaka ————▷ | (4) Refutation of Phenomenal Appearances |
| (3) Advanced Mahāyāna ——▷ | (5) Reveals the Nature |
| (4) Sudden | |
| (5) Perfect | |

The most telling difference, however, is Tsung-mi's omission of the Perfect Teaching, the teaching that Fa-tsang had ranked highest, and, in its stead, his raising to preeminence of the teaching that Fa-tsang had merely ranked third (i.e., the Advanced Teaching of the Mahāyāna). This shift is especially important for assessing Tsung-mi's revaluation of Hua-yen teachings because the teaching that is displaced is precisely that which Fa-tsang had taken to express the most profound insight of the Buddha, which was revealed exclusively in the *Hua-yen Sūtra* and was therefore the basis of the Hua-yen tradition's claim to represent the most exalted teaching of Buddhism. Textually, Tsung-mi's rearrangement of Buddhist teachings signals his displacement of the *Hua-yen Sūtra,* in favor of the *Awakening of Faith,* as the ultimate basis of Hua-yen thought. Doctrinally, it reveals his emphasis on the tathāgatagarbha as the most fundamental teaching of the Buddha.

To appreciate the significance of this shift, we must understand what Fa-tsang meant by the Perfect Teaching. The Perfect Teaching for Fa-tsang embodied the content of the Buddha's enlightenment,

7. I have discussed the reasons why Tsung-mi might have included the Teaching of Humans and Gods in his classification scheme in the *Inquiry* in "The Teaching of Men and Gods: The Doctrinal and Social Basis of Lay Buddhist Practice in the Hua-yen Traditon." I have discussed the reasons why he might have omitted the Sudden Teaching in chapter 5 of my *Tsung-mi and the Sinification of Buddhism.*

that which the Buddha experienced immediately after his enlightenment while in the samādhi of oceanic reflection (*hai-in san-mei* 海印三昧), the state in which he perceived the harmonious interrelation of all phenomena as if the entire universe were reflected on the surface of a vast ocean. It is this vision that is unique to the *Hua-yen Sūtra* and that therefore distinguishes the Perfect Teaching from all the other teachings of the Buddha and sets the Hua-yen tradition above all the other traditions of Buddhism. This vision came to be known in Hua-yen as the realm of unobstructed interrelation of each and every phenomenon (*shih-shih wu-ai* 事事無礙).

Whereas the Perfect Teaching had to do with the content of the Buddha's enlightenment, the Advanced Teaching (what Tsung-mi called the Teaching That Reveals the Nature) had to do with the ontological ground on which enlightenment was based, the intrinsically enlightened mind of the *Awakening of Faith*. It was the luminous quality of this mind that made possible the reflection of the harmonious interrelation of all phenomena on the surface of the Buddha's enlightened mind.[8]

The revision that Tsung-mi made in Hua-yen doctrinal classification can be understood as part of his effort to provide an ontological basis for Buddhist practice. His revalorization of Hua-yen thought, in turn, points back to his involvement with, and reaction to, various developments that had taken place within Ch'an.[9] The iconoclastic rhetoric of the radical movements that had gained currency within Chinese Ch'an during the latter part of the T'ang could easily be misinterpreted in antinomian ways that denied the need for spiritual cultivation and moral discipline. Having grown up and received his early Ch'an training in Szechwan, an area in which the most extreme of these movements flourished in the late eighth and early ninth centuries, Tsung-mi was particularly sensitive to such ethical dangers.

The two most important of these Szechwan Ch'an traditions were the Hung-chou and Pao-t'ang. The Hung-chou tradition derived from Ma-tsu Tao-i (709-788). The essential criticism that Tsung-mi leveled against the Hung-chou tradition in his *Ch'an Chart* was that its attitude that Ch'an practice consisted in "entrusting oneself to act freely according to the nature of one's feelings" had dangerous antinomian implications. Tsung-mi's sensitivity to

8. For a more extended treatment of this theme, see chapter 6 of my *Tsung-mi and the Sinification of Buddhism*.

9. See chapter 9 of my *Tsung-mi and the Sinification of Buddhism*.

such ethical concerns gains importance when seen in the context of his reaction to the Pao-t'ang tradition, which had, according to his account, interpreted Shen-hui's teaching of "no-thought" (*wu-nien* 無念) to entail the rejection of all forms of traditional Buddhist ethical practice and ritual observance. Tsung-mi saw a similarity in the ethical import of the Hung-chou line of Ch'an and the religious paradigm associated with the *Hua-yen Sūtra* (as embodied in Fa-tsang's Perfect Teaching), which helps explain why he displaced that text in favor of the *Awakening of Faith* in his systematic evaluation of Buddhist teachings.

Tsung-mi was drawn to Hua-yen because it provided him with a solid ontological rationale for Ch'an practice, and he accordingly adapted its theory as a buttress against the antinomian implications of these radical interpretations of Ch'an teaching. His critique of Hung-chou Ch'an, in particular, is important for establishing the ethical thrust behind his adaptation of Hua-yen metaphysics. The ethical tenor animating Tsung-mi's systematic classification of the teachings, moreover, reveals the importance of the Confucian moral vision that he had internalized in his youthful study of the classics.

The role of Confucianism in Tsung-mi's thought is far more extensive than his formal ranking of it would suggest. Even though he officially places Confucianism below the most elementary Buddhist teaching, the *Inquiry* articulates a larger framework in which Confucianism is integrated into a more encompassing Buddhist vision. As we shall see, Tsung-mi maintains that the difference among the three teaching of Buddhism, Taoism, and Confucianism is a matter of expedients. Their differences are a function of the particular historical circumstances in which the three teachings were taught and have nothing to do with level of understanding attained by each of the three sages (i.e., Buddha, Lao-tzu, and Confucius). Tsung-mi's inclusive approach is most clearly revealed in the concluding part of the *Inquiry,* in which he incorporates Confucianism and Taoism together with five levels of Buddhist teaching into an overarching explanation of the process by which the human condition comes into being.

Tsung-mi's attempt to elaborate a syncretic framework in which Confucian moral teachings could be integrated within Buddhism, his effort to clarify the underlying ontological basis for moral and religious action, and the ethical thrust of his criticism of the Hung-chou line of Ch'an all reveal his preoccupation with moral order. Tsung-mi's writings demonstrate his life-long effort to justify the values that he had learned as a youth in terms of the discrepant

claims of the religion to which he had converted as an adult. Here
it is important to note that his actual conversion to Buddhism occurred at the age of twenty-four. Even though Tsung-mi interrupted
his concentration on Confucian classics to read Buddhist texts for
a few years in his late adolescence, he did not take up the practice
of Buddhism until after his conversion in 804. That is, Tsung-mi began Buddhist practice at a time after which we can suppose that
his basic values would have already been formed—and the core of
those values were Confucian. What is significant in Tsung-mi's case
is that his conversion to Buddhism did not entail a rejection of his
early Confucian training.

## THE TEXT

Although it is impossible to date the *Inquiry into the Origin of Humanity* with precision, the evidence we do have suggests that it
was probably written sometime after 828 and before 835.

A comparison of the text of part 1 of the *Inquiry* with the corresponding section on Confucianism and Taoism in Tsung-mi's
*Commentary to the Scripture of Perfect Enlightenment,* completed
in 823, suggests that the *Inquiry* version represents a refinement of
the *Commentary* passage, which thus served as a draft. The prose
in the *Inquiry* is more polished, extraneous material has been eliminated, and unclear passages in the *Commentary* text have either
been clarified or deleted. More significantly, the *Inquiry* is not mentioned in the autobiographical section of Tsung-mi's *Subcommentary to the Scripture of Perfect Enlightenment,* which notes the dates
and circumstances under which he composed many other works.
Nor is it mentioned in the corresponding section of the *Yüan-chüeh
ching lüeh-shu ch'ao,* Tsung-mi's subcommentary to his abridged
commentary to the *Scripture of Perfect Enlightenment.* Although
neither the abridged commentary and its subcommentary are dated, both were written after his *Commentary,* indicating that at the
very least the *Inquiry* could not have been composed before 825.

The content and tone of the *Inquiry,* in which Tsung-mi, sure
of his own authority, elaborates his own, original assessment of the
teachings, suggests that it must have been a product of his maturity.
The style and content of the *Inquiry* suggest that it was written for
an audience well versed in the Confucian and Taoist classics, such
as would have been found among Tsung-mi's scholar-official
friends. The fact that it was included in Tsung-mi's *Collected Correspondence* (*Tao-su ch'ou-ta wen-chi*) compiled by his lay and

clerical followers after his death, together with Tsung-mi's deft use of classical allusions and his inclusion of Confucianism and Taoism within the compass of the essay, all suggest that the *Inquiry* was written for a lay follower to serve as a general overview of the main teachings of Chinese Buddhism. It is unlikely that Tsung-mi would have commanded such an audience before his invitation to the court. As we saw, Tsung-mi congratulated the emperor on his birthday in 828. Throughout the T'ang dynasty the imperial birthday was often the occasion for a debate among representatives of the three teachings (of Confucianism, Taoism, and Buddhism), such as the one in which Tsung-mi's friend Po Chü-i (772-846) took part in 827.[10] Perhaps such an occasion provided the stimulus for a request for Tsung-mi to write an essay upholding the position of Buddhism.

As has been frequently noted,[11] the title of Tsung-mi's *Inquiry* (*Yüan jen lun* 原人論) probably derives from an essay, or series of essays, by Han Yü (768-824). Tsung-mi's gloss on his title may even contain a veiled reference to Han Yü.[12] Although there is no evidence that Tsung-mi knew Han Yü personally, he must surely have known of him and his work. He was acquainted with several figures who would have moved in the same circles as Han Yü, most notably Liu Yü-hsi (772-842). Han Yü had earlier written a series of five essays whose titles all began with *yüan* 原 (on the origin of);[13]

10. See Arthur Waley, *Po Chü-i*, pp. 169-171.

11. See, for example, Kamata Shigeo's introduction to his translation of the *Yüan jen lun, Genninron*, p. 19.

12. See T 45.708c21-22, translated in the chapter on the Teaching of Human and Gods.

13. The *yüan* 原 here functions as a verb, as it also does in the title of Tsung-mi's essay. Tsung-mi's use of *yüan* as a verb is made clear in his Preface, where he writes: "I have studied for several decades without a constant teacher and have thoroughly examined the inner and outer [teachings] in order to find the origin of myself (*i yüan tzu-shen* 以原自身). I sought it without cease (*yüan chih pu-i* 原之不已) until I realized its origin" (707c29-708a2). When Tsung-mi refers to "the origin" as a noun, he uses a different character—*yüan* with the water radical (源).

In so using *yüan*, Tsung-mi probably had the following passage from the *Classic of Change* in mind: "[The sage] traces things back to their beginning (*yüan-shih* 原始), and follows them to their end (*fan-chung* 反終);—thus he knows what can be said about death and life (*ku chih ssu sheng chih shuo* 故知死生之説)" (as translated by James Legge in Sung, *The Text of the Yi King*, p. 278). This passage, which Tsung-mi quotes elsewhere, neatly encapsulates what he tries to do in the *Inquiry*. He "traces things

one of these was the *Yüan jen* 原人 (On the Origin of Humanity);
another was the *Yüan hsing* 原性, which discussed human nature.[14]
The topic of human nature was also the subject of Li Ao's famous
*Fu-hsing shu* (Essay on Returning to One's True Nature).[15] Not only
was human nature a topic of concern in the beginning of the ninth
century, the fact that Tsung-mi's essay took its title from Han Yü
also suggests that it was written in part as a response to Han Yü's
attacks on Buddhism. Han Yü's criticisms of Buddhism can be
found in many places, but the most well known are contained in
his *Yüan tao* 原道 (On the Origin of the Way),[16] written around
805, and his *Memorial on the Buddha's Bone,*[17] presented in 819.
Even though Han Yü's strident brand of Confucianism was an
anomaly within T'ang intellectual life, there is evidence that his
anti-Buddhist sentiments increasingly found favor at court in the
late 820s and early 830s.[18]

   As a response to renewed attacks against Buddhism, Tsung-
mi's *Inquiry* can be seen as the product of a long history of Buddhist polemical literature extending back to the introduction of
Buddhism in China. Yet, unlike earlier polemics, Tsung-mi's essay
is no mere apology for the faith seeking to refute the traditional

---

to their beginning" in the first three parts of the essay and "follows them
to their end" in the fourth, and he thus makes known the explanation of
life-and-death (*sheng-ssu* 生死, i.e., saṃsāra).

   The "Inquiry" in my translation of the title of Tsung-mi's essay is an
attempt to combine the verbal force of *yüan* 原 with a translation of *lun*
論 (treatise, essay, tract).

   14. The *Yüan hsing* has been translated by Wing-tsit Chan in his *A
Source Book of Chinese Philosophy,* pp. 451-453. The other three are *Yüan
kuei* 原鬼 (On the Origin of Ghosts), *Yüan hui* 原鬼 (On the Origin of
Slander), and *Yüan tao* 原道 (On the Origin of the Way). *Yüan hui* has
been translated by Rideout in Cyril Birch, ed., *Anthology of Chinese Literature,* pp. 255-257.

   15. For a definitive study and translation of this text see Timothy
Barrett, *Li Ao: Buddhist, Taoist, or NeoConfucian?*

   16. This work has been frequently translated; see, for example, Chan,
*A Source Book of Chinese Philosophy,* pp. 454-456; for a discussion of this
work, see Hartman, *Han Yü and the T'ang Search for Unity,* pp. 145-162.

   17. This memorial has also been frequently translated; see that by
James Hightower in Edwin Reischauer's *Ennin's Travels in T'ang China,*
pp. 221-224; see also Homer Dubs, "Han Yü and the Buddha Relic."

   18. See Weinstein, *Buddhism under the T'ang,* pp. 108-110.

array of Chinese objections to Buddhism. Rather, viewed from the perspective of the subsequent development of Neo-Confucianism in the Sung dynasty (960-1279), Tsung-mi's essay gains importance because it goes beyond the polemical intent of earlier works and, in so doing, shifts the field of controversy to a new and more philosophical level of debate, putting Buddhism, for the first time, in the position of determining the intellectual context in terms of which Confucianism was called upon to respond.

# A Note on the Translation

In preparing my translation of the *Yüan-jen lun* I have used the version of the text found in volume 45 of the *Taishō shinshū daizōkyō*. I have also consulted a number of traditional and modern commentaries in both Chinese and Japanese. The most useful of these have been the two Chinese commentaries found in volume 104 of the *Hsü tsang ching*: those of Ching-yüan 淨源 (1011-1088), the *Hua-yen yüan jen lun fa-wei lu* 華嚴原人論發微錄, and Yüan-chüeh 圓覺, the *Hua-yen yüan jen lun chieh* 華嚴原人論解.

There is also a large body of commentaries and annotated translations available in Japanese, many of them dating from the Meiji period (1868-1912), when the text became especially popular. Kamata Shigeo lists twenty-five Japanese commentaries in the introduction to his own annotated translation of the text. Without attempting an exhaustive search, I have come across the titles of some dozen others not listed by Kamata. Of these, I have made use of the following nine:

Atsuta Ryōchi 熱田靈知, *Genninron* 原人論 (1894).
Kamata Shigeo 鎌田茂男, *Genninron* 原人論 (1973).
Katō Kumaichirō 加藤熊一郎, *Genninron kōwa* 原人論講話 (1908).
Kimura Yoshiyuki 木村善之, *Genninron shinkō* 原人論新講 (1931).
Kishigami Kairyō 岸上恢嶺, *Kachū genninron kōgi* 科註原人論講義 (1891).
Ōtomo Tōtsu 大友洞達, *Genninron shōkai* 原人論詳解 (1921).
Ōuchi Seiran 大内青巒, *Genninron kōgi* 原人論講義 (1904).
Wada Ryūzō 和田龍造, *Genninron kōroku* 原人論講録 (1934).
Yusugi Ryōei 湯次了栄, *Kanwa taishō genninron shinshaku* 漢和対照原人論新釈 (1935).

The most valuable of the Japanese commentaries consulted were those of Ōtomo, Kimura, Yusugi, and Kamata. Nevertheless, they generally add little to what can be found in the two Chinese commentaries and are often not as extensive as that of Yüan-chüeh, which proved to be the most useful overall.

In addition to the Chinese and Japanese commentaries, there are five translations of Tsung-mi's text into Western languages. The earliest of these—which I have not consulted—was done into German by Hans Haas in 1909. The next to appear was that of Nukariya Kaiten, published as an appendix to his *The Religion of the Samurai: A Study of Zen Philosophy and Discipline in China and Japan* (originally issued in 1913, this work was reprinted in 1973). In 1915 Paul Masson-Oursel published a French translation of Tsung-mi's essay in the *Journal Asiatique*. Heinrich Dumoulin's German translation of the *Yüan-jen lun* appeared in the first volume of *Monumenta Nipponica* in 1938. This work was the result of the translator's participation in a seminar on the text led by Ui Hakuju in the previous year. Although Dumoulin's translation is more amply annotated than the earlier ones of Nukariya and Masson-Oursel, the translation itself is rendered so freely as to be of little more than a German paraphrase of the original.

The most recent translation of Tsung-mi's essay is that done by Yoshito Hakeda in *The Buddhist Tradition in India, China, and Japan,* published in 1969 under the general editorship of William T. deBary and subsequently reprinted in a paperback edition in 1972. Hakeda's translation, unfortunately, does not include Tsung-mi's own autocommentary, which forms an important part of the text. Its numerous minor and substantive errors also suggest that it was dashed off in haste in order to meet the deadline for inclusion in deBary's anthology. Even more critical, Hakeda's translation contains virtually no annotation. The conviction underlying my own translation is that the richness and texture of a text such as the *Inquiry into the Origin of Humanity,* composed over a thousand years ago in a culture far different from our own, is only dimly accessible to the contemporary reader in bare translation. Unless the many allusions that Tsung-mi employs so skillfully are noted, and their assumptions and implications spelled out, the meaning of the work will remain largely opaque. Likewise, without some knowledge of the doctrinal and historical issues behind his discussion of the various teachings, Tsung-mi's arguments are likely to appear simplistic, bizarre, or dead.

The most valuable resource in preparing my own translation of the *Yüan-jen lun* has been Tsung-mi's own writings, which have a remarkable consistency overall. One of my guiding principles has thus been, whenever possible, to turn to other works by Tsung-mi to elucidate and amplify passages in the *Inquiry*. Since Tsung-mi's formulations of his thought are surprisingly consistent throughout his opera and there are many passages in the *Inquiry* that parallel passages in other works by Tsung-mi, this method has proven to be both practicable and fruitful. The first part of the text, for example, in which Tsung-mi discusses Confucianism and Taoism, corresponds closely to a section of his *Commentary to the Scripture of Perfect Enlightenment*. This correspondence is particularly fortunate as Tsung-mi has written his own subcommentary to his *Commentary to the Scripture of Perfect Enlightenment*, and the pertinent sections of the subcommentary can thus be used as footnotes to elucidate this part of the *Inquiry*. Tsung-mi's discussion of the five Buddhist teachings, which comprise the second and third parts of the *Inquiry*, closely parallel sections of his *Ch'an Preface*. Segments of the concluding part of the *Inquiry*, moreover, parallel the concluding sections of the *Ch'an Preface* as well. In some instances the parallel passages in the *Ch'an Preface* are more detailed than those in the *Inquiry*, and they can thus be used to supplement the *Inquiry*.

Tsung-mi's autocommentary appears in small print within the body of the Taishō edition of the *Yüan jen lun*. In an effort to make the translation simulate the appearance of the original text, Tsung-mi's autocommentary will appear in small type within parentheses within the body of the translation. Material that appears in brackets represents my own interpolation. For easy reference, page, column, and line numbers for the Taishō edition of the *Yüan jen lun* are given at the beginning of the translation of each passage. The Chinese text that has been incorporated into the translation with commentary is based on the Taishō edition, although readers should note that I have made several minor emendations and have repunctuated the text to accord with the translation.

# RUNNING TRANSLATION

# Inquiry into the Origin of Humanity

by the Sramana Tsung-mi of the Ts'ao-t'ang Temple
on Mount Chung-nan

## PREFACE

[707c25] The myriad animate beings teeming with activity—all have
their origin. The myriad things flourishing in profusion—each returns to its root. Since there has never been anything that is without
a root or origin and yet has branches or an end, how much less
could [humanity,] the most spiritual among the three powers [of the
cosmos, i.e., heaven, earth, and humanity,] be without an original
source? Moreover, one who knows the human is wise, and one who
knows himself is illuminated. Now, if I have received a human body
and yet do not know for myself whence I have come, how can I
know whither I will go in another life, and how can I understand
human affairs of the past and present in the world? For this reason,
I have studied for several decades without a constant teacher and
have thoroughly examined the inner and outer [teachings] in order
to find the origin of myself. I sought it without cease until I realized
its origin.

[708a2] Now those who study Confucianism and Taoism merely
know that, when looked at in proximate terms, they have received
this body from their ancestors and fathers having passed down the
bodily essence in a continuous series. When looked at in far-reaching terms, the one pneuma of the primordial chaos divided into the
dyad of yin and yang, the two engendered the triad of heaven,
earth, and human beings, and the three engendered the myriad
things. The myriad things and human beings all have the pneuma
as their origin. [708a5] Those who study Buddhism just say that,
when looked at in proximate terms, they created karma in a previous
life and, receiving their retribution in accord with karma, gained
this human body. When looked at in far-reaching terms, karma, in

43

turn, develops from delusion, and ultimately the ālayavijñāna constitutes the origin of bodily existence. All [i.e., Confucianists, Taoists,
and Buddhists] maintain that they have come to the end of the
matter, but, in truth, they have not yet exhausted it.

[708a7] Still, Confucius, Lao-tzu, and Śākyamuni were consummate sages who, in accord with the times and in response to beings,
made different paths in setting up their teachings. The inner and
outer [teachings] complement one another, together benefiting the
people. As for promoting the myriad [moral and religious] practices,
clarifying cause and effect from beginning to end, exhaustively investigating the myriad phenomena, and elucidating the full scope
of birth and arising—even though these are all the intention of the
sages, there are still provisional and ultimate [explanations]. The
two teachings are just provisional, whereas Buddhism includes both
provisional and ultimate. Since encouraging the myriad practices,
admonishing against evil, and promoting good contribute in common to order, the three teachings should all be followed and practiced. If it be a matter of investigating the myriad phenomena,
fathoming principle, realizing the nature, and reaching the original
source, then Buddhism alone constitutes the definitive answer.

[708a13] Nevertheless, scholars today each cling to a single tradition. Even those who follow the Buddha as their teacher are often
deluded about the true meaning and therefore, in seeking the origin
of heaven, earth, humanity, and things, are not able to find the
ultimate source. I will now proceed to investigate the myriad phenomena by relying on the principles of the inner and outer teachings.
First, I will advance from the superficial to the profound. For those
who study provisional teachings, I will dig out their obstructions,
allowing them to penetrate through and reach the ultimate origin.
Later, I will demonstrate the meaning of phenomenal evolution by
relying on the ultimate teaching. I will join the parts together, make
them whole, and extend them back out to the branches ("branches"
refers to heaven, earth, humanity, and things). The treatise has four parts
and is entitled "Inquiry into the Origin of Humanity."

## I. Exposing Deluded Attachments

(For those who study Confucianism and Taoism)

[708a26] The two teachings of Confucianism and Taoism hold that human beings, animals, and the like are all produced and nourished by the great Way of nothingness. They maintain that the Way, conforming to what is naturally so, engenders the primal pneuma. The primal pneuma engenders heaven and earth, and heaven and earth engender the myriad things. [708a28] Thus dullness and intelligence, high and low station, poverty and wealth, suffering and happiness are all endowed by heaven and proceed according to time and destiny. Therefore, after death one again returns to heaven and earth and reverts to nothingness.

[708a29] This being so, the essential meaning of the outer teachings merely lies in establishing [virtuous] conduct based on this bodily existence and does not lie in thoroughly investigating the ultimate source of this bodily existence. The myriad things that they talk about do not have to do with that which is beyond tangible form. Even though they point to the great Way as the origin, they still do not fully illuminate the pure and impure causes and conditions of conforming to and going against [the flow of] origination and extinction. Thus, those who study [the outer teachings] do not realize that they are provisional and cling to them as ultimate.

### [Critique of the Way]

[708b4] Now I will briefly present [their teachings] and assess them critically. Their claim that the myriad things are all engendered by the great Way of nothingness means that the great Way itself is the origin of life and death, sageliness and stupidity, the basis of fortune and misfortune, bounty and disaster. Since the origin and basis are permanently existent, [it must follow that] disaster, disorder, misfortune, and stupidity cannot be decreased, and bounty, blessings, sageliness, and goodness cannot be increased. What use, then, are the teachings of Lao-tzu and Chuang-tzu? Furthermore, since the Way nurtures tigers and wolves, conceived Chieh and Chou, brought Yen Hui and Jan Ch'iu to a premature end, and brought disaster upon Po I and Shu Ch'i, why deem it worthy of respect?

## [Critique of Spontaneity]

[708b9] Again, their claim that the myriad things are all spontaneously engendered and transformed and that it is not a matter of causes and conditions means that everything should be engendered and transformed [even] where there are no causes and conditions. That is to say, stones might engender grass, grass might engender-humans, humans engender beasts, and so forth. Further, since they might engender without regard to temporal sequence and arise without regard to due season, the immortal would not depend on an elixir, the great peace would not depend on the sage and the virtuous, and benevolence and righteousness would not depend on learning and practice. For what use, then, did Lao-tzu, Chuang-tzu, the Duke of Chou, and Confucius establish their teachings as invariable norms?

## [Critique of the Primal Pneuma]

[708b13] Again, since their claim that [the myriad things] are engendered and formed from the primal pneuma means that a spirit, which is suddenly born out of nowhere, has not yet learned and deliberated, then how, upon gaining [the body of] an infant, does it like, dislike, and act willfully? If they were to say that one suddenly comes into existence from out of nowhere and is thereupon able to like, dislike, and so forth in accordance with one's thoughts, then it would mean that the five virtues and six arts can all be understood by according with one's thoughts. Why then, depending on causes and conditions, do we study to gain proficiency?

[708b17] Furthermore, if birth were a sudden coming into existence upon receiving the endowment of the vital force and death were a sudden going out of existence upon the dispersion of the vital force, then who would become a spirit of the dead? Moreover, since there are those in the world who see their previous births as clearly as if they were looking in a mirror and who recollect the events of past lives, we thus know that there is a continuity from before birth and that it is not a matter of suddenly coming into existence upon receiving the endowment of the vital force. Further, since it has been verified that the consciousness of the spirit is not cut off, then we know that after death it is not a matter of suddenly going out of existence upon the dispersion of the vital force. This is why the classics contain passages about sacrificing to the dead and beseeching them in prayer, to say nothing of cases, in both

present and ancient times, of those who have died and come back to life and told of matters in the dark paths or those who, after death, have influenced their wives and children or have redressed a wrong and requited a kindness.

[708b23] An outsider [i.e., a non-Buddhist] may object, saying: If humans become ghosts when they die, then the ghosts from ancient times [until now] would crowd the roads and there should be those who see them—why is it not so? I reply: When humans die, there are six paths; they do not all necessarily become ghosts. When ghosts die, they become humans or other forms of life again. How could it be that the ghosts accumulated from ancient times exist forever? Moreover, the vital force of heaven and earth is originally without consciousness. If men receive vital force that is without consciousness, how are they then able suddenly to wake up and be conscious? Grasses and trees also all receive vital force, why are they not conscious?

## [Critique of the Mandate of Heaven]

[708b28] Again, as for their claim that poverty and wealth, high and low station, sageliness and stupidity, good and evil, good and bad fortune, disaster and bounty all proceed from the mandate of heaven, then, in heaven's endowment of destiny, why are the impoverished many and the wealthy few, those of low station many and those of high station few, and so on to those suffering disaster many and those enjoying bounty few? If the apportionment of many and few lies in heaven, why is heaven not fair? How much more unjust is it in cases of those who lack moral conduct and yet are honored, those who maintain moral conduct and yet remain debased, those who lack virtue and yet enjoy wealth, those who are virtuous and yet suffer poverty, or the refractory enjoying good fortune, the righteous suffering misfortune, the humane dying young, the cruel living to an old age, and so on to the moral being brought down and the immoral being raised to eminence. Since all these proceed from heaven, heaven thus makes the immoral prosper while bringing the moral to grief. How can there be the reward of blessing the good and augmenting the humble, and the punishment of bringing disaster down upon the wicked and affliction upon the full? Furthermore, since disaster, disorder, rebellion, and mutiny all proceed from heaven's mandate, the teachings established by the sages are not right in holding human beings and not heaven responsible and in blaming people and not destiny. Nevertheless, the [*Classic of*]

*Poetry* censures chaotic rule, the [*Classic of*] *History* extols the kingly Way, the [*Book of*] *Rites* praises making superiors secure, and the [*Classic of*] *Music* proclaims changing [the people's] manners. How could that be upholding the intention of heaven above and conforming to the mind of creation?

## II. EXPOSING THE PARTIAL AND SUPERFICIAL
(For those who study the teachings of the Buddha whose meaning is not ultimate)

[708c12] The Buddha's teachings proceed from the superficial to the profound. Altogether there are five categories: (1) the Teaching of Humans and Gods, (2) the Teaching of the Lesser Vehicle, (3) the Teaching of the Phenomenal Appearances of the Dharmas within the Great Vehicle, (4) the Teaching That Refutes the Phenomenal Appearances within the Great Vehicle (the above four [teachings] are included within this part), and (5) the Teaching of the One Vehicle That Reveals the Nature (this one [teaching] is included within the third part).

### [1. The Teaching of Humans and Gods]

[708c15] 1. The Buddha, for the sake of beginners, at first set forth the karmic retribution of the three periods of time [i.e., past, present, and future] and the causes and effects of good and bad [deeds]. That is to say, [one who] commits the ten evils in their highest degree falls into hell upon death, [one who commits the ten evils] in their lesser degree becomes a hungry ghost, and [one who commits the ten evils] in their lowest degree becomes an animal. [708c17] Therefore, the Buddha grouped [the five precepts] with the five constant virtues of the worldly teaching and caused [beginners] to maintain the five precepts, to succeed in avoiding the three [woeful] destinies, and to be born into the human realm. [708c17] (As for the worldly teaching of India, even though its observance is distinct, in its admonishing against evil and its exhorting to good, there is no difference [from that of China]. Moreover, it is not separate from the five constant virtues of benevolence, righteousness, and so forth, and there is virtuous conduct that should be cultivated. For example, it is like the clasping of the hands together and raising them in this country and the dropping of the hands by the side in Tibet—both are [examples of] propriety. Not killing is benevolence, not stealing is righteousness, not committing adultery is propriety, not lying is trustworthiness, and, by neither drinking wine nor eating meat, the spirit is purified and one increases in wisdom.) [708c20] [One who] cultivates the ten good deeds

in their highest degree as well as bestowing alms, maintaining the precepts, and so forth is born into [one of] the six heavens of [the realm of] desire. [708c20] [One who] cultivates the four stages of meditative absorption and the eight attainments is born into [one of] the heavens of the realm of form or the realm of formlessness. [708c21] (The reason gods, [hungry] ghosts, and the denizens of hell are not mentioned in the title [of this treatise] is that their realms, being different [from the human], are beyond ordinary understanding. Since the secular person does not even know the branches, how much less could he presume to investigate the root thoroughly. Therefore, in concession to the secular teaching, I have entitled [this treatise] "An Inquiry into the Origin of Humanity." [However,] in now relating the teachings of the Buddha, it was, as a matter of principle, fitting that I set forth [the other destinies] in detail.) Therefore, [this teaching] is called the Teaching of Humans and Gods. (As for karma, there are three types: 1) good, 2) bad, and 3) neutral. As for retribution, there are three periods of time, that is to say, retribution in the present life, in the next life, and in subsequent lives.) According to this teaching, karma constitutes the origin of bodily existence.

[708c23] Now I will assess [this teaching] critically. Granted that we receive a bodily existence in [one of] the five destinies as a result of our having generated karma, it is still not clear who generates karma and who experiences its retribution. [708c25] If the eyes, ears, hands, and feet are able to generate karma, then why, while the eyes, ears, hands, and feet of a person who has just died are still intact, do they not see, hear, function, and move? If one says that it is the mind that generates [karma], what is meant by the mind? If one says that it is the corporeal mind, then the corporeal mind has material substance and is embedded within the body. How, then, does it suddenly enter the eyes and ears and discern what is and what is not of externals? If what is and what is not are not known [by the mind], then by means of what does one discriminate them? Moreover, since the mind is blocked off from the eyes, ears, hands, and feet by material substance, how, then, can they pass in and out of one another, function in response to one another, and generate karmic conditions together? If one were to say that it is just joy, anger, love, and hate that activate the body and mouth and cause them to generate karma, then, since the feelings of joy, anger, and so forth abruptly arise one moment and abruptly perish the next and are of themselves without substance, what can we take as constituting the controlling agent and generating karma?

[709a4] If one were to say that the investigation should not be pursued in a disconnected fashion like this, but that it is our body-and-mind as a whole that is able to generate karma, then, once this body has died, who experiences the retribution of pain and pleasure? If one says that after death one has another body, then how can the commission of evil or the cultivation of merit in the present body-and-mind cause the experiencing of pain and pleasure in another body-and-mind in a future life? If we base ourselves on this [teaching], then one who cultivates merit should be extremely disheartened and one who commits evil should be extremely rejoiceful. How can the holy principle be so unjust? Therefore we know that those who merely study this teaching, even though they believe in karmic conditioning, have not yet reached the origin of their bodily existence.

### [2. The Teaching of the Lesser Vehicle]

[709a11] 2. The Teaching of the Lesser Vehicle holds that from [time] without beginning bodily form and cognitive mind, because of the force of causes and conditions, arise and perish from moment to moment, continuing in a series without cease, like the trickling of water or the flame of a lamp. The body and mind come together contingently, seeming to be one and seeming to be permanent. Ignorant beings in their unenlightenment cling to them as a self. [709a14] Because they value this self, they give rise to the three poisons of greed (coveting reputation and advantage in order to promote the self), anger (being angry at things that go against one's feelings, fearing that they will trespass against the self), and delusion (conceptualizing erroneously). The three poisons arouse thought, activating body and speech and generating all karma. Once karma has come into being, it is difficult to escape. Thus [beings] receive a bodily existence (determined by individual karma) of pain and pleasure in the five destinies and a position (determined by collective karma) of superior or inferior in the three realms. In regard to the bodily existence that they receive, no sooner do [beings] cling to it as a self then they at once give rise to greed and so forth, generate karma, and experience its retribution. [709a18] In the case of bodily existence, there is birth, old age, sickness, and death; [beings] die and are born again. In the case of a world, there is formation, continuation, destruction, and emptiness; [worlds] are empty and are formed again.

[709a19] (As for the first formation of the world from the empty kalpa, a verse says that a great wind arises in empty space, its expanse is immeasurable,

its density is sixteen hundred thousand [leagues], and not even a diamond could harm it. It is called the wind that holds the world together. [709a20] In the light-sound [heaven] a golden treasury cloud spreads throughout the great chiliocosm. Raindrops [as large as] cart hubs come down, but the wind holds it in check and does not let it flow out. Its depth is eleven hundred thousand [leagues]. [709a20] After the diamond world is created, a golden treasury cloud then pours down rain and fills it up, first forming the Brahma [heavens, and then going on to form all the other heavens] down to the Yāma [heaven]. The wind stirs up the pure water, forming Mount Sumeru, the seven gold mountains, and so on. When the sediment forms the mountains, earth, the four continents, and hell, and a salty sea flows around their circumference, then it is called the establishment of the receptacle world. At that time one [period of] increase/decrease has elapsed. [709a22] Finally, when the merit of [beings in] the second meditation [heaven] is exhausted, they descend to be born as humans. They first eat earth cakes and forest creepers; later the coarse rice is undigested and excreted as waste, and the figures of male and female become differentiated. They divide the fields, set up a ruler, search for ministers, and make distinctions as to the various classes. [This phase] lasts nineteen periods of increase/decrease. Combined with the previous [period during which the receptacle world was formed] it makes twenty periods of increase/decrease and is called the kalpa of formation.

[709a23] [I will now] elaborate on [the above]. [The period of time] during the kalpa of empty space is what the Taoists designate as the Way of nothingness. However, since the essence of the Way is tranquilly illuminating and marvellously pervasive, it is not nothingness. Lao-tzu was either deluded about this or he postulated it provisionally to encourage [people] to cut off their human desires. Therefore he designated empty space as the Way. The great wind [that arises] in empty space corresponds to their one pneuma of the primordial chaos; therefore they say that the Way engenders the one. The golden treasury cloud, being the beginning of the pneuma's taking form, is the great ultimate. The rain coming down and not flowing out refers to the congealing of the yin pneuma. As soon as yin and yang blend together, they are able to engender and bring [all things] to completion. From the Brahma Kings' realm down to Mount Sumeru corresponds to their heaven, and the sediment corresponds to the earth, and that is the one engendering the two. The merits [of those in] the second meditation [heaven] being exhausted and their descending to be born refers to human beings, and that is the two engendering the three, and the three powers thus being complete. From the earth cakes to the various classes is the three engendering the myriad things. This corresponds to [the time] before the three kings when people lived in caves, ate in the wilderness, did not yet have the transforming power of fire, and so on. [709a27]

It is only because there were no written records at the time that the legendary accounts of people of later times were not clear; they became increasingly confused, and different traditions wrote up diverse theories of sundry kinds. Moreover, because Buddhism penetrates and illuminates the great chiliocosm and is not confined to China, the writings of the inner and outer teachings are not entirely uniform.

[709b1] "Continuation" refers to the kalpa of continuation; it also lasts for twenty [periods of] increase/decrease. "Destruction" refers to the kalpa of destruction; it also lasts for twenty [periods of] increase/decrease. During the first nineteen [periods of] increase/decrease sentient beings are destroyed; during the last [period of] increase/decrease the receptacle world is destroyed. That which destroys them are the three cataclysms of fire, water, and wind. "Empty" refers to the kalpa of emptiness; it also lasts for twenty [periods of] increase/decrease. During [the kalpa of] emptiness there is neither [receptacle] world nor sentient beings.)

[709b2] Kalpa after kalpa, birth after birth, the cycle does not cease; it is without end and without beginning, like a well wheel drawing up [water]. (Taoism merely knows of the single kalpa of emptiness when the present world had not yet been formed. It calls it nothingness, the one pneuma of the primordial chaos, and so forth, and designates it as the primeval beginning. It does not know that before [the kalpa of] empty space there had already passed thousands upon thousands and ten-thousands upon ten-thousands of [kalpas of] formation, continuation, destruction, and emptiness, which, on coming to an end, began again. Therefore we know that within the teaching of Buddhism even the most superficial Teaching of the Lesser Vehicle already surpasses the most profound theories of the outer canon.) All this comes about from [beings] not understanding that the body is from the very outset not the self. "Is not the self" refers to the fact that the body originally takes on phenomenal appearance because of the coming together of form and mind.

[709b6] If we now push our analysis further, form is comprised of the four great elements of earth, water, fire, and wind, whereas mind is comprised of the four aggregates of sensation (that which receives agreeable and disagreeable things), conceptualization (that which forms images), impulses (that which creates and shifts and flows from moment to moment), and consciousness (that which discriminates). If each of these were a self, then they would amount to eight selves. How much more numerous would [the selves] be among the earthly element! That is to say, each one of the three hundred sixty bones is distinct from the others; skin, hair, muscles, flesh, liver, heart, spleen, and kidneys are each not the other. Each of the various

mental functions are also not the same; seeing is not hearing, joy is not anger, and so on and so forth to the eighty-four thousand defilements. Since there are so many things, we do not know what to choose as the self. If each of them were a self, then there would be hundreds upon thousands of selves, and there would be the utter confusion of many controlling agents within a single body. Furthermore, there is nothing else outside of these [components]. When one investigates them inside and out, a self cannot be found in any of them. One then realizes that the body is just the phenomenal appearance of the seeming combination of various conditions and that there has never been a self.

[709b16] On whose account does one have greed and anger? On whose account does one kill, steal, give [alms], and maintain the precepts (knowing the truth of suffering)? Then, when one does not obstruct the mind in good and bad [deeds] that have outflows in the three realms (the truth of cutting off the accumulation [of suffering]) and only cultivates the wisdom of the view of no-self (the truth of the path), one thereby cuts off greed and so forth, puts a stop to all karma, realizes the reality of the emptiness of self (the truth of extinction), until eventually one attains arhatship: as soon as one makes one's body as ashes and extinguishes thought, one cuts off all suffering. According to this teaching, the two dharmas of form and mind, as well as greed, anger, and delusion, constitute the origin of the body of senses and the receptacle world. There has never been nor will ever be anything else that constitutes the origin.

[709b21] Now I will assess [this teaching] critically. That which constitutes the source of bodily existence in the experiencing of repeated births and the accumulation of numerous life-times must, in itself, be without interruption. [However], the present five [sense] consciousnesses do not arise in the absence of conditions (the sense organs, sense objects, and so forth constitute the conditions), there are times when consciousness does not operate (during unconsciousness, deep sleep, the attainment of extinction, the attainment of non-consciousness, and among the non-conscious gods), and the gods in the realm of formlessness are not comprised of the four great elements. How, then, do we hold on to this bodily existence life-time after life-time without ceasing? Therefore we know that those who are devoted to this teaching have also not yet reached the origin of bodily existence.

[3. The Teaching of the Phenomenal Appearances of the Dharmas]

[709b26] 3. The Teaching of the Phenomenal Appearances of the Dharmas within the Great Vehicle holds that all sentient beings from [time] without beginning inherently have eight kinds of consciousness. Of these, the eighth—the ālayavijñāna—is the fundamental basis. It instantaneously evolves into the body of the senses, the receptacle world, and the seeds, and transforms, generating the [other] seven consciousnesses. All [eight consciousnesses] evolve and manifest their own perceiving subject and perceived objects, none of which are substantial entities.

[709c1] How do they evolve? [The Ch'eng wei-shih lun] says: "Because of the influence of the karmically conditioned predispositions of the discrimination of self and things [in the ālayavijñāna], when the consciousnesses are engendered [from the ālayavijñāna], they evolve into the semblance of a self and things." The sixth and seventh consciousness, because they are obscured by ignorance, "consequently cling to [their subjective and objective manifestations] as a substantial self and substantial things."

[709c3] "It is like the case of being ill (in grave illness the mind is befuddled and perceives people and things in altered guise) or dreaming (the activity of dreaming and what is seen in the dream may be distinguished). Because of the influence of the illness or dream, the mind manifests itself in the semblance of the phenomenal appearance of a variety of external objects." When one is dreaming, one clings to them as substantially existing external things, but, as soon as one awakens, one realizes that they were merely the transformations of the dream. One's own bodily existence is also like this: it is merely the transformation of consciousness. Because [beings] are deluded, they cling to [these transformations] as existing self and objects, and, as a result of this, generate delusion and create karma, and birth-and-death is without end (as amply explained before). As soon as one realizes this principle, one understands that our bodily existence is merely the transformation of consciousness and that consciousness constitutes the root of bodily existence ([this teaching is of] non-final meaning, as will be refuted later).

[4. The Teaching That Refutes Phenomenal Appearances]

[709c9] 4. The Teaching of the Great Vehicle That Refutes Phenomenal Appearances refutes the attachment to the phenomenal appearances of the dharmas in the previous [teachings of] the Great

and Lesser Vehicles and intimates the principle of the emptiness and tranquility of the true nature in the later [teaching]. [709c10] (Discussions that refute phenomenal appearances are not limited to the various sections of the Perfection of Wisdom but pervade the scriptures of the Great Vehicle. [Although] the previous three teachings are arranged on the basis of their temporal order, [since] this teaching refutes them in accordance with their attachments, it [was taught] without a fixed time period. Therefore Nāgārjuna posited two types of wisdom: the first is the common, and the second is the distinct. The common refers to [that which the followers of] the two vehicles alike heard, believed, and understood, because it refuted the attachment to dharmas of [the followers of] the two vehicles. The distinct refers to [that which] only the bodhisattvas understood, because it intimated the Buddha-nature. [709c12] Therefore the two Indian śāstra-masters Śīlabhadra and Jñānaprabha each categorized the teachings according to three time periods, but in their placing of this teaching of emptiness, one said that it was before [the Teaching of] the Phenomenal Appearances of the Dharmas of consciousness-only, while the other said that it was after. Now I will take it to be after.)

[709c13] Wishing to refute [the Teaching of the Phenomenal Appearances of the Dharmas], I will first assess [the previous teaching] critically. Granted that the object that has evolved is illusory, how, then, can the consciousness that evolves be real? If one says that one exists and the other does not (from here on their analogy will be used to refute them), then the activity of dreaming and the things seen [in the dream] should be different. If they are different, then the dream not being the things [seen in the dream] and the things [seen in the dream] not being the dream, when one awakens and the dream is over, the things [seen in the dream] should remain. Again, the things [seen in the dream], if they are not the dream, must be real things, but how does the dream, if it is not the things [seen in the dream], assume phenomenal appearance? Therefore we know that when one dreams, the activity of dreaming and the things seen in the dream resemble the dichotomy of seeing and seen. Logically, then, they are equally unreal and altogether lack existence. [709c19] The various consciousnesses are also like this because they all provisionally rely on sundry causes and conditions and are devoid of a nature of their own. Therefore the *Middle Stanzas* says: "There has never been a single thing that has not been born from causes and conditions. Therefore there is nothing that is not empty." And further: "Things born by causes and conditions I declare to be empty." The *Awakening of Faith* says: "It is only on the basis of deluded thinking that all things have differentiations.

If one is free from thinking, then there are no phenemenal appearances of any objects." The [*Diamond*] *Sūtra* says: "All phenomenal appearances are illusory." Those who are free from all phenomenal appearances are called Buddhas. (Passages like these pervade the canon of the Great Vehicle.) Thus we know that mind and objects both being empty is precisely the true principle of the Great Vehicle. If we inquire into the origin of bodily existence in terms of this [teaching], then bodily existence is from the beginning empty, and emptiness itself is its basis.

[709c26] Now I will also assess this Teaching [That Refutes Phenomenal Appearances] critically. If the mind and its objects are both nonexistent, then who is it that knows they do not exist? Again, if there are no real things whatsoever, then on the basis of what are the illusions made to appear? Moreover, there has never been a case of the illusory things in the world before us being able to arise without being based on something real. [709c29] If there were no water whose wet nature were unchanging, how could there be the waves of illusory, provisional phenomenal appearances? If there were no mirror whose pure brightness were unchanging, how could there be the reflections of a variety of unreal phenomena? Again, while the earlier statement that the activity of dreaming and the dream object are equally unreal is indeed true, the dream that is illusory must still be based on someone who is sleeping. Now, granted that the mind and its objects are both empty, it is still not clear on what the illusory manifestations are based. Therefore we know that this teaching merely destroys feelings of attachment but does not yet clearly reveal the nature that is true and numinous. Therefore the *Great Dharma Drum Sūtra* says: "All emptiness sūtras are expositions that have a remainder." ("Having a remainder" means that the remaining meaning has not yet been fully expounded.) The *Great Perfection of Wisdom Sūtra* says: "Emptiness is the first gate of the Great Vehicle."

[710a6] When the above four teachings are compared with one another in turn, the earlier will be seen to be superficial and the later profound. If someone studies [a teaching] for a time, and oneself realizes that it is not yet ultimate, [that teaching] is said to be superficial. But if one clings to [such a teaching] as ultimate, then one is said to be partial. Therefore it is in terms of the people who study them that [the teachings] are spoken of as partial and superficial.

### III. DIRECTLY REVEALING THE TRUE SOURCE

(The true teaching of the ultimate meaning of the Buddha.)

## [5. The Teaching That Reveals the Nature]

[710a11] 5. The Teaching of the One Vehicle That Reveals the Nature holds that all sentient beings without exception have the intrinsically enlightened, true mind. From [time] without beginning it is permanently abiding and immaculate. It is shining, unobscured, clear and bright ever-present awareness. It is also called the Buddha-nature and it is also called the tathāgatagarbha. From time without beginning deluded thoughts cover it, and [sentient beings] by themselves are not aware of it. Because they only recognize their inferior qualities, they become indulgently attached, enmeshed in karma, and experience the suffering of birth-and-death. The great enlightened one took pity upon them and taught that everything without exception is empty. He further revealed that the purity of the numinous enlightened true mind is wholly identical with all Buddhas.

[710a16] Therefore the *Hua-yen Sūtra* says: "Oh sons of the Buddha, there is not a single sentient being that is not fully endowed with the wisdom of the Tathāgata. It is only on account of their deluded thinking and attachments that they do not succeed in realizing it. When they become free from deluded thinking, the all-comprehending wisdom, the spontaneous wisdom, and the unobstructed wisdom will then be manifest before them." [710a19] [The sūtra] then offers the analogy of a single speck of dust containing a sūtra roll [as vast as] the great chiliocosm. The speck of dust represents sentient beings, and the sūtra represents the wisdom of the Buddha. [710a20] [The *Hua-yen Sūtra*] then goes on to say: "At that time the Tathāgata with his unobstructed pure eye of wisdom universally beheld all sentient beings throughout the universe and said: 'How amazing! How amazing! How can it be that these sentient beings are fully endowed with the wisdom of the Tathāgata and yet, being ignorant and confused, do not know it and do not see it? I must teach them the noble path enabling them to be forever free from deluded thinking and to achieve for themselves the seeing of the broad and vast wisdom of the Tathāgata within themselves and so be no different from the Buddhas.'"

[710a24] [I will now] elaborate on [this teaching]. Because for numerous kalpas we have not encountered the true teaching, we have not known how to turn back and find the [true] origin of our

bodily existence but have just clung to illusory phenomenal appearances, heedlessly recognizing [only] our unenlightened nature, being born sometimes as an animal and sometimes as a human. When
we now seek our origin in terms of the consummate teaching, we
will immediately realize that from the very outset we are the Buddha.
Therefore, we should base our actions on the Buddha's action and
identify our minds with Buddha's mind, return to the origin and
revert to the source, and cut off our residue of ignorance, reducing
it and further reducing it until we have reached the [state of being]
unconditioned. Then our activity in response [to other beings] will
naturally be [as manifold as] the sands of the Ganges—that is called
Buddhahood. You should realize that delusion and enlightenment
alike are [manifestations of] the one true mind. How great the marvelous gate! Our inquiry into the origin of humanity has here come
to an end.

[710a29] (In the Buddha's preaching of the previous five teachings, some
are gradual and some are sudden. In the case of [sentient beings of] medium
and inferior capacity, [the Buddha] proceeded from the superficial to the profound, gradually leading them forward. He would initially expound the first
teaching [of Humans and Gods], enabling them to be free from evil and to
abide in virtue; he would then expound the second and third [teachings of the
Lesser Vehicle and the Phenomenal Appearances of the Dharmas], enabling
them to be free from impurity and to abide in purity; he would finally discuss
the fourth and fifth [teachings], those that Refute Phenomenal Appearances and
Reveal the Nature, subsuming the provisional into the true, [enabling them] to
cultivate virtue in reliance on the ultimate teaching until they finally attain
Buddhahood. [710b2] In the case of [sentient beings of] wisdom of the highest
caliber, [the Buddha] proceeded from the root to the branch. That is to say,
from the start he straightaway relied on the fifth teaching to point directly
to the essence of the one true mind. When the essence of the mind had
been revealed, [these sentient beings] themselves realized that everything
without exception is illusory and fundamentally empty and tranquil; that it
is only because of delusion that [such illusory appearances] arise in dependence upon the true [nature]; and that it is [thus] necessary to cut off evil
and cultivate virtue by means of the insight of having awakened to the true,
and to put an end to the false and return to the true by cultivating virtue.
When the false is completely exhausted and the true is present in totality,
that is called the dharmakāya Buddha.)

## IV. Reconciling Root and Branch

### [The Process of Phenomenal Evolution]

[710b4] (When [the teachings that] have been refuted previously are subsumed together into the one source, they all become true.) [710b5] Although the true nature constitutes the [ultimate] source of bodily existence, its arising must surely have a causal origin, for the phenomenal appearance of bodily existence cannot be suddenly formed from out of nowhere. It is only because the previous traditions had not yet fully discerned [the matter] that I have refuted them one by one. Now I will reconcile root and branch, including even Confucianism and Taoism.

[710b7] (At first there is only that which is set forth in the fifth teaching of the Nature. From the following section on, [each] stage [in the process of phenomenal evolution] will be correlated with the various teachings, as will be explained in the notes.) At first there is only the one true numinous nature, which is neither born nor destroyed, neither increases nor decreases, and neither changes nor alters. [Nevertheless], sentient beings are [from time] without beginning asleep in delusion and are not themselves aware of it. Because it is covered over, it is called the tathāgatagarbha, and the phenomenal appearance of the mind that is subject to birth-and-death comes into existence based on the tathāgatagarbha.

[710b10] (From here on corresponds to the fourth teaching, which is the same as [that which] Refuted the Phenomenal Appearances that are subject to birth-and-death.) The interfusion of the true mind that is not subject to birth-and-death and deluded thoughts that are subject to birth-and-death in such a way that they are neither one nor different is referred to as the ālayavijñāna. This consciousness has the aspects both of enlightenment and unenlightenment.

[710b13] (From here on corresponds to that which was taught in the third teaching of the Phenomenal Appearances of the Dharmas.) When thoughts first begin to stir because of the unenlightened aspect [of the ālayavijñāna], it is referred to as the phenomenal appearance of activity. Because [sentient beings] are also unaware that these thoughts are from the beginning nonexistent, [the ālayavijñāna] transforms into the manifestation of the phenomenal appearance of a perceiving subject and its perceived objects. Moreover, being unaware that these objects are deludedly manifested from their own mind, [sentient beings] cling to them as fixed existents, and that is referred to as attachment to things.

[710b16] (From here on corresponds to that which was taught in the second teaching of the Lesser Vehicle.) Because they cling to these, [sentient beings] then perceive a difference between self and others and immediately form an attachment to the self. Because they cling to the phenomenal appearance of a self, they hanker after things that accord with their feelings, hoping thereby to enhance themselves, and have an aversion to things that go against their feelings, fearing that they will bring harm to themselves. Their foolish feelings thus continue to escalate ever further.

[710b19] (From here on corresponds to that which was taught in the first teaching of Humans and Gods.) Therefore, when one commits [evil deeds] such as murder or theft, one's spirit, impelled by this bad karma, is born among the denizens of hell, hungry ghosts, or animals. Again, when one who dreads suffering or is virtuous by nature practices [good deeds] such as bestowing alms or maintaining the precepts, one's spirit, impelled by this good karma, is transported through the intermediate existence into the mother's womb (from here on corresponds to that which was taught in the two teachings of Confucianism and Taoism) and receives an endowment of vital force and material substance. ([This] incorporates their statement that the vital force constitutes the origin.)

[710b23] The moment there is vital force, the four elements are fully present and gradually form the sense organs; the moment there is mind, the four [mental] aggregates are fully present and form consciousness. When ten [lunar] months have come to fruition and one is born, one is called a human being. This refers to our present body-and-mind. Therefore we know that the body and mind each has its origin and that as soon as the two interfuse, they form a single human. It is virtually the same as this in the case of gods, titans, and so forth.

[710b26] While one receives this bodily existence as a result of one's directive karma, one is in addition honored or demeaned, impoverished or wealthy, long or short lived, ill or healthy, flourishes or declines, suffers or is happy, because of one's particularizing karma. That is to say, when the respect or contempt shown [to others] in a previous existence serves as the cause, it determines the result of one's being honored or demeaned in the present, and so on and so forth to the humane being long-lived, the murderous short-lived, the generous wealthy, and the miserly impoverished. The various types of individual retribution [are so diverse that they] could not be fully enumerated. Therefore, in this bodily existence,

while there may be cases of those who are without evil and even so suffer disaster, or those who are without virtue and even so enjoy bounty, or who are cruel and yet are long-lived, or who do not kill and yet are short-lived, all have been determined by the particularizing karma of a previous lifetime. Therefore the way things are in the present lifetime does not come about from what is done spontaneously. Scholars of the outer teachings do not know of previous existences but, relying on [only] what is visible, just adhere to their belief in spontaneity. ([This] incorporates their statement that spontaneity constitutes the origin.)

[710c5] Moreover, there are those who in a previous life cultivated virtue when young and perpetuated evil when old, or else were evil in their youth and virtuous in their old age; and who hence in their present lifetime enjoy moderate wealth and honor when young and suffer great impoverishment and debasement when old, or else experience the suffering of impoverishment in youth and enjoy wealth and honor in old age. Thus scholars of the outer teachings just adhere to their belief that success and failure are due to the sway of fortune. ([This] incorporates their statement that everything is due to the mandate of heaven.)

[710c8] Nevertheless, the vital force with which we are endowed, when it is traced all the way back to its origin, is the primal pneuma of the undifferentiated oneness; and the mind that arises, when it is thoroughly investigated all the way back to its source, is the numinous mind of the absolute. In ultimate terms, there is nothing outside of mind. The primal pneuma also comes from the evolution of mind, belongs to the category of the objects that were manifested by the previously evolved consciousness, and is included within the objective aspect of the ālaya[vijñāna]. From the phenomenal appearance of the activation of the very first thought, [the ālayavijñāna] divides into the dichotomy of mind and objects. The mind, having developed from the subtle to the coarse, continues to evolve from false speculation to the generation of karma (as previously set forth). Objects likewise develop from the fine to the crude, continuing to evolve from the transformation [of the ālayavijñāna] into heaven and earth. (The beginning for them starts with the grand interchangeability and evolves in five phases to the great ultimate. The great ultimate [then] produces the two elementary forms. Even though they speak of spontaneity and the great Way as we here speak of the true nature, they are actually nothing but the subjective aspect of the evolution [of the ālayavijñāna] in a single moment of thought; even though they talk of the primal pneuma as we here

speak of the initial movement of a single moment of thought, it is actually nothing but the phenomenal appearance of the objective world.) When karma has ripened, then one receives one's endowment of the two vital forces from one's father and mother, and, when it has interfused with activated consciousness, the human body is completely formed. According to this, the objects that are transformed from conscious-ness immediately form two divisions: one division is that which interfuses with consciousness to form human beings, while the other division does not interfuse with consciousness and is that which forms heaven and earth, mountains and rivers, and states and towns. The fact that only humans among the three powers [of heaven, earth, and humanity] are spiritual is due to their being fused with spirit. This is precisely what the Buddha meant when he said that the internal four elements and the external four elements are not the same.

[710c21] How pitiable the confusion of the false attachments of shallow scholars! Followers of the Way, heed my words: If you want to attain Buddhahood, you must thoroughly discern the coarse and the subtle, the root and the branch. Only then will you be able to cast aside the branch, return to the root, and turn your light back upon the mind source. When the coarse has been exhausted and the subtle done away with, the numinous nature is clearly manifest and there is nothing that is not penetrated. That is called the dhar-makāya and sambhogakāya. Freely manifesting oneself in response to beings without any bounds is called the nirmāṇakāya Buddha.

# ANNOTATED TRANSLATION
# AND COMMENTARY

# Tsung-mi's Preface

All indications suggest that the *Inquiry into the Origin of Humanity* was written for one of Tsung-mi's lay disciples or scholar-official friends. It at once affords a broad overview of different Buddhist teachings in terms that could be understood by someone unfamiliar with the technicalities of Buddhist scholastic thought at the same time that it provides a context in which Confucian and Taoist teachings could be evaluated in the same framework as Buddhist teachings. In the essay Tsung-mi adopts the framework of doctrinal classification from Buddhist scholastic literature but goes beyond earlier Buddhist classification schemes in including Confucianism and Taoism within his overall purview—a move that makes sense in light of the literati audience to which it is addressed. In this context it is also important to note that in the Preface Tsung-mi begins by defining the basic problematic of his work in terms drawn from the Chinese classical tradition. The Preface is written in an elegant classical style, in which Tsung-mi demonstrates his virtuosity in making deft use of classical allusions—a skill that would not have been lost on a literati audience. The allusions to Confucian and Taoist texts would have struck a ready chord among such readers, who would have known the texts in question by heart. The opening paragraph, for example, contains allusions to the *Lao-tzu, Classic of Change, Analects,* and *Classic of History.* These allusions would have evoked a chain of associations that would have given rhetorical force to Tsung-mi's argument, and it is only by elucidating them that we can clarify the invisible web of associations that would have linked them together in the minds of his readership.

The Preface can be divided into four sections. The first formulates the fundamental problem Tsung-mi addresses in the *Inquiry,* the second mentions some provisional answers, the third introduces the hermeneutical principle by which the different teachings (Buddhist and non-Budddhist alike) are organized, and the fourth outlines the structure of the essay. The subheadings I have accordingly supplied in this chapter are my own and do not appear in the original text.

### THE FUNDAMENTAL PROBLEM

What is particularly noteworthy is that instead of posing the problem of the origin of humanity from the Buddhist perspective of causes and conditions, Tsung-mi begins his essay by stating the fundamental issue in terms that were of paramount significance in Chinese thought prior to the introduction of Buddhism.

> [707c25] 萬靈蠢蠢皆有其本。萬物芸芸各歸其根。未有無根本而有枝末者也、況三才中之最靈而無本源乎。且知人者智、自知者明。今我稟得人身而不自知所從來、曷能知他世所趣乎、曷能知天下古今之人事乎。故數十年中學無常師、博攷內外以原自身。原之不已果得其本。

[707c25] The myriad animate beings teeming with activity—all have their origin. The myriad things flourishing in profusion—each returns to its root. Since there has never been anything that is without a root or origin and yet has branches or an end, how much less could [humanity,] the most spiritual among the three powers [of the cosmos, i.e., heaven, earth, and humanity,] be without an original source? Moreover, one who knows the human is wise, and one who knows himself is illuminated. Now, if I have received a human body and yet do not know for myself whence I have come, how can I know whither I will go in another life, and how can I understand human affairs of the past and present in the world? For this reason, I have studied for several decades without a constant teacher and have thoroughly examined the inner and outer [teachings] in order to find the origin of myself. I sought it without cease until I realized its origin.

The parallel structure of the first two sentences in this passage indicates that the first is modeled after the second, which is quoted from chapter 16 of the *Lao-tzu*. The *Lao-tzu* passage continues: "Returning to one's root is called stillness. This is what is meant by returning to one's destiny. Returning to one's destiny is called the eternal. Knowing the eternal is called illumination."[1] Tsung-mi's

---

1. Cf. the translation of Lau, p. 72.

quotation of this passage thus sets up the association for the quotation from chapter 33 of the *Lao-tzu* that occurs two sentences later ("one who knows the human is wise, and one who knows himself is illuminated").[2] Knowing the root from which all things issue and to which all things return is illumination, and illumination is no other than knowing oneself. The eternal, of course, refers to the Way (*tao* 道), which throughout the *Lao-tzu* is described as the original source and progenitor of all things.[3]

Knowing whence one has come and whither one will go in another life thus corresponds to knowing oneself, and knowing human affairs of the past and present in the world corresponds to knowing the human. As Yüan-chüeh remarks in his commentary, the first constitutes knowing the root (*pen* 本), while the second constitutes knowing the branches (*mo* 末), and one cannot truly know the branches until one knows the root.[4]

Root and branch(es) form a conceptual pair that is fundamental for understanding Tsung-mi's thought as presented in his *Inquiry*. The root stands for the ultimate ontological basis on which all phenomenal things (i.e., the branches) are grounded and out of which all phenomenal things evolve. The branches are thus nothing but phenomenal manifestations of the root. "Root" refers to what is primary, absolute, unchanging, unconditioned, eternal, and profound, whereas "branch" refers to what is derivative, relative, variable, conditioned, transient, and superficial. Root and branch thus correlate with other conceptual pairs used throughout the *Inquiry,* the most important of which are nature (*hsing* 性) and phenomenal appearances (*hsiang* 相).[5] In the succeeding parts of the *Inquiry,* Confucianism, Taoism, and various teachings of Buddhism are all ranked according to the relative degree of profundity with which they answer the question of the ultimate ontological basis of human

2. Although the *chih jen* 知人 in the quotation from chapter 33 of the *Lao-tzu* is usually rendered as "knowing others," it has here been translated as "knows the human" because this sentence serves as the basis for the one that follows. Cf. Lau's translation, p. 92.

3. Although Tsung-mi later criticizes the view of the Way as eternal (*ch'ang* 常), universal (*pien* 遍), and being able to engender all things (*neng-sheng* 能生), no criticism is intended at this point.

4. *Chieh* 110a.

5. Root and branch would further correspond respectively to essence (*t'i* 體) and function (*yung* 用), and absolute (*li* 理) and phenomenal (*shih* 事).

existence. Only that teaching that penetrates to the root of the question is ultimate, all the others are provisional.

According to the *Classic of Change,* the "three powers" (*san-ts'ai* 三才) that Tsung-mi refers to in the third sentence of the opening section are heaven, earth, and humanity.[6] The most spiritual (*ling* 靈) among them refers to humanity, as is stated in the *Classic of History:* "Heaven and earth are the father and mother of the myriad things, and it is humanity that is [the most] spiritual of the myriad things."[7]

Tsung-mi's claim that he "studied for several decades without a constant teacher" alludes to a passage in the *Analects* that was frequently cited by his literati contemporaries:

> Kung-sun Ch'ao of Wei asked Tzu-kung: "From whom did Chung-ni [Confucius] learn?" Tzu-kung replied: "The Way of [kings] Wen and Wu has not yet fallen to the ground and is to be found among men. The worthy recognize what is of major significance, and the unworthy recognize what is of minor significance. There are none who do not possess the Way of Wen and Wu within themselves. From whom, then, does the master not learn? What need did he thus have for a constant teacher?"[8]

In his "Discourse on Teachers," for example, Han Yü alludes to this passage when he writes: "A sage has no constant teacher."[9]

The "inner" (*nei* 內) and "outer" (*wai* 外) teachings that Tsung-mi mentions at the end of the opening section of the Preface refer to Buddhism, on the one hand, and Confucianism and Taoism, on the other.[10] The designation of the two teachings of Confucianism

6. See Sung, *The Text of the Yi King,* 333 and 340.

7. Cf. Legge's translation in *The Chinese Classics* 3.283; elsewhere I translate *ling* 靈 as "numinous."

8. 19.22, as translated by Legge, *The Chinese Classics* 1.346 (the transliterated Chinese that appears in parentheses in the original has been omitted).

9. Charles Hartman, *Han Yü and the T'ang Search for Unity,* p. 164. Hartman goes on to comment that Han Yü's emphasis that the sage had no constant teacher was a natural corollary to his egalitarianism (p. 166). Tsung-mi's use of this phrase may also more distantly resonate with the wisdom that is without a teacher (*wu-shih-chih* 無師智) found in Buddhist texts.

10. *Wai* (outer) is an abbreviation of *wai-tao* 外道, which was used to translate the Sanskrit term *tīrthika,* meaning an adherent of another (i.e., non-Buddhist) school.

and Taoism as "outer" not only means that they are outside of the Buddhist tradition but also connotes the Buddhist judgment of them as inferior for dealing only with "outer"—that is, external and therefore superficial or worldly—matters (such as human affairs in the past and present). The scale on which Tsung-mi ranks the various teachings he considers within his *Inquiry* can thus be seen as moving from outer to inner—hence the inner/outer polarity overlaps with that of root/branch.

### PROVISIONAL EXPLANATIONS

The second section of the Preface anticipates some of the major points that Tsung-mi develops in the first two parts of his essay— those dealing with Confucianism and Taoism, on the one hand, and those dealing with the first three Buddhist teachings, on the other.

[708a2]　然今習儒道者、祇知近則乃祖乃父、傳體相續
受得此身。遠則混沌一氣剖為陰陽之二、二生天地人三、
三生萬物。萬物與人皆氣為本。

[708a2] Now those who study Confucianism and Taoism merely know that, when looked at in proximate terms, they have received this body from their ancestors and fathers[11] having passed down the bodily essence in a continuous series. When looked at in far-reaching terms, the one pneuma of the primordial chaos divided into the dyad of yin and yang, the two engendered the triad of heaven, earth, and human beings, and the three engendered the myriad things. The myriad things and human beings all have the pneuma as their origin.

In most superficial terms, Confucians explain our present human existence as a biological inheritance from our ancestors. Elsewhere Tsung-mi notes: "What the outer teachings take as their cardinal principle is that humans have material form as their basis and pass down their bodily essence in a continuous series."[12] This idea is echoed in the *Classic of Filiality*: "The son derives his life from his parents and no greater gift could possibly be transmit-

---

11. The expression *nai tsu nai fu* 乃祖乃父 comes from the *Shu ching;* cf. Legge's translation in *The Chinese Classics* 3.239 and 240.

12. *Yü-lan-p'en ching shu,* T 39.508a11.

ted."[13] In more profound terms, Taoists explain human existence and that of the manifold universe as being based on the Way. The present passage from the Preface alludes to the cosmogony contained in chapter 42 of the *Lao-tzu:* "The Way engenders the one; the one engenders the two; the two engender the three; and the three engender the myriad things." This cosmogonic scenario is combined with another that pictures the universe as beginning in a state of undifferentiatedness, which divides into a primal polarity of yang and yin, the masculine and feminine forces (of heaven and earth, light and dark, active and passive, and so forth) that emerge when the primordial chaos (*hun-tun* 混沌) split; the universe of diversified phenomena was generated through their intercourse and continues to operate according to the rhythms of their dynamic interaction.[14]

"Pneuma" here renders the Chinese *ch'i* 氣, a notoriously difficult term to translate[15] because it overlaps categories that we tend to think of as distinct—such as energy and matter, or mental and physical. Etymologically it traces back to a graph meaning "breath," "air," and "vapor."[16] A. C. Graham indicates the range of meaning encompassed by this term:

> *Ch'i,* a common and elusive word in ordinary Chinese speech as well as in philosophy, covers a number of concepts for which we have different names in English or none at all. Unlike the abstract *li* [理, principle] . . . , *ch'i* is quite concrete; it really is, among other things, the breath in our throats. It is the source of life, dispersing into the air at death; we breathe it in and out, and feel it rising and ebbing in our bodies as physical energy, swelling when we are angry, failing in a limb which grows numb; we smell it as odours, feel it as heat or cold, sense it as the air or atmosphere of a person or a place, as the vitality of a poem,

---

13. *Hsiao ching* 4/9/5, as translated by Legge in *The Sacred Books of China* 1.479.

14. For a discussion of the importance of the theme of primordial chaos (*hun-tun*) in Chinese cosmogonic myths, see Girardot, *Myth and Meaning in Early Taoism.* See also the reviews by Hal Roth and Sarah Allan.

15. As a philosophical concept, it has been variously rendered as "vital force" (Bodde), "material force" (Chan), "ether of materialization" (Metzger), "pneuma" (Needham, Schafer), "ether" (Graham), "breath" (Watson), etc.

16. See Bernhard Karlgren, *Analytic Dictionary of Chinese and Sino-Japanese,* p. 120.

or as the breath of spring which quickens and the breath of autumn which withers; we even see it condensing as vapour or mist.[17]

When *ch'i* is used to designate a cosmogonic force (i.e., *yüan-ch'i* 元氣 or *i-ch'i* 一氣), I have translated it as "pneuma." "Pneuma" is at once faithful to the etymological meaning of *ch'i* as well as being sufficiently vague to intimate the elusive and metaphysical character of *ch'i* as a cosmogonic term. When Tsung-mi uses *ch'i* to refer to an individual's endowment of life, however, I have translated it as "vital force."

Tsung-mi goes on to mention various Buddhist theories of the origin of human existence.

[708a5] 習佛法者、但云近則前生造業隨業受報得此人身。遠則業又從惑展轉乃至阿賴耶識為身根本。皆謂已窮而實未也。

[708a5] **Those who study Buddhism just say that, when looked at in proximate terms, they created karma in a previous life and, receiving their retribution in accord with karma, gained this human body. When looked at in far-reaching terms, karma, in turn, develops from delusion, and ultimately the ālayavijñāna constitutes the origin of bodily existence. All [i.e., Confucianists, Taoists, and Buddhists] maintain that they have come to the end of the matter, but, in truth, they have not yet exhausted it.**

Tsung-mi here mentions the basic explanations of the origin of human existence offered by the first three Buddhist teachings he discusses in the *Inquiry,* and they will accordingly be treated in detail in later chapters. "Karma" (*yeh* 業) means "action" or "deed" and is broadly construed in Buddhism to include physical, verbal, or mental actions. Karma is the central content of the most elementary Buddhist teaching, the Teaching of Humans and Gods, which explains how good and bad actions in one lifetime lead to pleasurable or woeful rebirth in different modes of existence in a future life.

17. *Two Chinese Philosophers,* p. 31. In his *A Source Book in Chinese Philosophy,* Wing-tsit Chan notes: "*ch'i* as opposed to *li* (Principle) means both energy and matter. . . . In many cases, especially before the Neo-Confucian doctrine of *li* developed, *ch'i* denotes the psycho-physiological power associated with blood and breath. As such it is translated as 'vital force' or 'vital powers'" (p. 784).

Karma, of course, arises from delusion, and delusion arises from attachment. According to the Buddhist understanding of the human condition, the fundamental delusion is that there is an autonomous self (*ātman; wo* 我) that is separate from everything else. The very notion of self is predicated on a bifurcation of experience into subject and object, which leads to attachment to "self" and "things" (*dharma; fa* 法).[18] The attachment to the self as a substantial entity is eliminated by the second teaching, that of the Lesser Vehicle, whose teaching of conditioned origination (*pratītyasamutpāda; yüan-ch'i* 緣起) undermines beings' belief in a substantial self by showing that what they cling to as their "self" is really only a complex of factors that provisionally come together as a result of various causes and conditions. The attachment to things (dharmas) as substantial entities is overcome by the next teaching, that of the Phenomenal Appearances of the Dharmas. This teaching reveals that the false concepts of self and things that beings cling to are merely projections of an underlying consciousness, the ālayavijñāna, and thus have no independent reality of their own. The ālayavijñāna is one of the most difficult terms that Tsung-mi uses in his *Inquiry,* and its meaning will be more fully explained in the chapter on the Teaching of the Phenomenal Appearances of the Dharmas. For now it should suffice to note that "ālaya" means "store," "receptacle," or "repository." The ālayavijñāna is thus the consciousness in which all experiences are stored as karmically-charged "seeds," which, under the proper conditions, "ripen" as actions (whether mental, verbal, or physical), which in turn create new seeds. Hence the ālayavijñāna designates the underlying consciousness on which the process of delusion is based.[19]

18. The term *dharma* (*fa* 法) has a broad range of meanings in Buddhism. Most generally it refers to the teaching of the Buddha and, by extension, the eternal truth (the Buddha's enlightenment consisted in his insight into the dharma). Often it is simply used to mean "thing." It is also used in a more technical sense, as developed in the dharma theory of the Abhidharma literature: the dharmas are the elementary categories into which all experience can be analyzed.

19. In his commentary to this passage, Yüan-chüeh gives a more technical amplification of this process. He explains that just as karma develops from delusion, so delusion arises from attachment. Moreover, there are two types of attachment: the attachment to a self as a substantial entity (*ātmagrāha; wo-chih* 我執), and the attachment to things (dharmas) as substantial entities (*dharmagrāha; fa-chih* 法執). The delusion that arises

Here it is important to note a point whose significance will only become fully clear later. In his summary of various provisional explanations above, Tsung-mi does not mention the fourth Buddhist teaching (that which Refutes Phenomenal Appearances) because its teaching of emptiness has no positive content and thus can say nothing about the origin of human existence; as we shall see, for Tsung-mi its function is purely negative—to destroy deluded attachments.

Tsung-mi concludes this passage by noting that none of the Confucian, Taoist, or Buddhist teachings mentioned so far are ultimate, thereby laying the ground for the distinction between the provisional (*ch'üan* 權) and ultimate (*shih* 實) teachings that he introduces at the end the following section of the Preface. Tsung-mi uses "provisional" and "ultimate" synonymously with a different set of terms for a distinction made early in the history of Buddhism between teachings of "nonultimate meaning" (*neyārtha; pu-liao-i* 不了義) and those of "ultimate meaning" (*nītārtha; liao-i* 了義).[20] This distinction, in turn, was related to that between conventional (*samvṛti; su* 俗) and ultimate (*paramārtha; chen* 眞) truth, and as such was also connected with expedient means (*upāya; fang-pien* 方便), the hermeneutical principle that Tsung-mi uses to organize

---

on account of attachment to self is the obstruction of the defilements that cause rebirth (*kleśāvaraṇa; fan-nao chang* 煩惱障); the delusion that arises on account of attachment to things is the obstruction that hinders knowledge (*jñeyāvaraṇa; so-chih chang* 所知障). Yüan-chüeh goes on to comment that the Teaching of the Lesser Vehicle (Hīnayāna) merely cuts off attachment to self and the obstruction of the defilements whereas that of the Great Vehicle (Mahāyāna) cuts off both kinds of obstructions resulting from both kinds of attachment. Furthermore, self (*ātman; wo* 我) and things (*dharma; fa* 法) are merely representations based on the transformation of consciousness; the fundamental consciousness from which all the others evolve is the ālayavijñāna. See *Chieh* 110d-111a.

20. *Nītārtha* consists of two elements: *nīta* and *artha* (meaning). *Nīta* is the past participle of *nī*, "to lead." The compound thus literally means "the meaning that has been led to." *Neyārtha* also consists of two elements: *neya* and *artha*. *Neya* is the future passive participle of *nī*. The compound thus literally means "the meaning that is to be led to." See Edgerton, *Buddhist Hybrid Sanskrit Dictionary*, pp. 310b and 311b, and Monier-Williams, *A Sanskrit-English Dictionary*, pp. 565a and 596b. The Pāli terms—*nītattha* and *neyattha*—can be analyzed in the same way; see Rhys Davids and Stede, *Pāli-English Dictionary*, pp. 310b and 311b.

the different teachings into a coherent whole. Those teachings taught by the Buddha as expedients to prepare his followers for his ultimate message are all provisional.

## ORGANIZING PRINCIPLE

The next section of the Preface introduces the main principle according to which Tsung-mi's *Inquiry* is organized.

> [708a7] 然孔老釋迦皆是至聖、隨時應物設教殊塗。内
> 外相資共利群庶。策勤萬行、明因果始終、推究萬法、彰
> 生起本末、雖皆聖意而有實有權。二教唯權、佛兼權實。
> 策萬行懲惡勸善同歸於治、則三教皆可遵行。推萬法窮理
> 盡性至於本源、則佛教方為決了。

[708a7] Still, Confucius, Lao-tzu, and Śākyamuni were consummate sages who, in accord with the times and in response to beings, made different paths in setting up their teachings. The inner and outer [teachings] complement one another, together benefiting the people. As for promoting the myriad [moral and religious] practices, clarifying cause and effect from beginning to end, exhaustively investigating the myriad phenomena, and elucidating the full scope of birth and arising—even though these are all the intention of the sages, there are still provisional and ultimate [explanations]. The two teachings are just provisional, whereas Buddhism includes both provisional and ultimate. Since encouraging the myriad practices, admonishing against evil, and promoting good contribute in common to order, the three teachings should all be followed and practiced. If it be a matter of investigating the myriad phenomena, fathoming principle, realizing the nature, and reaching the original source, then Buddhism alone constitutes the definitive answer.

Without explicitly mentioning it by name, this section introduces the doctrine of expedient means and illustrates its double function. That is, expedient means provides a rationale for subordinating some teachings to others at the same time that it provides a framework in which all those teachings can be integrated into a single, conceptually coherent whole. In most simple terms, the doctrine of expedient means holds that different teachings could be interpreted properly only by understanding the context in which they were preached. Accordingly, the Buddha, in expounding the eternal dharma, always expressed his teaching in terms that could be understood by his listeners within their own particular context. In this way, the many different and sometimes even conflicting doctrines, all of which were believed to have been taught by the Buddha, could be seen as a reflection of the differences in the capacities of his audience rather than differences in the eternal dharma itself.

In China, the same rubric was extended to the Chinese sages, as Tsung-mi does in the present passage. The differences between Confucianism and Taoism, on the one hand, and Buddhism, on the other, could thus be explained as arising out of the limitations set by the particular historical circumstances in which Confucius, Lao-tzu, and the Buddha lived and taught, rather than from any difference in the level of understanding attained by them. In this manner, the doctrine of expedient means serves as the major structuring device that enables Tsung-mi to arrange the different teachings he discusses in the *Inquiry* into a hierarchical order.

Yüan-chüeh's commentary illustrates how this doctrine works. He writes that since people's capacities had not yet matured in the time of Confucius and Lao-tzu, and they were thus not yet ready to hear even the most elementary teaching of cause and effect, how much less were they prepared to hear the ultimate teaching of Bud-dha-nature. Therefore Confucius first used the moral teaching of benevolence (*jen* 仁) and righteousness (*i* 義) to lead them gradu-ally forward, and Lao-tzu pointed to the primal pneuma as the or-igin. Yüan-chüeh goes on to say that even during the first part of the Buddha's teaching career the capacities of his disciples were not yet matured and they were also not yet ready to hear the ulti-mate teaching of Buddha-nature. Only after forty years of preparing them by expounding provisional teachings was the Buddha able to deliver his ultimate message.[21]

Tsung-mi was not the first to extend the rubric of expedient means to Chinese sages. It was a ploy that had long been used by Buddhist apologists in China. In the fourth century, for instance, Sun Ch'o had written in his *Essay on the Clarification of the Way* (*Yü-tao lun*):

> [The teachings of] the Duke of Chou and Confucius are identical to [those of] the Buddha, and [the teachings of] the Buddha are identical to [those of] the Duke of Chou and Confucius, for [the difference between] the inner and outer

21. *Chieh* 111b.

[teachings] is merely a matter of name. . . . [One who] responds to the world and guides beings is also [one who] accords with the times. The Duke of Chou and Confucius rescued [the world] from extreme evil, whereas the Buddha only taught and elucidated the fundamental. Together [the teachings of the Duke of Chou and Confucius and those of the Buddha] comprise head and tail and do not differ in their purpose.[22]

Nor was the idea that different teachings were expedient devices geared to fit the historical circumstances under which they were propounded exclusively found in Buddhism. Neo-Taoists of the third century had already developed their own version of this idea to account for the differences in the teachings of Confucius and Lao-tzu, both of whom they revered as sages. Zürcher rightly points out Sun Ch'o's equal debt to the Neo-Taoists:

By manipulating Hsiang Hsiu's distinction between *chi* 迹 "(manifested) traces (of the Saint)" and *so i chi* 所以迹 "(the Saint's inner nature) by which the traces are made," the author reduces all contrasts between Buddhism and Confucianism to a mere difference in expedient means. The "traces," i.e., the manifested doctrines of the Confucian sages and the Buddha, diverge on account of the different circumstances under which they were revealed and to which they were adapted, but the inner nature of these saints, the source and motive power of their teachings, is one and the same.[23]

The third section of the Preface is also particularly interesting because it reveals the ease and skill with which Tsung-mi was able to draw from his early education in the Confucian classics. The phrase "fathoming principle, realizing the nature, and reaching the ultimate source" (*ch'iung-li chin-hsing chih yü pen-yüan* 窮理盡性 至於本源), for instance, is modeled after the following passage from the *Classic of Change:* "By fathoming principle, [the sages] realized their nature and thereby reached what was appointed for it [by heaven]" (*ch'iung-li chin-hsing i chih yü ming* 窮理盡性以至於命).[24] Tsung-

---

22. T 52.17a7-11; for a study and translation of Sun Ch'o's treatise, see Arthur Link and Tim Lee, "Sun Ch'o's *Yü-tao-lun*."

23. *The Buddhist Conquest of China* 1.133.

24. For the Chinese text and Legge's translation, see Sung, *The Text of the Yi King,* pp. 338-339. As Hartman has discussed at length, the phrase

mi's phrase "contribute in common to order" (*t'ung-kuei yü chih* 同歸於治) is drawn from the *Classic of History:* "Acts of goodness are different, but they contribute in common to order. Acts of evil are different, but they contribute in common to disorder."[25] Tsung-mi's use of the phrase "contribute in common" (*t'ung-kuei* 同歸), moreover, recalls another pasage from the *Classic of Change:* "In all [the processes taking place] under heaven, what is there of thinking? What is there of anxious scheming? They all come to the same [successful] issue (*t'ung-kuei*), though by different paths (*shu-t'u* 殊塗); there is one result, though there might be a hundred anxious schemes."[26] The *Classic of Change* passage is of further importance in that it connects Tsung-mi's use of the phrase "contribute in common" (*t'ung-kuei*) with the phrase "different paths" (*shu-t'u*), which he used in the previous quotation when he said that the three sages "made different paths in setting up their teachings." Taken together, the phrase *shu-t'u t'ung-kuei* 殊塗同歸—which can be freely rendered as "the different paths ultimately lead to the same goal"—was used by Chinese Buddhists to characterize the universal teaching of the one vehicle associated with the *Lotus Sūtra,* according to which the teachings of the three vehicles (i.e., those of the śrāvaka, pratyekabuddha, and bodhisattva) were all subsumed into one all-inclusive vehicle of salvation.[27] Dharma master Chi of the Liu-Sung dynasty (420-479), for instance, classified the teaching of the *Lotus Sūtra* as the universal teaching (*t'ung-kuei chiao* 同歸教) because "it subsumes the three into the one" (*hui-san kuei-i* 會三歸一).[28] The phrase "the different paths ultimately lead to the same goal" thus provided Chinese Buddhists with a convenient formula for es-

---

*ch'iung-li chin-hsing* 窮理盡性 had a long history of use in Buddhist apologetics and was used by Han Yü and his contemporaries to articulate their new conception of the absolute; see his *Han Yü and the T'ang Search for Unity,* pp. 191-198.

25. I have slightly altered the translation by Legge in *The Chinese Classics* 3.490.

26. As translated by Legge in Sung, *The Text of the Yi King,* p. 316.

27. See especially chapters 2 and 3 (T 9.5b-16b; cf. Hurvitz, trans., *Scripture of the Lotus Blossum of the Fine Dharma,* pp. 22-83). Without going into the complexities of the terms here, suffice it to say that the first two vehicles (i.e., those of the śrāvaka and pratyekabuddha) refer to Hīnayāna or the Lesser Vehicle, while the third vehicle (i.e., that of the bodhisattva) refers to Mahāyāna or the Great Vehicle.

28. See T 35.508c21-23.

tablishing the ultimate identity of all the different teachings of the
Buddha. By the same token, the phrase was also used to assert the
ultimate identity of the three teachings and seems to have enjoyed
currency in this usage during the second half of the eighth century.[29]
Tsung-mi's use of the phrases "different paths" (*shu-t'u*) and "contribute in common" (*t'ung-kuei*) thus indicates that he thought of
the teaching of Buddhism—or, more accurately, the ultimate teaching of Buddhism—as embodying the universal truth toward which
all the other teachings lead and into which all the other teachings
are ultimately subsumed. It also reveals the sophistication with
which he was able to utilize classical allusions to establish a synthetic framework in which the teachings of Buddhism, Confucianism, and Taoism could be seen as but different expressions of the
one universal truth.[30]

### Structure of the Essay

The final section of the Preface outlines the structure of the *Inquiry*.

[708a13]　然當今學士各執一宗。就師佛者、仍迷實義、
故於天地人物不能原之至源。余今還依內外教理推窮萬
法。初從淺至深。於習權教者、斥滯令通而極其本。後依
了教、顯示展轉生起之義。會偏令圓而至於末（末即天地
人物）。文有四篇、名原人也。

[708a13] Nevertheless, scholars today each cling to a single
tradition.[31] Even those who follow the Buddha as their
teacher are often deluded about the true meaning and therefore, in seeking the origin of heaven, earth, humanity, and
things, are not able to find the ultimate source. I will now
proceed to investigate the myriad phenomena by relying on
the principles of the inner and outer teachings. First, I will

29. As seen, for example, in Chan-jan's *Chih-kuan fu-hsing chuan
hung-chüeh,* see T 46.441a8-9.

30. For Tsung-mi's explanation of *shu-t'u t'ung-kuei* 殊塗同歸, see
TSC 240b16-c2 (commenting on TS 112b6), which he quotes from Ch'eng-
kuan's *Yen-i ch'ao,* T 36.39b2-8 (see T 35.508a10). See also references to
the phrase in *Hung-ming chi,* T 52.43a16 and 72c14.

31. The word translated as "tradition" (*tsung* 宗) covers a wide
range of meaning. In the present case it also connotes the idea of the
"cardinal principle" on which different lineages or teaching traditions
base themselves.

advance from the superficial to the profound. For those who study provisional teachings, I will dig out their obstructions, allowing them to penetrate through and reach the ultimate origin. Later, I will demonstrate the meaning of phenomenal evolution by relying on the ultimate teaching. I will join the parts together, make them whole, and extend them back out to the branches ("branches" refers to heaven, earth, humanity, and things). The treatise has four parts and is entitled "Inquiry into the Origin of Humanity."

The first part of this passage describes what Tsung-mi does in the first three parts of his *Inquiry*. Part 1 deals with the teachings of Confucianism and Taoism; part 2 deals with the teachings of Humans and Gods, the Lesser Vehicle, the Phenomenal Appearances of the Dharmas, and the Refutation of Phenomenal Appearances. All of these teachings are provisional in that they fail to discern the ultimate origin of humanity. Their arrangement, nevertheless, describes a process that, in a step-by-step manner, proceeding "from the superficial to the profound," comes ever closer to fathoming the ultimate origin, and that naturally leads to the fifth teaching, the subject of part 3. This teaching, which Tsung-mi refers to as the Teaching That Reveals the Nature, represents the ultimate teaching of the Buddha because it reveals the ultimate origin of phenomenal existence—i.e., the intrinsically enlightened true mind, which Tsung-mi also refers to as the Buddha-nature or, more technically, the tathāgatagarbha.

The second part of this passage describes what Tsung-mi does in the fourth and final part of the *Inquiry,* which he entitles "Reconciling Root and Branches." Having traced the ultimate origin of phenomenal existence in the previous three parts, Tsung-mi then moves from the ontological ground of being (*pen* 本) back out to its phenomenal manifestation (*mo* 末) by outlining the process of phenomenal evolution. Since enlightenment, for Tsung-mi, consists in a direct insight into the ultimate origin, the arrangement of the teachings in the first three parts also describes a process of soteriological progress. Moreover, since the ultimate origin is the absolute mind that is intrinsically enlightened, the first three parts can also be seen as answering the question of how, in spite of the suffering and delusion that characterize the human condition, enlightenment is possible. Part 4 can thus be seen as answering the question of how, if the ontological ground of being is pure and enlightened, delusion comes about in the first place.

# Part 1 Exposing Deluded Attachments
## Confucianism and Taoism

The first main part of the *Inquiry into the Origin of Humanity,* entitled "Exposing Deluded Attachments,"[1] is addressed to "those who practice Confucianism and Taoism." Tsung-mi's lumping of Confucianism and Taoism together under the rubric of the two teachings, of course, ignores the profound differences between them. Many Confucians during his time would have been more apt to put Buddhism and Taoism together in the same category than they would have been to identify with Taoism in contrast with Buddhism. Tsung-mi's treatment of the two teachings together, however, makes sense from the point of view of his agenda, where his emphasis is on their difference from Buddhist teachings. He does not attempt to give a comprehensive account of the teachings of Confucianism and Taoism in his essay, and in this regard his treatment of the two teachings differs from his treatment of the five Buddhist teachings he also discusses in the *Inquiry*—that is, he presumes a familiarity with Confucianism and Taoism that he does not presume in the case of the Buddhist teachings. This difference is understandable in the context of the literati audience to whom the essay is directed. After all, part of the purpose of Tsung-mi's discussion of the different Buddhist teachings is pedagogical: to provide an account of their basic tenets to those with only a limited familiarity with Buddhism. In the case of Confucianism and Taoism, however, he is less concerned with being informative than he is with critically assessing them.

Considered within the general context of Chinese Buddhist scholastic literature, Tsung-mi's *Inquiry* is remarkable in that it extends the problematic of doctrinal classification to Confucianism

1. Given the ambiguity of Chinese grammar, *ch'ih mi chih* 斥迷執 could also be translated as "Exposing Delusions and Attachments."

and Taoism. Whatever the particular scheme by which the teachings were classified, doctrinal classification was typically an enterprise that applied exclusively to the Buddha's teachings. Even though, as "outer" teachings, Tsung-mi does not include Confucianism and Taoism within his fivefold categorization—which only applies to the "inner" teachings of Buddhism—he does, nonetheless, extend the problematic of doctrinal classification to the two teachings, something that is only possible because he places Confucius and Lao-tzu on a par with the Buddha. As we saw in the Preface, Tsung-mi uses the Buddhist rubric of expedient means to account for the differences among the three teachings.

Although it should be no surprise that Tsung-mi regards Buddhism as a higher level of teaching than either Confucianism or Taoism, what is especially noteworthy is that his attitude toward the two teachings is sympathetic and inclusive. Even though his designation of them as exclusively provisional places them in a category inferior to the Buddhist teachings, it also—and far more significantly—places them within the same realm of discourse. Its concrete forms of expression may differ, but the truth realized by the three sages is universal. Tsung-mi's originality thus does not lie in the mere reshuffling of the traditional repertoire of Buddhist teachings to devise a new classificatory arrangement; it lies in extending the scope of doctrinal classification itself.

Despite the polemical edge to his discussion of the two teachings, Tsung-mi's treatment of them is far more accommodating than those of his Buddhist predecessors had been. His Hua-yen mentor, Ch'eng-kuan (738-839), for example, had excoriated those who tried to accommodate Confucianism and Taoism with Buddhism by claiming (as Tsung-mi did) that the three teachings of Buddhism, Taoism, and Confucianism were essentially one. "Those who go too far and equate [false teachings] with Buddhism," he wrote, "are all outside the teaching of the Buddha."[2] He goes on to liken the Buddha's teaching to cow's milk, from which the ghee of liberation can be obtained; the teachings of non-Buddhists, however, are likened to donkey's milk, from which ghee can never be

---

2. *Hua-yen ching shu,* T 35.521b15-16. Ch'eng-kuan goes on at length in his subcommentary to elaborate ten major points of difference that distinguish Buddhism from Confucianism and Taoism (see *Yen-i ch'ao,* T 36.106a27-107a13); see also my *Tsung-mi and the Sinification of Buddhism,* pp. 258-260, and Kamata, *Chūgoku kegon shisōshi no kenkyū,* pp. 273-285.

obtained: they lack the taste of liberation and can only be made into urine and ordure.[3] Further, he says that the gap between Buddhism and the two teachings is "so vast that even a thousand leagues would not seem far."[4] He concludes his invective with the following admonition:

> Do not seek after the trivial reputation of a single age and confuse the three teachings as one. Studying the poisonous seeds of false views is a deep cause for being born in hell, opens up the wellspring of ignorance, and blocks off the road to omniscience. Take heed! Take heed![5]

Part 1 of Tsung-mi's *Inquiry* is divided into two main sections. The first consists of a brief synopsis of Confucianism and Taoism, followed by a general critique. The second singles out four major concepts to subject to more detailed scrutiny and criticism. These are the Way (*tao* 道), spontaneity (*tzu-jan* 自然), the primal pneuma (*yüan-ch'i* 元氣), and the mandate of heaven (*t'ien-ming* 天命). This part is modelled after an earlier discussion of the two teachings that had appeared in Tsung-mi's *Commentary to the Scripture of Perfect Enlightenment*,[6] and the close correspondence of the two versions means that the pertinent sections of Tsung-mi's *Subcommentary to the Scripture of Perfect Enlightenment* can be used as "footnotes" to amplify his discussion of Confucianism and Taoism in the *Inquiry*.

3. *Yen-i ch'ao*, T 36.106a7-12. Ch'eng-kuan's remark is based on a parable from the *Nirvāṇa Sūtra* (see T 12.381c-282b), which he cites in full in the preceding passage (see 105b17-106a5). In this parable, which is related to illustrate the difference between the Buddha's teaching and the worldly teachings, the Buddha recounts the story of a man who had a herd of cows. He kept them and saw that they were well tended in order to have ghee made out of their milk. When the man died, the whole herd was stolen by a band of thieves, who also wanted to make ghee from the milk. However, since they did not know how to churn the milk to make cream, they could not make it thicken. They then added water to it, hoping thereby to make ghee, but only ruined the milk. The Buddha then explains that even though the common man has access to the Buddha's most excellent teaching, he does not know how to use it to attain liberation, just as the thieves did not know how to use the cow's milk to make ghee.

4. Ibid., 107a7-8.

5. Ibid., 107a11-13.

6. Kamata has conveniently collated the two versions of Tsung-mi's discussion of Confucianism and Taoism in his *Shūmitsu*, pp. 115-117.

## GENERAL CRITIQUE

Tsung-mi's general summary and critique of the two teachings introduces the themes that he examines in more detail in the second section of this part and intimates some of the criticisms developed there. He begins by summarizing the cosmogonic basis of Confucianism and Taoism:

[708a26]　儒道二教説、人畜等類皆是虚無大道生成養育。謂道法自然生於元氣。元氣生天地、天地生萬物。

[708a26] The two teachings of Confucianism and Taoism hold that human beings, animals, and the like are all produced and nourished by the great Way of nothingness. They maintain that the Way, conforming to what is naturally so,[7] engenders the primal pneuma. The primal pneuma engenders heaven and earth, and heaven and earth engender the myriad things.

7. *Tao fa tzu-jan* 道法自然 is a reference to *Lao-tzu* 25: "Man models himself on earth, earth on heaven, heaven on the Way, and the Way on that which is naturally so" (as translated by Lau, p. 82). The Japanese commentaries maintain that there are two traditions on the reading of this sentence. The first, that of Ching-yüan, takes *fa* 法 to function as a verb—as it does in the *Lao-tzu* passage. The second, that of Yüan-chüeh, supposedly takes *fa* as a noun and thus understands the sentence to read: "The principle of the Way (*tao fa* 道法) spontaneously engenders the primal pneuma." This second line of interpretation is the one followed by all the Japanese commentators consulted, with the sole exception of Katō (p. 25). However, it is not at all clear that Yüan-chüeh does, in fact, take *fa* as a noun as the Japanese commentators all claim. Moreover, since Ching-yüan's interpretation is itself based on Tsung-mi's comment on this passage in his *Subcommentary,* I have translated this sentence in accordance with the first line of interpretation. Tsung-mi writes: "*Fa* 法 means 'to imitate' (*fang-hsiao* 倣效) or 'to hold [something] before one as a model' (*ch'ü ch'ien tse* 取前則). . . . The great Way's being without a place from which it comes is called 'of itself so' (*tzu-jan* 自然). It is not that there is a separately existing self-so (*tzu-jan* 自然) that causes the great Way to take it as a model. It is only in thoroughly investigating the source of the great Way that one realizes that it is of itself so and nothing else. Further, since it is without an origin or cause, it says 'conforms to' (*fa chih* 法之)" (TSC 413d–414a). This passage makes it clear that Tsung-mi understands *fa* to be functioning as a verb. Even though *tzu-jan* is the object of *fa,* it still is not something that is ontologically prior to the Way—rather, it is precisely that characteristic of the Way that indicates that there is nothing ontologically antecedent to the Way itself.

Tsung-mi's account draws on a series of allusions to the *Lao-tzu*. Chapter 51, for example, states: "The Way gives them life and rears them; brings them up and nurses them; brings them to fruition and maturity; feeds and shelters them."[8] Chapter 25 says: "Humans model themselves on earth, earth on heaven, heaven on the Way, and the Way on that which is naturally so."[9] In his *Subcommentary*,[10] Tsung-mi links the process of cosmogony here described with that found in chapter 42 of the *Lao-tzu:* "The Way engenders the one; the one engenders the two; the two engender the three; and the three engender the myriad things."[11] The Way's engendering of the primal pneuma[12] thus corresponds to the Way's engendering of the one; the primal pneuma's engendering of heaven and earth, to the one's engendering of the two; and so forth. He goes on to identify the primal pneuma's engendering of heaven and earth with the great ultimate's (*t'ai-chi* 太極) engendering of the two elementary forms (*liang-i* 兩儀) as recounted in the Great Appendix of the *Classic of Change*.[13] In so doing Tsung-mi is following the officially-sanctioned tradition of K'ung Ying-ta (574-648), who, in his subcommentary to this line, linked the cosmogonic process described in the *Classic of Change* passage with that given in *Lao-tzu* 42.[14] Elsewhere in his *Subcommentary*,[15] Tsung-mi quotes a lengthy passage from Ch'eng-kuan's *Yen-i ch'ao*[16] that cites both Han K'ang-po's (332-380) commentary and K'ung Ying-ta's subcommentary to the *Classic of Change*. The *Yen-i ch'ao* passage goes on to cite the *I kou-ming chüeh*, which further connects the cosmogonic process found in the Great Appendix with that given in the first chapter of the *Lieh-tzu*.[17] That work analyzes

8. As translated by Lau, p. 112.

9. Cf. translation by Lau, p. 82.

10. TSC 414a.

11. Cf. Lau, p. 103. Tsung-mi had already alluded to this passage in the Preface to the *Inquiry;* see 708a3-5: "The one pneuma of the primordial chaos divided into the dyad of yin and yang, the two engendered the triad of heaven, earth, and man, and the three engendered the myriad things."

12. See the passage in *Lao-tzu* 25 quoted in the previous chapter.

13. See Sung, *The Text of the Yi King,* p. 299.

14. See *Chou-i chu-shu* 7.17a.

15. TSC 352c.

16. See T 36.104b. Jan Yün-hua discusses this passage at length in "Tsung-mi's Questions Regarding the Confucian Absolute," but fails to note that it is quoted in its entirety from Ch'eng-kuan.

17. In answer to the question: "From what were heaven and earth born?" Lieh-tzu answers: "There was the great interchangeability (*t'ai-i* 太易),

the cosmogonic process into five phases, the first four corresponding to those enumerated in the first chapter of the *Lieh-tzu* (i.e., the great interchangeability, the great antecedence, the great initiation, and the great simplicity) and the fifth referring to the great ultimate of the Great Appendix. Such a five-phase theory must have enjoyed wide currency in the T'ang, for we find it referred to in other works as well.[18] Tsung-mi evidently had this scheme in mind when, in the conclusion to the *Inquiry,* he wrote: "The beginning for them starts with the great interchangeability and evolves in five phases to the great ultimate."[19]

Tsung-mi's synopsis of the two teachings continues, pointing out the consequences of such a cosmogony:

[708a28]　故愚智貴賤貧富苦樂、皆禀於天、由於時命。
故死後却歸天地、復其虛無。

[708a28] Thus dullness and intelligence, high and low station, poverty and wealth, suffering and happiness are all en-

---

there was the great antecedence (*t'ai-ch'u* 太初), there was the great initiation (*t'ai-shih* 太始), and there was the great simplicity (*t'ai-su* 太素). The great interchangeability refers to the time when the pneuma was not yet visible. The great antecedence refers to the beginning of the pneuma. The great initiation refers to the beginning of form. The great simplicity refers to the beginning of material substance" (*Lieh-tzu* 1.6-7; cf. Graham, pp. 18-19).

18. The *Pien-cheng lun* by Fa-lin (572-640) (see T 52.490b), for instance, quotes the following passage from the *I kou-ming chüeh:* "Before heaven and earth divided, there was the great interchangeability, there was the great antecedence, there was the great initiation, there was the great simplicity, and there was the great ultimate, which formed five phases. Before pneuma had taken form as phenomena is what is referred to as the great interchangeability. The first stirrings of the primal pneuma is what is referred to as the great antecedence. The sprouting of the pneuma into form is what is referred to as the great initiation. The transformation of form into material substance is what is referred to as the great simplicity. The complete development of material substance and form is what is referred to as the great ultimate. [These terms] are thus designated as the five phases." This scheme is also quoted in the *Pei-shan lu* (T 52.573b24-26). Other works, such as the *T'ai-p'ing yü-lan,* divide the cosmogonic process into a series of six phases by designating the primal pneuma as the first phase, which is even prior to the grand initiation. For a discussion of these terms see Schafer, *Pacing the Void,* pp. 25-29.

19. T 45.710c15.

> dowed by heaven and proceed according to time and
> destiny. Therefore, after death one again returns to heaven
> and earth and reverts to nothingness.[20]

Tsung-mi here makes two points that will prove central for his
critique of Confucianism and Taoism. The first has to do with the
relationship of the Way or heaven, as the ultimate basis of phenomenal reality, with the evident inequalities that pertain in the world.
This point is connected with what could be broadly characterized
as the problem of theodicy, which Tsung-mi raises as part of his
more pointed criticism of the Way and the mandate of heaven in
the second section of this part. It is significant because it reveals
that as far as Tsung-mi is concerned the standard by which cosmogonic theories are to be measured has to do with their ability to
clarify the ontological basis of ethical action. The second point has
to do with the dispersion of the vital force (ch'i 氣) after death. In
his *Subcommentary*, Tsung-mi quotes a passage from the *Book of
Rites* that says that at death "the intelligent spirit (hun-ch'i 魂氣) returns to heaven, and the material soul (p'o 魄) returns to the earth."[21]
Tsung-mi focuses on the implications of this point in his critique of
the primal pneuma, where he mounts a forceful defense of the
Buddhist theory of rebirth. This point, then, is related to Tsung-mi's
general criticism of the two teachings for their ignorance of the
process of rebirth. These two points, moreover, are connected by
the Buddhist teaching of karma, which, as embodied in the Teaching
of Humans and Gods, supersedes Confucianism and Taoism in
Tsung-mi's scheme of things. The teaching of karma both clarifies
the relationship between cause and effect, on which ethical action
must depend, and explains how the process of rebirth operates.

Tsung-mi goes on to give the following general critique of the
two teachings:

> [708a29]　然外教宗旨、但在乎依身立行、不在究竟身之
> 元由。所説萬物不論象外。雖指大道為本而不備明順逆起
> 滅染淨因緣。故習者不知是權、執之為了。

> [708a29] This being so, the essential meaning of the outer
> teachings merely lies in establishing [virtuous] conduct
> based on this bodily existence and does not lie in thoroughly

20. Cf. TS 163a9-10.
21. See *Li chi* 8.11b; adapted from Legge's translation, *Book of Rites*
1.444. Tsung-mi quotes this passage in his TSC 414b2-3.

investigating the ultimate source of this bodily existence. The myriad things that they talk about do not have to do with that which is beyond tangible form. Even though they point to the great Way as the origin, they still do not fully illuminate the pure and impure causes and conditions of conforming to and going against [the flow of] origination and extinction. Thus, those who study [the outer teachings] do not realize that they are provisional and cling to them as ultimate.

Here there are several points to note. The first and second sentences are related to what Tsung-mi sees as the short-sightedness of Confucianism and Taoism for their failure to understand human existence in terms that go beyond this single bodily existence. Elsewhere Tsung-mi characterizes the essential meaning of Confucianism as lying in its moral teaching of loyalty, filial piety, benevolence, and righteousness and that of Taoism, in its life-nurturing practices.[22] In either case, the purview of the two teachings does not extend beyond the present existence. As Tsung-mi stated in the Preface to the *Inquiry,* followers of the two teaching merely know that "they have received this body from their ancestors and fathers having passed down the bodily essence in a continuous series."[23] The two teachings are thus inferior to even the most superficial Buddhist teaching, whose theory of karma presupposes a series of lifetimes in which the retribution for good and bad actions can be worked out. Furthermore, just as the two teachings are unaware that this life is but a single moment in an innumerable series of lives, so Taoism is ignorant of the fact that this cosmos is but a momentary pulse in a beginningless and endless series of cosmic cycles, as Tsung-mi later makes clear in the section on the Teaching of the Lesser Vehicle.[24]

"The pure and impure causes and conditions of conforming to and going against [the flow of] origination and extinction" (*shun-ni ch'i-mieh jan-ching yin-yüan* 順逆起滅染淨因緣) refers to the reciprocal processes of pure and impure conditioned origination. The first two terms, *shun* 順 and *ni* 逆 (Skt., *anuloma* and *pratiloma*), refer to the processes of conforming to and going against the flow of birth-and-death. "Conforming to" (*shun*) designates the

22. See TSC 352a17-b1.
23. T 45.708a2-3.
24. See below T 45.709b3-5.

process by which beings become increasingly enmeshed in the continuous cycle of suffering that is saṃsāra, while "going against" (*ni*) designates the process by which beings reverse the momentum of their karma and move towards nirvāṇa. "Origination" (*ch'i* 起) refers to the process by which the suffering attendant upon birth, sickness, old age, and death comes into existence, while "extinction" (*mieh* 滅) refers to the process by which it is eliminated. Pure causes and conditions lead to extinction, and impure causes and conditions lead to further involvement in the process of origination. The process of conforming to birth-and-death is a case of impure causes and conditions, whereas that of going against birth-and-death is a case of pure causes and conditions.[25]

The importance of the reciprocality of the processes of conforming to and going against the flow of birth-and-death lies in their soteriological implications. Understanding the cosmogonic process by which beings become enmeshed in saṃsāra provides a map for reversing the process and attaining liberation. Tsung-mi is here pointing to the ethical failure of the Confucian and Taoist cosmogonic theory to articulate such a map, and for Tsung-mi it is the coherence and profundity of such a map by which different teachings are to be judged.

### DETAILED CRITIQUE

The moral thrust behind Tsung-mi's critique of Confucianism and Taoism can most clearly be seen in his raising, *mutatis mutandis,* the issue of theodicy. Whereas in a Christian context the question of theodicy asks how there can be evil in a world where God is at once all good and all powerful, the question in a Confucian context revolves around the existence of social inequity and injustice in an universe that functions in accord with the Confucian moral order.

[708b4]　今略舉而詰之。所言萬物皆從虛無大道而生
者、大道即是生死賢愚之本、吉凶禍福之基。基本既其常
存、則禍亂凶愚不可除也、福慶賢善不可益也。何用老莊
之教耶。又道青虎狼胎桀紂、夭顏冉禍夷齊、何名尊乎。

[708b4] Now I will briefly present [their teachings] and assess them critically. Their claim that the myriad things are all engendered by the great Way of nothingness means that the great

25. See Ching-yüan's comment on this passage (*Chieh* 93a).

Way itself is the origin of life and death, sageliness and stupidity, the basis of fortune and misfortune, bounty and disaster. Since the origin and basis are permanently existent, [it must follow that] disaster, disorder, misfortune, and stupidity cannot be decreased, and bounty, blessings, sageliness, and goodness cannot be increased. What use, then, are the teachings of Lao-tzu and Chuang-tzu? Furthermore, since the Way nurtures tigers and wolves, conceived Chieh and Chou, brought Yen Hui and Jan Ch'iu to a premature end, and brought disaster upon Po I and Shu Ch'i, why deem it worthy of respect?

In the corresponding section of his *Commentary* and *Subcommentary*, Tsung-mi cites passages from the *Lao-tzu, Chuang-tzu,* and *Lieh-tzu* that, he claims, mean that there is nothing anywhere that is not the Way of nothingness.[26] Tsung-mi concludes this passage on a rhetorical note with a series of historical references that would have been well-known to his readers. Chieh and Chou were the last rulers of the Hsia and Shang. They became archetypes of the wicked last ruler whose crimes against heaven and tyranny against the people caused the downfall of their dynasties.[27] Yen Hui and Jan Ch'iu were two of Confucius' disciples who died at an early age;[28] Yen Hui, in particular, was held up as a paragon of moral virtue. Po I and Shu Ch'i were upright and loyal followers of the Shang who, in protest over what they regarded as the unjust usurpation by King Wu, refused to eat the grain of the new Chou dynasty and withdrew to Mount Shou-yang, where they starved to death.[29]

26. See TS 163a, where he says that since the Way is nothingness (*hsü-wu* 虛無) and is neither existent nor a thing, it is said to be mysterious (*yao-jan* 杳然) and obscure (*ming-jan* 冥然), which he elucidates in his *Subcommentary* (TSC 414b) by referring to the following passage in *Lao-tzu* 14: "What cannot be seen is called evanescent; what cannot be heard is called rarified" (Lau, p. 70). His *Commentary* then goes on to quote *Lao-tzu* 40: "Being is engendered by non-being" (cf. Lau, p. 101); *Chuang-tzu* 33/13/7: "Emptiness, stillness, limpidity, silence, inaction are the root of the ten thousand things" (Watson, p. 168); *Lieh-tzu* 1.6: "All that has shape was born from the shapeless" (Graham, p. 18); and *Wen-tzu:* "The full emerges from the empty" (I have not been able to locate the original).

27. For Chieh see *Shih-chi* 2; for Chou see *Shih-chi* 3 and *Shu ching,* chapter five, "The Books of Chou" (*The Chinese Classics* 3.284-285).

28. Their biographies may be found in *Shih-chi* 67.

29. See *Shih-chi* 61; cf. Watson, *Records of the Historian,* pp. 11-15. After relating the story of Po I and Shu Ch'i, Ssu-ma Ch'ien mentions the

### Critique of Spontaneity

Tsung-mi's critique of spontaneity (*tzu-jan* 自然) is based on a more complex series of arguments, which also have implications for his critique of the Way. Nevertheless, like his critique of the Way, the thrust of his criticism of spontaneity focuses on its moral implications.

> [708b9]　又言萬物皆是自然生化非因緣者、則一切無因
> 緣處悉應生化。謂石應生草、草或 [應] 生人、人生畜等。
> 又應生無前後、起無早晚、神仙不藉丹藥、太平不藉賢
> 良、仁義不藉教習。老莊周孔何用立教為軌則乎。

[708b9] Again, their claim that the myriad things are all spontaneously engendered and transformed and that it is not a matter of causes and conditions means that everything should be engendered and transformed [even] where there are no causes and conditions. That is to say, stones might engender grass, grass might engender humans,[30] humans engender animals, and so forth. Further, since they might engender without regard to temporal sequence and arise without regard to due season, the immortal would not depend on an elixir, the great peace would not depend on the sage and the virtuous, and benevolence and righteousness would not depend on learning and practice. For what use, then, did Lao-tzu, Chuang-tzu, the Duke of Chou, and Confucius establish their teachings as invariable norms?

Tsung-mi interprets the cosmogonic significance of spontaneity as meaning that all things come into existence in a haphazard way

---

fate of Yen Hui, who, although virtuous in deed, suffered severe hardship throughout his short life. He then tells of Robber Chih, who, although he terrorized the world and ate the flesh of the innocent people he killed, lived to a ripe old age. These flagrant examples of injustice prompt Ssu-ma Ch'ien to ask the same question that Tsung-mi here raises: how can the way of heaven be just in the face of such obvious instances of injustice in the world?

30. Both the Taishō text and that followed by Ching-yüan read *ts'ao huo sheng jen* 造或生人. I am here following the reading found in the Yüan-chüeh commentary and the corresponding passage in Tsung-mi's *Commentary,* which both have *ying* 應 in place of *huo* 或. In any case, either reading hardly affects the meaning of the passage.

in total disregard of any causal process.[31] Spontaneity is thus an acausal (*wu-yin* 無因) cosmogonic principle. Tsung-mi develops this theme in the corresponding section of his *Commentary*.[32] There he explains spontaneity by making reference to the *Chuang-tzu* passage that says: "The snow goose needs no daily bath to stay white; the crow needs no daily inking to stay black."[33] In his *Sub-commentary*,[34] he elaborates his interpretation of spontaneity by piecing together a wide selection of passages from the *Chuang-tzu*.[35] He concludes that what these passages all add up to is that

31. See TS 145a.

32. TS 163b.

33. 39/14/58-59; as translated by Watson, p. 163.

34. TSC 416c-d.

35. He writes: "Birth and death, rising and falling, all emerge from nothingness and are completed by non-action. Therefore their emerging without a place from which they come forth is called indistinct and shadowy; their being engendered without a place from where they are born is called mysterious and obscure." He then quotes the following passage from the *Chuang-tzu:* "There is no trace of its coming, no limit to its going. Gateless, roomless, it is airy and open as the highways of the four directions. . . . Heaven cannot help but be high, earth cannot help but be broad, the sun and moon cannot help but revolve, the ten thousand things cannot help but flourish. Is this not the Way?" (58/22/31-33; as translated by Watson, p. 239). "Therefore," Tsung-mi continues, quoting again from the *Chuang-tzu,* "'it comes out from no source, it goes back in through no aperture' [63/23/54-55; as translated by Watson, p. 256]. It is born of itself without a source; it dies of itself without an aperture. That which is without a source or aperture is nothingness. Nothingness does not act and yet is born of itself, does nothing and yet comes forth of itself. Therefore [the *Chuang-tzu*] says: '[Wonderfully, mysteriously, there is no place they come up out of. . . .] Each thing minds its business and all grow [out of inaction. So I say, heaven and earth do nothing and there is nothing that is not done]' [46/18/13-14; as translated by Watson, p. 191]. Since this is so, non-action is the activity of heaven and nothingness is the gate of heaven."

"The gate of heaven" is an allusion to another passage from the *Chuang-tzu:* "In the coming out and going back its form is never seen. This is called the heavenly gate. The heavenly gate is non-being. The ten thousand things come forth from non-being" (63/23/56-57; as translated by Watson, pp. 256-257). Tsung-mi continues: "The heavenly gate is non-being and cannot be sought for in being; the heavenly activity is non-action and cannot be looked for in action. Because it does not act, there is nothing that is not done; because it is without being, there is nothing that does not exist. Therefore 'it transports and weighs the ten thousand things without ever failing them' [*Chuang-tzu* 59/22/35; as translated by Watson, p. 239]."

what is spontaneously so (*tzu-jan* 自然) does not depend on being made, and what is transformed of itself does not depend on causes and conditions but always emerges forth from nothingness and is engendered by non-action (*wu-wei* 無為). Being completed by non-action, it does not labor with compass and square, and emerging forth from nothingness, it does not avail itself of curve and plumb line.[36]

Tsung-mi is here alluding to another passage from the *Chuang-tzu:*

If we must use curve and plumb line, compass and square to make something right, this means cutting away its inborn nature; if we must use cords and knots, glue and lacquer to make something firm, this means violating its natural virtue. . . . Where there is constant naturalness (*ch'ang tzu-jan* 常自然), things are arced not by the use of the curve, straight not by the use of the plumb line, rounded not by compass, squared not by T squares, joined not by glue and lacquer, bound not by ropes and lines.[37]

The soteriological implication of such passages is in Tsung-mi's opinion clear and damning:

If the principle of heaven is spontaneity (*tzu-jan*) and does not depend upon cultivation and study, then, if one were to cultivate and study it, it would be the action of human beings and not the action of heaven. It would be like using a plumb line to make something straight, using a curve to make an arc, using glue to join, or using ropes to bind—there would be no difference. . . . Since one violates heaven by using a plumb line, one should not use a plumb line. One who does not use a plumb line trusts in its being straight of itself in accord with the condition of heaven.[38]

According to such a rationale, the purposeful cultivation of moral virtues such as benevolence (*jen* 仁) and righteousness (*i* 義) is fundamentally misguided. Tsung-mi concludes by saying that this is why the *Lao-tzu* contends that "in pursuit of the Way one does less every day"[39] and admonishes people to "exterminate the sage" and "discard the wise."[40] Tsung-mi never questions that moral and spiritual endeav-

36. TSC 416d2-4.
37. 21/8/13-16; as translated by Watson, pp. 100-101.
38. TSC 416d7-12.
39. Chapter 48; cf. Lau, p. 109.
40. Chapter 19; cf. Lau, p. 75.

or is meaningful and necessary. Since such a conclusion cannot be countenanced, the premises that lead to it must be rejected as false.

Against such an acausal theory, Tsung-mi argues that, if the existence of things did not depend on causes and conditions, anything could be produced anywhere and anytime. In his *Subcommentary,* he points out that supposing that things are engendered and transformed in the absence of causes and conditions is a case of what he refers to as "the error of universally engendering" (*pien-sheng chih kuo* 遍生之過). He likens it to grain's growing without either a seed (its cause) or water, soil, and human cultivation (its conditions). He goes on to draw out the absurd consequences entailed by such a theory: everything from the physical environment throughout the entire universe to the thousands of varieties of animate and inanimate things within it should all be spontaneously engendered at once without any causes or conditions. He concludes that, since nothing can be engendered or transformed without causes and conditions, the principle of spontaneity is thereby refuted.[41]

Tsung-mi continues, claiming that the example of stones engendering grass, which he employs to illustrate the implications of such a theory, goes against the principle that the causes and conditions of one thing do not also engender another thing and that the causal process does not act wantonly.[42] The example of things engendering one another without regard to temporal sequence is a case of what Tsung-mi refers to as "the error of constant engendering" (*ch'ang-sheng chih kuo* 常生之過), which has consequences equally absurd as the error of universally engendering. It would mean, for instance, that grain, wheat, hemp, beans, and other crops might all come up at the same time on the first of the year and that there would be no need to wait until the third or fourth month for grain, the sixth of seventh month for beans, or the ninth or tenth month for wheat.[43]

41. TSC 417a2-9. See T. R. V. Murti, *The Central Philosophy of Buddhism,* p. 172, n. 4, for an example of a stone producing a plant.

42. See TSC 417c9-15. This passage throws light on the reasoning behind Tsung-mi's statement elsewhere (TS 145a and TSC 353a) that a single cause cannot engender various different effects. A specific set of causes and conditions is necessary for the engendering of each individual thing. Since this set of causes and conditions is specific to each individual thing, it is thus impossible for one universal cause to engender the variegated and everchanging phenomena of the manifold universe.

43. See TSC 417a15-d1.

Elsewhere Tsung-mi goes on to point out that spontaneity (*tzu-jan*) can also be interpreted as an underlying ontological principle—"something existing separately of itself." If such an interpretation were adopted, spontaneity would then be a case of erroneous causality, and the same argument that is used against an eternal and universal Way would apply. In charging that the Confucian and Taoist cosmogonic theories are examples of either acausality or erroneous causality,[44] Tsung-mi is following Ch'eng-kuan.[45] In either case—whether spontaneity be interpreted as a case of acausality or erroneous causality—there is no scope for moral and spiritual striving.[46]

44. See TS 145a.

45. Who had made the same charge in his commentary and subcommentary to the *Hua-yen Sūtra;* see *Hua-yen ching shu,* T 35.52lb and *Yen-i ch'ao,* T 36.104b.

46. This latter argument ultimately derives from the *Ch'eng wei-shih lun,* as Tsung-mi makes clear in his *Subcommentary* (TSC 353a). The argument in the *Ch'eng wei-shih lun* is directed against those who believe that the manifold universe is created by a single god, Maheśvara, whose substance is real (*shih* 實), universal (*pien* 遍), eternal (*ch'ang* 常), and capable of engendering all things (*neng-sheng* 能生). This theory is in error because something that is capable of engendering other things cannot be eternal. Following K'uei-chi's commentary, Tsung-mi points out that although the four great elements of earth, water, fire, and wind are not eternal, they are capable of engendering everything (TSC 352d). He then quotes K'uei-chi's comment that things that are capable of engendering other things must themselves be engendered by other things (T 43.262b3-4). The *Ch'eng wei-shih lun* argument continues: what is not eternal cannot be universal, and what is not universal is not truly real. If Maheśvara's substance were eternal and universal, then he should have all the energies and capacities necessary to engender all things all at once in all places and times ( T 31.3b7-11; cf. La Vallée Poussin, 1.30 and Wei Tat, pp. 38-39). The argument is an old one as La Vallée Poussin notes. Woodward, for instance, translates the *Aṅguttara-nikāya* passage cited by La Vallée Poussin as follows:

So then, owing to the creation of a Supreme Deity, men will become murderers, thieves, unchaste, liars, slanderers, abusive, babblers, covetous, malicious, and perverse in view. Thus for those who fall back on the creation of a Supreme Deity as the essential reason there is neither desire to do, nor effort to do, nor necessity to do this deed or abstain from that deed.

So then, owing to no cause or condition at all, men will become murderers, . . . and perverse in view. Thus for those who fall back on the uncaused and unconditioned as the essential, there is neither

### Critique of the Primal Pneuma

Tsung-mi's main objection to the primal pneuma (*yüan-ch'i* 元氣)
is that it cannot, on the one hand, account for the predispositions
inherited at birth, nor, on the other hand, can it account for the
existence of spirits of the dead (*kuei-shen* 鬼神). In the corresponding sections of his *Commentary* and *Subcommentary to the Scripture
of Perfect Enlightenment,* Tsung-mi adduces a number of examples
of the existence of spirits of the dead, drawing from a body of largely
Confucian historical literature, to support his contention that death
is not a mere cessation of existence. Again, the thrust of his critique
is ethical. After all, without the mechanism of rebirth supplied by
the teaching of karmic retribution, there would be no impelling
reason for people to behave morally. Ample cases of the wicked
prospering with impunity and the good suffering unjustly could be
cited from both history and the contemporary world. If, upon death,
their "spirits" simply dispersed into nothingness and there were no
punishment or reward in a future state, then why should people
behave morally, especially in cases where moral behavior demand-
ed that they act contrary to their own immediate interests?

Tsung-mi's detailed critique of the primal pneuma in the *Inquiry* begins:

[708b13] 又言皆從元氣而生成者、則欻生之神未曾習慮、
豈得嬰孩便能愛惡驕恣焉。若言欻有自然便能隨念愛惡等
者、則五德六藝悉能隨念而解、何待因緣學習而成。

---

desire to do, nor effort to do, nor necessity to do this deed or to
abstain from that deed (*Gradual Sayings* 1.158; cf. T 1.435b15-c9).

Tsung-mi was not the first to see the applicability of this argument to
Confucian and Taoist cosmogonic theories—it had already been pointed
out by K'uei-chi in his commentary on the *Ch'eng wei-shih lun* (see T
43.262c9-11). In the *Inquiry* passage, however, Tsung-mi has shifted the
context of the *Ch'eng wei-shih lun* argument from being directed against
a theory of erroneous causality to one of acausality.

Although Tsung-mi's analysis of such mistaken causal theories derives
from the *Ch'eng wei-shih lun* and K'uei-chi's commentary, the arguments
on which it is based have a long history in Buddhist polemics. As these
earlier examples demonstrate, Buddhists have traditionally criticized the
causal theories of their opponents on moral grounds. For all of the ways
in which his highly sinified interpretation of Buddhism differs from that of
India, Tsung-mi's emphasis on soteriology is part of a continuous concern
that goes back as far as we can trace Buddhist teachings.

[708b13] Again, since their claim that [the myriad things] are engendered and formed from the primal pneuma means that a spirit, which is suddenly born out of nowhere,[47] has not yet learned and deliberated, then how, upon gaining [the body of] an infant, does it like, dislike, and act willfully? If they were to say that one suddenly comes into existence from out of nowhere and is thereupon able to like, dislike, and so forth in accordance with one's thoughts, then it would mean that the five virtues and six arts can all be understood by according with one's thoughts. Why then, depending on causes and conditions, do we study to gain proficiency?

In this passage Tsung-mi raises the same general objection that he had raised against spontaneity as an acausal principle. In the corresponding section of his *Commentary*, he alludes to a series of passages from the *Chuang-tzu*, *Huai-nan-tzu*, and *Classic of Change* that claim that life consists in a coming together of the vital force (*ch'i* 氣) and that death consists in its dispersion.[48] He goes on to argue that feelings such as attraction and aversion do not suddenly arise out of nowhere but are the result of the reactivation of residual conditioning acquired in previous lives. Such residual conditioning lies latent within the ālayavijñāna as seeds lie in the ground awaiting the proper set of

47. In his *Subcommentary* (TSC 417c13) Tsung-mi defines *hu* 欻 as "to come into existence suddenly *ex nihilo*."

48. See *Chuang-tzu* 58/22/11: "Man's life is a coming together of breath (*ch'i*). If it comes together, there is life; if it scatters, there is death" (as translated by Watson, p. 235); *Chuang-tzu* 46/18/18: "In the midst of the jumble of wonder and mystery a change took place and she had a spirit (*ch'i*). Another change and she had a body. Another change and she was born" (as translated by Watson, p. 192); *Chuang-tzu* 58/22/12-13: "The ten thousand things are really one. . . . You have only to comprehend the one breath (*i-ch'i* 一氣) that is the world. The sage never ceases to value oneness" (as translated by Watson, p. 236); *Huai-nan-tzu*: "The heavenly pneuma (*t'ien-ch'i* 天氣) constitutes the spiritual soul (*hun* 魂) and the earthly pneuma (*ti-ch'i* 地氣) constitutes the material soul (*p'o* 魄)" (9.1b); and *I ching*: "[The sage] traces things to their beginning and follows them to their end;—thus he knows what can be said about death and life. (He perceives how the union of) essence and breath form things, and the (disappearance or) wandering away of the soul produces the change (of their constitution);—thus he knows the characteristics of the anima and animus" (as translated by Legge in Sung, *The Text of the Yi King*, p. 278).

conditions to germinate. Only when the proper set of conditions occurs do feelings such as attraction and aversion become manifested.[49] The five constant virtues, of course, refer to benevolence (*jen* 仁), righteousness (i 義), propriety (*li* 禮), wisdom (*chih* 智), and trustworthiness (*hsin* 信), and the six arts refer to the rites, music, archery, charioteering, composition, and arithmetic.

In the corresponding section of his *Commentary*,[50] Tsung-mi gives two further arguments that do not appear in the *Inquiry*. Both are directed against the view that one is born upon receiving one's endowment of vital force (*ch'i*) and that one's nature is originally quiescent and only changes from its original state of quiescence when it is stimulated by external things. Tsung-mi contends that the alarm and fear of a one-month old infant gives rise, in turn, to the greed, anger, and willfulness of the infant in his first, second, and third year without these emotions ever having been learned from another person. How then, he asks, can such emotions arise in response to external stimulation? His point is that such feelings develop out of an internal causal process within the ālayavijñāna. Whereas his first argument is based on a Yogācāra understanding of mind and mental processes, the second is based on a Chinese understanding of the meaning of the nature (*hsing* 性) of a thing as referring to its inherent potential or tendency. The second argument runs as follows: since it is the nature of falcons and dogs to seize their prey, it is possible to train them to hunt. If it were the case that they were originally without this nature and only learned to hunt and seize their prey by being taught to do so, then why cannot doves and sheep be trained to hunt and seize prey?

Tsung-mi's continues his critique in the *Inquiry:*

[708b17]　又若生是稟氣而欻有、死是氣散而欻無、則誰為鬼神乎。且世有鑒達前生追憶往事、則知生前相續、非稟氣而欻有。又驗鬼神靈知不斷、則知死後非氣散而欻無。故祭祀求禱、典籍有文、況死而蘇者説幽途事、或死後感動妻子儻報怨恩、今古皆有耶。

[708b17] Furthermore, if birth were a sudden coming into existence upon receiving the endowment of the vital force and death were a sudden going out of existence upon the dispersion of the vital force, then who would become a spir-

49. TSC 417c.
50. TS 163c.

it of the dead? Moreover, since there are those in the world who see their previous births as clearly as if they were looking in a mirror and who recollect the events of past lives, we thus know that there is a continuity from before birth and that it is not a matter of suddenly coming into existence upon receiving the endowment of the vital force. Further, since it has been verified that the consciousness of the spirit is not cut off, then we know that after death it is not a matter of suddenly going out of existence upon the dispersion of the vital force. This is why the classics contain passages about sacrificing to the dead and beseeching them in prayer, to say nothing of cases, in both present and ancient times, of those who have died and come back to life and told of matters in the dark paths or those who, after death, have influenced their wives and children or have redressed a wrong and requited a kindness.

The corresponding sections of Tsung-mi's *Commentary* and *Subcommentary* contain a wealth of fascinating material culled from a variety of historical sources as "proof" for the existence of the spirits of the dead and their effect on the living.[51] One example should

51. As examples of people who have recollected their past lives, Tsung-mi recounts the cases Yang Hu, T'an-ti, and Pao Ching, which can be found in *Chin shu* 34.1023-1024, *Kao-seng chuan,* T 50.370c24-371a16, and *Chin shu* 95.2482 (see TSC 418b). As examples of cases proving that the consciousness of the spirit is not cut off after death, Tsung-mi recounts those of Chiang Chi, Su Shao, and the favorite concubine, which can be found in *San-kuo chih* 14.454-455 (the story that Tsung-mi gives in the TSC is a somewhat abridged version of one that appears in a biographical collection of marvelous tales, the *Lieh-i chüan,* which is quoted by Pei Sung-chih in his commentary on Chiang Chi's biography in the *San-kuo chih*); what Tsung-mi erroneously claims to be the *Chin shu* (I have been unable to locate the source; a different version of this story can be found in the *Meng-ch'iu* 1.41a, a popular collection of supernatural tales, which were grouped together by category with rhyming four character headings and was compiled during the T'ang by Li Han); and the *Tso-chüan,* the fifteenth year of Duke Hsüan (see Legge, *The Chinese Classics* 5.328b) (see TSC 418b-d). Tsung-mi recounts the details of Liu Ts'ung's son's journey to the realm of the dead, derived from the biography of Liu Ts'ung in *Chin shu* 102.2673-2677, in TSC 419a-b. His reference to sacrifices to the dead is based on the *Li chi;* see chapters 23, 24, and 25 of the *Li-chi* (chapters 20, "The Law of Sacrifices"; 21, "The Meaning of Sacrifices"; and 22, "A Summary Account of Sacrifices" in Legge's translation). His allusion to beseeching them in

suffice to indicate the flavor of such evidence. This is the case of Tou Ying, who distinguished himself as the general in charge of suppressing the revolt of Wu and Ch'u in 154 B.C.[52] His character, however, was inflexible, and he was apt to offend others by his self-righteous behavior. Tou Ying's tragic demise grew out of his rivalry with T'ien Fen, who was a generation younger than Tou Ying and was related to the imperial house by marriage. With the death of Emperor Ching, T'ien Fen's influence began to rival, and then eclipse, that of Tou Ying. As his political fortunes waxed, T'ien Fen's behavior is depicted as becoming increasingly arrogant and ostentatious. While out of favor in retirement at his villa, Tou Ying befriended Kuan Fu, a general who had earlier distinguished himself by his daring feats of bravery during the suppression of the Wu-Ch'u revolt. Kuan Fu is described as stubborn and outspoken, especially when in his cups. Through a series of increasingly acrimonious encounters, the rivalry between Tou Ying and T'ien Fen finally reached its crescendo at a banquet celebrating the marriage of T'ien Fen in 131, when Kuan Fu brazenly insulted one of T'ien Fen's guests and was arrested for his outburst of disrespect. Tou Ying tried to intercede with the emperor in behalf of Kuan Fu, but the empress favored T'ien Fen, who succeeded in having charges trumped up that implicated Tou Ying in the affair and led to his execution following that of Kuan Fu. Shortly thereafter, T'ien Fen fell ill and spent his time crying out that he was at fault and begging for forgiveness. When the emperor summoned a shaman who could see ghosts, he reported that he saw Tou Ying and Kuan Fu watching over the bed, preparing to kill T'ien Fen. T'ien Fen died soon thereafter.

A few pages later Tsung-mi's *Subcommentary* goes on to refute the objections against the existence of the spirits of the dead raised by Wang Ch'ung's first-century treatise, *Lun-heng,* famous for the skeptical attitude it takes toward many traditional beliefs. There

---

prayer is drawn from the *Shu ching;* see "The Metal-Bound Coffer" chapter of the *Shu ching* (*The Chinese Classics* 3.351ff). Tsung-mi gives seven different examples of people who either redressed a wrong or requited a kindness after they died (see TSC 419b-420d), the most noteworthy of which is the case of Tou Ying.

52. Tou Ying's biography can be found in *Han shu* 52 and *Shih chi* 107, the latter of which has been translated by Burton Watson in *Records of the Grand Historian of China* 2.109-129. The particular episode concerning Tou Ying's ghost occurs at *Han shu* 52.10a and *Shih chi* 107.10a-b (see Watson, pp. 127-128).

Tsung-mi cites two passages in which Wang Ch'ung offers a psychological explanation for the belief in the existence of ghosts. In the first passage,[53] Wang Ch'ung refers to Tou Ying, contending that T'ien Fen's mind had become so deranged by animosity that he hallucinated, and did not actually see, the ghosts of Tou Ying and Kuan Fu. In the second passage,[54] Wang Ch'ung gives a generic explanation for such phenomena, arguing that ghosts are products of a deranged imagination: when people become seriously ill, they become anxious and afraid, and their anxiety and fear work on their imagination to produce hallucinations. In response, Tsung-mi asks how, if the apparition of Tou Ying and Kuan Fu were merely a hallucination, could the shaman also have seen their ghosts? Was his mind similarly deranged by fever? Even if the shaman's mind were also deranged, Tsung-mi continues, he surely would not have seen the same apparition as the ailing T'ien Fen.[55]

Tsung-mi's critique in the *Inquiry* also implicitly takes aim at Wang Ch'ung.

> [708b23]　外難曰、若人死為鬼、則古來之鬼填塞巷路、
> 合有見者、如何不爾。答曰、人死六道、不必皆為鬼。鬼
> 死復為人等。豈古來積鬼常存耶。且天地之氣本無知也、
> 人禀無知之氣、安得歘起而有知乎。草木亦皆禀氣、何不
> 知乎。

[708b23] An outsider [i.e., a non-Buddhist] may object, saying: If humans become ghosts when they die, then the ghosts from ancient times [until now] would crowd the roads and there should be those who see them—why is it not so? I reply: When humans die, there are six paths; they do not all necessarily become ghosts. When ghosts die, they become humans or other forms of life again. How could it be that the ghosts accumulated from ancient times exist forever? Moreover, the vital force of heaven and earth is originally without consciousness. If human beings receive vital force that is without consciousness, how are they then able suddenly to wake up and be conscious? Grasses and trees also all receive vital force, why are they not conscious?

53. 21.10a; see Alfred Forke, trans., *Lun-Heng* 1.217-218.
54. 22.10a; see Forke, *Lun-Heng* 1.239.
55. See TSC 420d18-421a10.

In his *Subcommentary*,[56] Tsung-mi quotes the original passage from the *Lun-heng:*

> If everyone who dies becomes a ghost, there should be a ghost at every pace of the road. If people see ghosts when they are about to die, they should see millions and millions filling the hall and crowding the road instead of only one or two.[57]

To this objection, Tsung-mi gives the Buddhist answer that not everyone who dies becomes a ghost. There are six possible paths of rebirth (*gati; tao* 道 or *ch'ü* 趣): one may be reborn as a god, human, animal, titan, hungry ghost, or denizen of hell.[58] Moreover, even those who are reborn as ghosts do not remain ghosts forever. When the particular karma that has caused them to be reborn as ghosts is exhausted, they reenter the cycle to be reborn in another form.

Underlying the different arguments he employs, the thrust of Tsung-mi's critique of the two teachings focuses on their ethical implications. What is especially significant about Tsung-mi's critique of Confucianism and Taoism is that it is carried out within the framework of the moral vision of Confucianism. This moral vision itself is not challenged; it is only the ability of Confucianism and Taoism to provide a coherent ontological basis for that vision that is disputed. It is in this context that the Teaching of Humans and Gods takes on importance as its teaching of karmic retribution provides a way in which the Confucian moral vision can be preserved, for it is precisely the teaching of karmic retribution that is needed to explain the apparent cases of injustice in the world. If the good suffer hardship and die young, it is because they are reaping the consequences

---

56. TSC 421a.

57. 20.10b; Chan, *Source Book,* p. 301.

58. Sometimes the destiny of titan (*asura; a-hsiu-lo* 阿修羅) is deleted, as Tsung-mi does later in his discussion of the Teaching of Humans and Gods. It seems that the destiny of titan was added to an original set of five in order to accommodate a number of different hybrid beings introduced into the Buddhist pantheon. With few exceptions the *Nikāyas* refer to only five destinies, and some of the sectarian traditions (such as the Theravādins and Sarvāstivādins) remained faithful to the traditional number of five; other sects (such as the Andhakas, Uttarāpathakas, Mahāsāṃghikas, and Vātsīputrīyas) included the titans as a sixth destiny (see Lamotte, *History of Indian Buddhism,* pp. 629-630). The *Abhidharmakośabhāsya,* which Tsung-mi follows in his accounts of the Teaching of Humans and Gods and the Teaching of the Lesser Vehicle, enumerates only five destinies.

of evil committed in a former life. If the wicked prosper with impunity, it is because they are enjoying the rewards of good deeds done in a former life.

## Critique of the Mandate of Heaven

Tsung-mi raises the issue of theodicy again in his critique of the mandate of heaven. According to Confucian mythology tracing back to the *Classic of History* and the *Classic of Poetry,* heaven—whether conceived as a personal godlike agency or as an impersonal natural force—is that which monitors the socio-political world of human endeavor to ensure that it resonates with the larger rhythms of a universe functioning in natural harmony with Confucian moral principles.[59] Heaven is thus a providential moral force that intervenes in human history, as it did paradigmatically in the founding of the Chou dynasty. As it became translated into a theory of dynastic cycles, this myth held that whenever a ruler became tyrannical or otherwise morally unfit to exercise rule, heaven would display its disfavor by manifesting ominous portents and natural disasters. If the situation became critical enough, heaven would withdraw its mandate, disorder would increase, and the political order would fall into chaos. Out of the ensuing turmoil and strife, heaven would select the most worthy upon whom to confer a new mandate to rule, and peace and order would once again be restored.

Thus, according to this myth, heaven was seen as a cosmic moral force, or, as stated in the more straightforward words of the *Classic of History:* "The Way of heaven is to bless the good and punish the bad."[60] At the same time, other Confucian texts of equally hallowed provenance maintained that the individual's lot in life was determined by heaven. Tsung-mi cites the *Analects,* which quotes Confucius as saying: "Death and life have their determined appointment, riches and honor depend upon heaven."[61] If this is so, Tsung-mi reasons, then heaven must also be responsible for the manifold examples of injustice so apparent in the world. How then, he asks, can it be moral? As he puts the case in his critique of the mandate of heaven in the *Inquiry:*

59. See Herrlee Creel, *The Origins of Statecraft in China,* vol. 1, chapter 5, "The Mandate of Heaven," pp. 81-100.

60. *The Chinese Classics* 3.186. Tsung-mi cites this passage in his notes to his critique of the decree of heaven; see TSC 415d1-2.

61. *The Chinese Classics* 1.253. Tsung-mi cites this passage in the corresponding section of his TS 163b3-4.

[708b28] 　又言貧富貴賤賢愚善惡吉凶禍福皆由天命者、
則天之賦命奚有貧多富少賤多貴少、乃至禍多福少。苟多
少之分在天、天何不平乎。況有無行而貴、守行而賤、無
德而富、有德而貧。逆吉義凶仁夭暴壽、乃至有道者喪、
無道者興。既皆由天、天乃興不道而喪道。何有福善益謙
之賞、禍淫害盈之罰焉。又既禍亂反逆皆由天命、則聖人
設教、責人不責天、罪物不罪命、是不當也。然則詩刺亂
政、書讚王道、禮稱安上、樂號移風。豈是奉上天之意、
順造化之心乎。是知專此教者、未能原人。

[708b28] Again, as for their claim that poverty and wealth, high and low station, sageliness and stupidity, good and evil, good and bad fortune, disaster and bounty all proceed from the mandate of heaven, then, in heaven's endowment of destiny, why are the impoverished many and the wealthy few, those of low station many and those of high station few, and so on to those suffering disaster many and those enjoying bounty few? If the apportionment of many and few lies in heaven, why is heaven not fair? How much more unjust is it in cases of those who lack moral conduct and yet are honored, those who maintain moral conduct and yet remain debased, those who lack virtue and yet enjoy wealth, those who are virtuous and yet suffer poverty, or the refractory enjoying good fortune, the righteous suffering misfortune, the humane dying young, the cruel living to an old age, and so on to the moral being brought down and the immoral being raised to eminence. Since all these proceed from heaven, heaven thus makes the immoral prosper while bringing the moral to grief. How can there be the reward of blessing the good and augmenting the humble, and the punishment of bringing disaster down upon the wicked and affliction upon the full? Furthermore, since disaster, disorder, rebellion, and mutiny all proceed from heaven's mandate, the teachings established by the sages are not right in holding human beings and not heaven responsible and in blaming people and not destiny. Nevertheless, the [*Classic of*] *Poetry* censures chaotic rule, the [*Classic of*] *History* extols the kingly Way, the [*Book of*] *Rites* praises making superiors secure, and the [*Classic of*] *Music* proclaims changing [the people's]

manners. How could that be upholding the intention of heaven above and conforming to the mind of creation?

In the notes to the corresponding passage in his *Commentary to the Scripture of Perfect Enlightenment,* Tsung-mi also quotes the following passage from the *Classic of Change:* "It is the way of heaven to diminish the full and augment the humble."[62] Tsung-mi's reference to the morally transforming power of the rites and music derives from the *Classic of Filiality:* "For changing [the people's] manners and altering their customs there is nothing better than music; for securing the repose of superiors and good order of the people there is nothing better than the rules of propriety."[63]

62. As translated by Legge in Sung, *The Text of the Yi King,* p. 71; see TSC 415d.

63. *Hsiao ching* 4/12/1, as translated by Legge in *The Sacred Books of China* 1.481-482.

# Part 2 Exposing the Partial and Superficial
## Introduction

The second main division of the *Inquiry into the Origin of Humanity,* "Exposing the Partial and Superficial" (*ch'ih p'ien ch'ien* 斥偏淺), is devoted to the first four teachings that Tsung-mi includes within his classification of Buddhist teachings; the fifth and highest teaching is reserved for the next part. As Tsung-mi notes under the heading for this part, it is addressed to "those who study the teachings of the Buddha whose meaning is not ultimate (習佛不了義教者)."

[708c12]　佛教自淺之深。略有五等、一人天教、二小乘教、三大乘法相教、四大乘破相教 (上四在此篇中)。五一乘顯性教 (此一在第三篇中)。

[708c12] **The Buddha's teachings proceed from the superficial to the profound. Altogether there are five categories: (1) the Teaching of Humans and Gods, (2) the Teaching of the Lesser Vehicle, (3) the Teaching of the Phenomenal Appearances of the Dharmas within the Great Vehicle, (4) the Teaching That Refutes the Phenomenal Appearances within the Great Vehicle** (the above four [teachings] are included within this part), **and (5) the Teaching of the One Vehicle That Reveals the Nature** (this one [teaching] is included within the third part).

Tsung-mi's division of the five Buddhist teachings into two separate parts of his essay emphasizes that the first four are all provisional, whereas the fifth alone is ultimate. That is, each of the first four teachings comes successively closer to clarifying the ultimate ground of existence, but the fifth alone succeeds in revealing its nature. The criterion according to which the different teachings are arranged is thus determined by their ability to answer the cosmogonic question that Tsung-mi frames in terms of the origin of humanity.

The doctrinal classification scheme that Tsung-mi uses in the *Inquiry* is virtually identical to that of the *Ch'an Preface*. Even the wording in his accounts of the various teachings is largely the same in both works. The most notable difference between them is that, whereas Tsung-mi uses a fivefold scheme in the *Inquiry,* he uses a threefold one in the *Ch'an Preface*. This difference, however, is more apparent than real, as Tsung-mi includes the first three teachings of the *Inquiry* in the first category of teaching in the *Ch'an Preface,* which thus treats the same five teachings that he deals with in the *Inquiry*. The relationship between the classification schemes used in these two works can thus be represented as follows:

COMPARISON OF CLASSIFICATION SCHEMES
IN *INQUIRY* AND *CH'AN PREFACE*

| *INQUIRY* | *CH'AN PREFACE* |
|---|---|
| | 1. Hidden Intent That Set Forth the Phenomenal Appearances That are Based on the Nature 密意依性說相教 |
| 1. Humans and Gods 人天教 | A. Causes and Effects of Humans and Gods 人天因果教 |
| 2. Lesser Vehicle 小乘教 | B. Extinction of Suffering by Cutting Off Defilements 斷惑滅苦教 |
| 3. Phenomenal Appearances 法相教 | C. Refutation of Objects by Means of Consciousness 將識破境教 |
| 4. Refutation of Phenomenal Appearances 破相教 | 2. Hidden Intent That Refutes Phenomenal Appearances to Reveal the Nature 密意破相顯性教 |
| 5. Revelation of the Nature 顯性教 | 3. Direct Revelation That the Mind Is the Nature 顯示眞心即性教 |

The close correspondence between the contents of Tsung-mi's description of Buddhist teachings in two works means that the *Ch'an Preface* can be used to elucidate and amplify the second and third parts of the *Inquiry,* much as Tsung-mi's discussion of Confucianism and Taoism in his commentary and subcommentary to the *Scripture of Perfect Enlightenment* proved useful for understanding his discussion of those two teachings in the previous part. A comparison with the *Ch'an Preface* is also useful on another count: it makes explicit a second rationale behind Tsung-mi's classification of the teachings that is implicit in the *Inquiry*. This rationale is particularly important for understanding the role of emptiness (as represented in the Teaching That Refutes Phenomenal Appearances) within Tsung-mi's classification scheme because that teaching is otherwise an anomaly within his cosmogonic framework. This second ordering principle is reflected in the three major headings Tsung-mi uses to classify the teachings in the *Ch'an Preface*.

Tsung-mi refers to the first category of teachings in the *Ch'an Preface* as "the Teachings of Hidden Intent That Set Forth the Phenomenal Appearances That Are Based on the Nature" (*mi-i i-hsing shuo-hsiang chiao* 密意依性説相教). He gives the following explanation of this designation:

> The Buddha saw that the three realms [of existence] and six paths [of rebirth] were all phenomenal appearances of the true nature. [Phenomenal appearances] have no separate essence of their own but only arise because sentient beings are deluded about their nature. Hence [the designation of this teaching] says "based on the nature." Because its explanation does not reveal [the nature], it is said to be of "hidden intent."[1]

Tsung-mi subdivides this teaching into three further categories, corresponding to the first three teachings in the *Inquiry*. He refers to them as: the "Teaching of the Causes and Effects of [being born as] Humans and Gods" (*jen-t'ien yin-kuo chiao* 人天因果教), the "Teaching of Extinguishing Suffering by Cutting Off the Defilements" (*tuan-huo mieh-k'u chiao* 斷惑滅苦教),[2] and the "Teaching That Refutes Objects by Means of Consciousness" (*chiang-shih p'o-ching chiao* 將識破境教).

He refers to the second category of teaching in the *Ch'an Preface* as "the Teaching of Hidden Intent That Refutes Phenomenal Appearances in Order to Reveal the Nature" (*mi-i p'o-hsiang hsien-hsing chiao* 密意破相顯性教), whose designation he explains as follows:

> According to the true ultimate meaning, since deluded thoughts are originally empty, there is nothing that can be negated. All dharmas, being without defilement, are originally the true nature, and its marvelous functioning-in-accord-

---

1. T 48.403a16-18; K 103; cf. B 157.
2. *Huo* 惑 = *kleśa*.

with-conditions is not only never interrupted but also cannot be negated. It is only because a class of sentient beings clings to unreal phenomenal appearances, obscures their true nature, and has difficulty attaining profound enlightenment that the Buddha provisionally negated everything without distinguishing between good and bad, tainted and pure, or the nature and its phenomenal appearances. Although he did not regard the true nature and its marvelous functioning to be non-existent, because he provisionally said they were non-existent, [this teaching] is designated as being of "hidden intent." Furthermore, though his intention lay in revealing the nature, because his words thus negated phenomenal appearances and his intent was not expressed in words, they are referred to as "hidden."[3]

This category of teaching corresponds to the teaching of emptiness expounded in the Perfection of Wisdom scriptures and the Madhyamaka treatises that Tsung-mi classifies as the fourth teaching in the *Inquiry*.

Both of the first two main categories of teaching are characterized as being of "hidden intent" (*mi-i* 密意) because in neither is the Buddha's ultimate intent revealed. In this way Tsung-mi indicates that the first two levels of teaching are *neyārtha* (*pu-liao-i* 不了義), that is, not those of ultimate meaning. The second, however, is the more profound of the two because it does "intimate" (*mi-hsien* 密顯) it.[4]

The third teaching is ultimate (*nītārtha; liao-i* 了義) because, in contrast to the previous two, it "directly reveals" (*hsien-shih* 顯示) the essence. Tsung-mi thus refers to it as "the Teaching That Directly Reveals That the True Mind Is the Nature" (*hsien-shih chen-hsin chi hsing chiao* 顯示眞心即性教).

Because [this category of teaching] directly points to the fact that one's very own mind is the true nature, neither revealing it in terms of the appearances of phenomena nor revealing in terms of the refutation of phenomenal appearances (*p'o-hsiang* 破相), it has "is the nature" [in its name]. Because its intent is not hidden by expedients, it is said to "reveal it directly."[5]

3. T 48.404a7-9; K 121; cf. B 176.
4. See TS 121b and TSC 285b.
5. T 48.404b26-27; K 131; cf. B 188.

Tsung-mi's explanation of the three categories of teachings in the *Ch'an Preface* is thus significant for revealing a rationale within his ordering of the teachings that parallels and partially overlaps the cosmogony-derived rationale so prominent in the *Inquiry*. The progression of the teachings in both works begins with the naive affirmation of apparent reality in the Teaching of Humans and Gods, whose successive negation by each subsequent teaching culminates in the thoroughgoing negation of the teaching of emptiness, which exhausts deluded attachments and thereby makes possible the revelation of the true nature of reality in the Teaching that Reveals the Nature. This rationale clarifies the soteriological role that the teaching of emptiness plays within Tsung-mi's classification scheme and compensates for its anomalous status in his cosmogony-derived ordering.

# The Teaching of
# Humans and Gods

In terms of the overall structure of the *Inquiry into the Origin of Humanity*, the Teaching of Humans and Gods serves as the crucial link relating the teachings of Confucianism and Taoism to those of Buddhism. On the one hand, it serves a polemical purpose by subordinating the two teachings to even the most elementary and superficial teaching of Buddhism. On the other hand, it serves a broader and more synthetic purpose. The teaching of karmic retribution, by resolving the dilemma of theodicy,[1] preserves the Confucian belief in a moral universe. It also opens the way for Confucian moral practices to be incorporated into Buddhism by assimilating the five constant virtues of Confucianism into the five precepts of Buddhism. Even though in Tsung-mi's terms Confucianism cannot provide a convincing metaphysical rationale for the moral functioning of the universe, the moral practices that it advocates—being, in essence, no different from those advocated in Buddhism—are still meritorious and can lead to a good future birth in the human realm.[2]

1. The ability of karma theory to resolve the problem of theodicy has frequently been noted. Max Weber, for one, has argued that the Buddhist teaching of karma represents "the most complete formal solution of the problem of theodicy" (see his "Theodicy, Salvation, and Rebirth" in *The Sociology of Religion*, p. 145). Peter Berger, who uses Weber's discussion as the starting point for his own treatment of theodicy in *The Sacred Canopy*, regards "the *karma-samsara* complex" as "the most rational" theodicy (p. 65), claiming that "Buddhism probably represents the most radical rationalization of the theoretical foundations of the *karma-samsara* complex" (p. 67). See also Gananath Obeyesekere, "Theodicy, Sin and Salvation in a Sociology of Buddhism," and Arthur Herman, *The Problem of Evil and Indian Thought*.

2. The Teaching of Humans and Gods is notably absent in the classification schemes of Tsung-mi's Hua-yen predecessors; for a discussion of this teaching within the context of Hua-yen doctrinal categories, see my

110

The Teaching of Humans and Gods consists in the simple moral teaching of karmic retribution. It is so called because it teaches people how they can gain a propitious birth as a human or a god by maintaining the five precepts prescribed for lay people and by practicing the ten good deeds.[3] The Teaching of Humans and Gods generally corresponds to the teaching for the laity as propounded in such early Indian Buddhist scriptures as the *Discourse on the Lesser Analysis of Deeds* and *Discourse on the Greater Analysis of Deeds*.[4] In the first of these, for example, a young brahmin asks the Buddha why human beings live in such a variety of circumstances, some being short-lived while others are long-lived, some suffering many illnesses while others enjoy good health, some being impoverished while others are wealthy, some being born into families of low station while others are born into families of high station, and so forth. The Buddha answers that the discrepancies seen in human life are all due to karma. He then elaborates, saying that those who kill other living creatures, if they are reborn as humans in their next life, will be short-lived and those who abstain from killing other living creatures, if they are reborn as humans in their next life, will be long-lived. Similarly, in their next life, those who mistreat living creatures will suffer many illnesses, those who are kind to living creatures will enjoy good health, those who are stingy will be impoverished, those who are generous will be wealthy, those who are arrogant will be born into families of low station, and those who are humble will be born into families of high station.

Although the teaching of karma was basic to all forms of Buddhism, it seems to have formed the central focus of the teaching

---

"The Teaching of Men and Gods: The Doctrinal and Social Basis of Lay Buddhist Practice in the Hua-yen Tradition," especially pp. 278-296, in which I contend that Tsung-mi's inclusion of this teaching within his classification system reflects the growing importance of lay Buddhist societies in the late eighth and early ninth centuries.

3. The ten good deeds (*daśakuśala*) are not to commit the ten evil deeds (*daśākuśala*), viz., 1) killing, 2) stealing, 3) adultery, 4) lying, 5) slander, 6) harsh speech, 7) frivolous chatter, 8) covetousness, 9) malice, and 10) false views.

4. The *Cūlakammavibhaṅga-sutta* and *Mahākammavibhaṅga-sutta* in *Majjhima-nikāya* 3.202-206 and 207-215, translated by Horner in *The Middle Length Sayings* 3.248-253 and 254-262; cf. *Ying-wu ching* and *Fen-pieh ta-yeh ching*, nos. 170 and 171 of the *Chung a-han ching*, T 1.703c-706b and 706b-708c.

directed to the laity, especially as it dealt with the causal link between various actions or types of action and specific forms of rebirth. While lay practice centered around the maintenance of the five precepts, it was always justified in terms of the good consequences to be experienced in the future, either later in one's present lifetime or in a subsequent rebirth.[5] We find the Buddha in numerous other early scriptures exhorting lay people to practice almsgiving (*dāna*) with the promise that their generosity will lead to a desirable rebirth in a heavenly realm.

Although the Teaching of Humans and Gods thus seems to correspond to the teaching for lay people in the Indian Buddhist tradition, it was not referred to as a particular category of teaching by this name in Indian Buddhism. Rather, the term "the Teaching of Humans and Gods" seems to have been coined by Chinese Buddhists during the second half of the fifth century in an effort to accommodate Buddhism to the needs of its growing number of lay adherents by adapting it to the more socially-oriented concerns of Confucianism. The first mention of the Teaching of Humans and Gods occurs in the doctrinal classification scheme of Liu Ch'iu (438-495), a lay Buddhist recluse in the south, who divided the Buddha's teachings into two general types, the sudden and gradual. Liu went on to divide the gradual teachings into five, the first of which was that of humans and gods, as taught in the *T'i-wei Po-li ching* (The Scripture of Trapuṣa and Bhallika).

The *T'i-wei Po-li ching*,[6] the scripture on which the Teaching of Humans and Gods is based, was composed in northern China

---

5. In his *Indian Buddhism* (p. 187), Warder notes that the standard course of instruction for lay disciples comprised discourses on giving (*dāna*), morality (*śīla*), and heaven (*svarga*); the disadvantage, vanity, and depravity of sense pleasures; and the advantage of renunciation (see, for instance, *Dīgha-nikāya* 1.110, translated by Rhys Davids in *Dialogues of the Buddha* 1.134-135, and *Majjhima-nikāya* 1.379, translated by Horner in *The Middle Length Sayings* 2.45).

6. Tsukamoto Zenryū has gathered together the various fragments of the *T'i-wei Po-li ching* that are quoted in other sources and has published them in his *Shina bukkyōshi kenkyū, Hokugi hen*, pp. 293-353; reprinted in *Tsukamoto Zenryū chosaku shū* 2.189-240. The second fascicle of this text (Stein no. 2051) was among the works found at Tun-huang and has been published by Makita Tairyō in his "Tonkōbon *Daiikyō* no kenkyū," pp. 137-185. See also Whalen Lai, "The Earliest Folk Buddhist Religion in China: *T'i-wei Po-li ching* and Its Historical Significance." While there is nothing, in

around 460 by T'an-ching.[7] It fit in well with the widescale ideological use of Buddhism on the part of the Northern Wei state in
its efforts both to control a people of mixed ethnic stock, in whom
Confucian moral teachings had not yet been deeply ingrained, and
to mobilize the general population for the restoration of Buddhism
on a massive scale after the persecution of 446. This text purports
to have been taught on the seventh day after the Buddha's enlightenment to a group of five hundred merchants led by Trapuṣa (T'i-
wei) and Bhallika (Po-li). It exhorts them to take the triple refuge
in the Buddha, dharma, and sangha, to maintain the five precepts,
and to practice the ten good deeds so as to ensure a good future
birth as a human or a god. The five precepts are given special emphasis and are even accorded cosmological significance. They are
said to be

> . . . the root of heaven and earth and the source of all spiri-
> tual beings. When heaven observes them, yin and yang are
> harmonized; when earth observes them, the myriad crea-
> tures are engendered. They are the mother of the myriad
> creatures and the father of the myriad spirits, the origin of
> the great Way and the fundamental basis of nirvāṇa.[8]

The five precepts are homologized with other sets of five in
Chinese cosmology—such as the five elemental phases, five planets,

---

terms of content, comparable to the *T'i-wei Po-li ching* in Indian Buddhist
literature, the *Aṅguttara-nikāya* does contain a *Tapussa-sutta* (translated by
Hare in *The Book of Gradual Sayings* 4.293-295) whose resemblance to the
*T'i-wei Po-li ching*, however, does not go beyond its title. The earliest account
of Trapuṣa and Bhallika occur in the Vinaya section of the Tripiṭaka, where
they offer the Buddha his first meal after his enlightenment, take refuge in
the Buddha and dharma (the sangha still not having been formed), and
become the Buddha's first lay disciples (see Horner's translation in *The Book
of Discipline* 1.5-6; cf. *Ssu-fen lü*, T 22.103a; *Jui-ying pen-ch'i ching*, T 3.479a;
*Pen-hsing chi ching*, T 3.801a; and *P'u-yao ching*, T 3.526b).

7. At the end of the biography of T'an-yao, the famous Superintendent
of Monks who set the course for the revival of Buddhism after the Northern Wei persecution of 446, Tao-hsüan adds a brief note on T'an-ching,
which links the composition of the *T'i-wei Po-li ching* with the restoration
of Buddhism (see *Hsü kao-seng chuan*, T 50.428a10-12). He writes that
since the former translations had been burned up during the persecution,
some basis for guiding the people was urgently needed, and T'an-ching
accordingly composed the *T'i-wei Po-li ching* to make up for this deficiency.

8. Fragment 6, quoted in *Tsukamoto chosaku shū* 2.203.

five emperors, five sacred peaks, five internal organs, five colors, and five virtues[9]—and the failure to maintain them consequently has cosmic reverberations throughout the various spheres with which they correspond. Most significantly for Chinese lay Buddhist practice, the Buddha matches the five Buddhist precepts for lay people with the five constant virtues of Confucianism. Thus the Buddhist precept not to take life is paired with the Confucian virtue of benevolence (*jen* 仁); not to take what is not given, with righteousness (*i* 義); not to engage in illicit sexual activity, with propriety (*li* 禮); not to drink intoxicating beverages, with wisdom (*chih* 智); and not to lie, with trustworthiness (*hsin* 信).[10]

Whereas the *T'i-wei Po-li ching* couches Buddhist moral injunctions within the framework of Chinese cosmological thought, Tsung-mi's version of the Teaching of Humans and Gods in the *Inquiry* rationalizes the teaching of karmic retribution with Buddhist cosmology as systematically developed in the Abhidharma literature. In Tsung-mi's account all of the practices whose karmic fruits still involve beings in the various realms of birth are encompassed within the purview of the Teaching of Humans and Gods. Thus, although the Teaching of Humans and Gods generally refers to the lay teaching within Buddhism, the more advanced stages of meditation included within Tsung-mi's version of this teaching go beyond the usual sphere of lay Buddhist practice.

Tsung-mi gives a condensed account of this teaching in his *Ch'an Preface:*

> The teaching of the causes and effects of [being born as] humans and gods, teaching the karmic retribution of good and bad, enables [beings] to know that there is no discrepancy between cause and effect, to dread the suffering of the three [woeful] destinies, to seek the joy of [being reborn as] humans and gods, to cultivate all good practices—such as giving, maintaining the precepts, and practicing meditation—and thereby gain birth in the destinies of humans and gods and even the realms of form and the formlessness.[11]

9. See fragment 8, ibid. 2.204.

10. See fragment 9, ibid. 2.204. The way in which the five precepts are paired with the five constant virtues differs in different fragments of the text quoted by Tsukamoto. For a discussion of these see Ch'en, *The Chinese Transformation of Buddhism,* pp. 57-59.

11. T 48.403a18-21; K 103; cf. B 157-158.

As a final comment on the Teaching of Humans and Gods in the *Ch'an Preface,* Tsung-mi adds a critical note on this teaching that points to the way in which it is superseded by the next level of Buddhist teaching, that of the Lesser Vehicle. He says that the Teaching of Humans and Gods only explains "worldly causes and effects" and not "the causes and effects of transcending the world."

> It merely causes [beings] to have an aversion for the lower [realms] and to take delight in the higher [realms], not yet teaching that the three realms are all afflictions that should be renounced. It also has not yet destroyed [the belief in] the self.[12]

## SYNOPSIS

Tsung-mi gives a more detailed explanation of the workings of karmic retribution in the *Inquiry,* connecting various types of moral and spiritual action with birth in specific realms described in Buddhist cosmology. Accordingly, the commission of the ten evil deeds leads to birth in the three woeful destinies. The commission of the ten evil deeds in their highest degree leads to birth in hell; in their lesser degree, to birth as a hungry ghost; and in their lowest degree, to birth as an animal.

[708c15] 一佛為初心人且説三世業報善惡因果。謂造上品十惡死墮地獄、中品餓鬼、下品畜生。

[708c15] The Buddha, for the sake of beginners, at first set forth the karmic retribution of the three periods of time [i.e., past, present, and future] and the causes and effects of good and bad [deeds]. That is to say, [one who] commits the ten evils in their highest degree falls into hell upon death, [one who commits the ten evils] in their lesser degree becomes a hungry ghost, and [one who commits the ten evils] in their lowest degree becomes an animal.[13]

---

12. T 48.403b7; K 104; cf. B 161.

13. Yüan-chüeh's commentary on this passage (*Chieh* 120b-c) says that all good and evil deeds have three degrees, which, in turn, can be analyzed from three perspectives—i.e., in regard to the object, the state of mind of the perpetrator, and the three periods of time. In regard to the object, the killing of a person is a case of an evil in its highest degree; the killing of an animal is a case of an evil in its lesser degree; and the killing of an insect is a case of an evil in its lowest degree. In regard to the state

The maintenance of the five precepts, on the other hand, enables people to avoid birth in the three woeful destinies and to gain
birth as a human.

[708c17]　故佛且類世五常之教、令持五戒、得免三途生
人道中。

[708c17] Therefore, the Buddha grouped [the five pre-
cepts] with the five constant virtues of the worldly teaching
and caused [beginners] to maintain the five precepts, to
succeed in avoiding the three [woeful] destinies, and to be
born into the human realm.

---

of mind of the perpetrator, the commission of an evil deed with malicious
intent is a case of an evil in its highest degree; the commission of an evil
deed with only some deliberation is a case of an evil in its lesser degree;
and the commission of an evil deed unintentionally is a case of an evil in
its lowest degree. Finally, in regard to the three periods of time, the commission of an evil deed without any sense of contrition in any of the three
periods of time (i.e., before, during, and after) is a case of an evil in its
highest degree; the commission of an evil deed with a sense of contrition
in any one of the three periods of time is a case of an evil in its lesser
degree; and the commission of an evil deed with a sense of contrition in
two of the three periods of time is a case of an evil in its lowest degree.
　The idea that there are degrees of good and evil can be found in the
*Daśabhūmika* chapter of the *Hua-yen Sūtra*. In the section dealing with
the second *bhūmi,* the Śikṣānanda translation says: "The course of the ten
evil deeds is the cause of being born in [the realm of] hell, animals, and
hungry ghosts. The course of the ten good deeds is the cause of being
born in [the realm of] humans and gods up to the pinnacle of existence"
(T 10.185c1-3). And further: "As for the course of the ten evil deeds, the
highest [degree] is the cause of [being born as] a denizen of hell, the lesser
[degree] is the cause of [being born as] an animal, and the lowest [degree]
is the cause of [being born as] a hungry ghost" (185c16-18). (For the corresponding passages in the Buddhabhadra translation, see T 9.549a14-15
and 26-28.) It should be noted that Tsung-mi's ranking of the different
realms of woeful existence differs from that of the *Hua-yen Sūtra*. Whereas the passage from the *Hua-yen Sūtra* says that evils of a lesser degree
are a cause for being born as an animal and that evils of the lowest degree
are a cause for being born as a hungry ghost, the passage from the *Inquiry*
says that evils of a lesser degree are a cause for being born as a hungry
ghost and that evils of the lowest degree are a cause for being born as an
animal. Tsung-mi's position agrees with that of the *Abhidharmakośabhāṣya*,
which also ranks birth as an animal below that as a hungry ghost.

In his note to this passage, Tsung-mi goes on to pair the five precepts with the five constant virtues in the same manner in which
they had been paired with one another in the *T'i-wei Po-li ching.*

[708c17] （天竺世教儀式雖殊、懲惡勸善無別。亦不離仁義等
五常、而有德行可修。例如此國斂手而舉吐番散手而垂、皆為
禮也。不殺是仁、不盜是義、不邪淫是禮、不妄語是信、不飲
噉酒肉神氣清潔益於智也。）[14]

[708c17] (As for the worldly teaching of India, even though its observance is distinct, in its admonishing against evil and its exhorting to
good,[15] there is no difference [from that of China]. Moreover, it is not
separate from the five constant virtues of benevolence, righteousness,
and so forth, and there is virtuous conduct that should be cultivated.[16]
For example, it is like the clasping[17] of the hands together and raising
them in this country and the dropping of the hands by the side in Tibet—
both are [examples of] propriety. Not killing is benevolence, not stealing
is righteousness, not committing adultery is propriety, not lying is trustworthiness, and, by neither drinking wine nor eating meat, the spirit is
purified and one increases in wisdom.)

The practice of the ten good deeds and the six perfections,[18] moreover, leads to birth in one of the six heavens of the realm of desire.[19]

14. Note that I have slightly rearranged the order of the Chinese text
to make it conform to the translation.
15. The wording here (*ch'eng-o ch'üan-shan* 懲惡勸善) is the same
as that used in the passage in the Preface that says: "encouraging the myriad practices, admonishing against evil, and promoting good contribute in
common to order" (708a11-12).
16. The punctuation of the Taishō text is in error. The punctuation
should come after *hsiu* 修, as should be clear from Yüan-chüeh's commentary (*Chieh* 121b). *Li* 例 ("for example") begins the next sentence. The Japanese commentators also read the text in this way.
17. The Taishō text has *han* 斂. Following Kamata (*Genninron,* p. 60),
I have emended *han* to read *lien* 斂. Morohashi notes that *han* is often
written for *lien* (6.6362c).
18. That is, giving (*dāna*), morality (*śīla*), patience (*kṣānti*), vigor
(*vīrya*), concentration (*dhyāna*), and wisdom (*prajñā*).
19. Which constitute the upper levels of the realm of desire or *kāmadhātu.* They are, according to the *Abhidharmakośabhāṣya,* 1) the heaven
of the retainers of the four great kings (*caturmahārājakāyika-deva*), 2) the
heaven of the thirty-three gods (*trāyastriṃśa-deva*), 3) the heaven of the
yāmas (*yāma-deva*), 4) the heaven of the satisfied (*tuṣita-deva*), 5) the

[708c20]　修上品十善及施戒等生六欲天。

[708c20] [One who] cultivates the ten good deeds in their highest degree as well as bestowing alms, maintaining the precepts, and so forth is born into [one of] the six heavens of [the realm of] desire.

All of the destinies enumerated so far fall within the realm of desire (*kāmadhātu; yü-chieh* 欲界), the first and lowest of the three realms of birth in Buddhist cosmology. Birth into the next two realms is only possible through the development of various stages of meditative absorption.

[708c20]　修四禪八定生色界無色界天。

[708c20] [One who] cultivates the four stages of meditative absorption and the eight attainments is born into [one of] the heavens of the realm of form or the realm of formlessness.

Although the early Indian Buddhist scriptures do contain examples of laymen who succeeded in being born into these higher realms through the practice of meditation,[20] such cases are the exception

---

heaven of those who delight in their own creations (*nirmāṇarati-deva*), and 6) the heaven of those who delight in the creations of others (*paranirmitavaśavartin-deva*) (T 29.41a; cf. La Vallée Poussin 2.1 and Pruden 2.365). The same enumeration can be found in earlier texts; cf. *Majjhima-nikāya* 2.194 and 3.100 (translated by Horner in *The Middle Length Sayings* 2.377 and 3.139-140) and *Dīgha-nikāya* 1.216 (translated by Rhys Davids in *Dialogues of the Buddha* 1.280-281). For a more detailed discussion of these six heavens, see Mochizuki 4.3770b-3771b and La Vallée Poussin, "Cosmogony and Cosmology (Buddhist)," pp. 134-135.

20. In the *Dhānañjāni-sutta* of the *Majjhima-nikāya* (translated by Horner in *The Middle Length Sayings* 2.372-379), the brahmin Dhānañjāni succeeds in gaining birth in the heaven of Brahma as a result of having practiced the meditation of suffusing the universe with friendliness, compassion, sympathic joy, and equanimity. In the *Anāthapiṇḍikovāda-sutta* (translated by Horner in *The Middle Length Sayings* 3.309-315), the pious layman and *dānapati* Anāthapiṇḍika succeeds in being born in the Tuṣita heaven as a result of having heard Sāriputta discourse on the course of mental discipline usually taught to monks. As a final example, Ānanda, following instructions of the Buddha, explains the four stages of meditative absorption to a group of laymen in the *Sekha-sutta* (translated by Horner in *The Middle Length Sayings* 2.18-25), concluding his sermon with the assertion that even householders can achieve nirvāṇa.

rather than the rule. In general, the moral practices usually taught to the laity would only lead to birth in the higher spheres of the realm of desire. Birth into the next realm, the realm of form (*rūpadhātu; se-chieh* 色界), is attained through the mastery of the four stages of meditative absorption (*dhyāna; ch'an* 禪), and birth into the highest realm, the realm of formlessness (*arūpadhātu; wu-se-chieh* 無色界), is attained through the mastery of the four formless attainments (*samāpatti; ting* 定). The "eight attainments" that Tsung-mi refers to comprise the four stages of meditative absorption and the four formless attainments. They form part of the heritage of yogic practices that were incorporated into Buddhism, and together they comprise a stock set found throughout the Buddhist tradition.[21]

The eight attainments belong to the enstatic[22] pole of Buddhist meditation practice, which is associated with the cultivation of calming (*śamatha; chih* 止) as distinguished from the cultivation of insight (*vipaśyanā; kuan* 觀). Many scholars have seen these two meditational approaches as representing fundamentally different soteriological orientations and goals, which underlies the tension between them in the Buddhist tradition.[23] Whereas the cultivation of insight leads to the discernment of things as they really are, the cultivation of calming entails the mastery of a progressive series of states in which the contents and faculties of consciousness are systematically eliminated. Sometimes a ninth state, that of the cessation of conceptualization and sensation, is added to the eight attainments to comprise an ascending series of meditational stages known as the attainments of the nine successive stages.[24]

21. For an excellent presentation of traditional meditation theory and practice according to the Pāli Canon and the Theravāda tradition, see Paravahera Vajrañāṇa Mahāthera, *Buddhist Meditation in Theory and Practice;* see also Winston King, *Theravāda Meditation.*

22. "The term 'enstatic' is derived from the Greek *en-stasis* meaning 'standing within', and etymologically is the opposite of 'ecstatic'—'standing without'" (Griffiths, *On Being Mindless,* p. 148n27).

23. The first to call attention to this tension was La Vallée Poussin in his "Musīla et Nārada;" for a more recent elaboration of this tension see Griffiths, "Concentration or Insight;" see also Sponberg, "Meditation in Fa-hsiang Buddism," for an insightful discussion of Buddhist meditation terms.

24. The *navānupūrva-vihāra-samāpatti,* which are enumerated in the *Aṅguttara-nikāya* 4.409 (translated by Hare in *The Book of the Gradual Sayings* 4.276-277) and elsewhere in the Pāli Canon. For a detailed discussion

The four stages of meditative absorption correspond to the four main heavens within the realm of form, and mastery of each stage thus gives access to the corresponding heaven.[25] The standard formula says that having become free of sense-desires and unwholesome states, one enters the first stage of meditative absorption, which is accompanied by applied and discursive thought, born of detachment, rapturous, and joyful. From the appeasing of applied and discursive thought, one enters the second stage of meditative absorption, where the inward heart is serene and uniquely exalted, and which is devoid of applied and discursive thought, born of concentration, rapturous, and joyful. Through distaste for rapture, one dwells evenmindedly, mindful and clearly conscious, and enters

---

of this ninth state (*saṃjñā-vedayita-nirodha-samāpatti*), and the philosophical problems that it posed for Buddhist theory, see Griffiths, *On Being Mindless*. Although Tsung-mi does not mention the attainment of the cessation of conceptualization and sensation here, he does later in his critique of the Teaching of Humans and Gods, where he cites it for the particular problem that it poses for Hīnayāna theory in accounting for mental continuity in the absence of any underlying substratum of consciousness.

25. The realm of form (*rūpadhātu*), located above the six heavens of desire, is comprised for four main heavens. The number of heavens within these four main heavens, however, varies with different texts. According to the *Abhidharmakośabhāṣya* (T 29.41a; cf. La Vallée Poussin 2.2-4 and Pruden 2.366), the first three meditation heavens are each comprised of three heavens while the fourth is comprised of eight. The first meditation heaven is inhabited by gods in the retinue of Brahma (*brahmakāyika*), the Brahma chaplains (*brahmapurohita*), and the great Brahmas (*mahābrahma*). The second meditation heaven is inhabited by gods of limited splendor (*parīttābha*), of immeasurable splendor (*apramāṇābha*), and of radiance (*ābhāsvara*). The third meditation heaven is inhabited by gods of limited beauty (*parīttaśubha*), of immeasurable beauty (*apramāṇāśubha*), and of complete beauty (*śubhakṛtsna*). The fourth meditation heaven is inhabited by gods who are cloudless (*anabhraka*), merit born (*puṇyaprasava*), of abundant fruit (*bṛhatphala*), effortless (*avṛha*), of no heat (*atapa*), beautiful (*sudṛśa*), well-seeing (*sudarśana*), and sublime (*akaniṣṭha*). All of the gods dwelling in the heavens of the realm of form, being wholly beyond sense-desires, are without sexual characteristics and are born by apparitional birth without the intermediacy of parents; their bodies are luminous and of a subtle substance, which feeds on joy. For a more detailed discussion of these heavens and their inhabitants, see Mochizuki 4.3770a-3775a and La Vallée Poussin, "Cosmogony and Cosmology," pp. 135-136.

the third stage of meditative absorption, experiencing with one's body that joy of which the saints declare, "joyful lives one who is evenminded and mindful." From the forsaking of joy, from the forsaking of pain, from the going to rest of one's former gladness and sadness, one enters the fourth stage of meditative absorption, which is neither painful nor pleasurable, and which is the utter purity of evenmindedness and mindfulness.[26]

Access to the four stages of meditative absorption is made possible by focusing on an object of concentration. This object, belonging to the realm of form, must be dispensed with to enter into the four formless attainments, which represent a successive diminution of the content and functioning of consciousness. The four formless attainments likewise correspond to the four heavens within the formless realm, and mastery of each stage thus gives access to the corresponding heaven. Being totally beyond the realm of form, the formless heavens are wholly immaterial and thus do not exist in space. They are those of infinite space (*ākāśānantyāyatana; k'ung-wu-pien-ch'u* 空無邊處), infinite consciousness (*vijñānānantyāyatana; shih-wu-pien-ch'u* 識無邊處), nothingness (*ākiṃcanyāyatana; wu-ch'u-yu-ch'u* 無處有處), and neither conceptualization nor non-conceptualization (*naivasaṃjñānasaṃjñāyatana; fei-hsiang-fei-fei-hsiang-ch'u* 非想非非想處).[27]

---

26. Adapted from Conze's translation of the formula from the *Visuddhimagga* in his *Buddhist Meditation,* pp. 113-118. This standard description of the four stages of meditative absorption can be found in numerous places throughout the Pāli Canon; see, for example, *Dīgha-nikāya* 1.73-75, 182-183, and 2.314 (translated by Rhys Davids in *The Dialogues of the Buddha* 1.84-86, 248-249, and 2.345) and *Majjhima-nikāya* 1.174 (translated by Horner in *The Middle Length Sayings* 1.218). The paramount importance of the four stages of meditative absorption in Buddhism is established by the fact that it was only after passing through all four stages that the Buddha experienced enlightenment; see *Bhayabherava-sutta* ("Discourse on Fear and Dread," translated by Horner in *The Middle Length Sayings* 1.27-29) and *Mahāsac-caka-sutta* ("Greater Discourse to Saccaka," translated by Horner in *The Middle Length Sayings* 1.301-303). Mastery of the four stages of meditative absorption is also the necessary precondition for developing various supernormal powers (such as clairvoyance, clairaudience, telepathy, etc.). For a standard scholastic analysis of the four stages of meditation, see *Visuddhimagga* 4, translated by Ñāṇamoli in *The Path of Purification,* pp. 144-175.

27. For a detailed discussion of the four formless attainments, see *Visuddhimagga* 10 (translated by Ñāṇamoli in *The Path of Purification,* pp. 354-

### TSUNG-MI'S SCHEME OF KARMIC RETRIBUTION

| ACTION (*karma*) | DESTINY (*gati*) | | REALM (*dhātu*) |
|---|---|---|---|
| Four Formless Attainments | Gods | Four Formless Heavens | Formlessness (*arūpadhātu*) |
| Four Stages of Meditation | Gods | Four Heavens of Form | Form (*rūpadhātu*) |
| Ten Good Deeds | Gods | Six Heavens of Desire | Desire (*kāmadhātu*) |
| Five Precepts | Humans | | |
| Ten Evil Deeds | Hungry Ghosts, Animals, Hell Dwellers | Three Woeful Destinies | |

Tsung-mi's mention of the various modes of rebirth raises the question of why he only mentions the human in the title of his treatise.

[708c21] （題中不標天鬼地獄者、界地不同、見聞不及、凡俗尚不知末、況肯窮本。故對俗教且標原人。今敍佛經[教]、理宜具列。）故名人天教也。（然業有三種、一惡、二善、三不動。報有三時、謂現報、生報、後報。）據此教中、業為身本。

**[708c21] (The reason gods, [hungry] ghosts, and the denizens of hell are not mentioned in the title [of this treatise] is that their realms, being different [from the human], are beyond ordinary understanding. Since the secular person does not even know the branches, how much less could he presume to investigate the root thoroughly. Therefore, in concession to the secular[28] teaching, I have entitled [this treatise] "Inquiry into the Origin of Humanity."[29] [However,] in now relating the teachings of the Buddha, it was, as a matter of principle,[30] fitting that I set forth [the other destinies] in detail.)** Therefore, [this teaching]

371). According to *Ariyapariyesana-sutta* ("Discourse on the Ariyan Quest"), the teaching of two of the Buddha's teacher, Āḷāra Kālāma and Uddaka Rāmaputta, culminated, respectively, in the seventh and eighth attainments. Since the attainment of neither one of these stages frees one from the cycle of rebirth, they were rejected as not being ultimate by the Buddha (see the translation by Horner in *The Middle Length Sayings* 1.208-210).

28. *Su* 俗 has a range of connotations that cannot be captured by a single English word. In a Buddhist context, it means 'lay', whereas in a Confucian context, it is often used to mean 'vulgar'.

29. Could Tsung-mi possibly be alluding to Han Yü here?

30. The punctuation of the Taishō text is in error. The editors of the Ching-yüan commentary (98c), as well as all the Japanese commentaries

is called the Teaching of Humans and Gods. (As for karma, there are three types: 1) good, 2) bad, and 3) neutral. As for retribution, there are three periods of time, that is to say, retribution in the present life, in the next life, and in subsequent lives.) According to this teaching, karma constitutes the origin of bodily existence.

## CRITIQUE

Although this teaching enables one to escape birth in one of the woeful modes of existence and to gain a desirable birth as a human or a god, it still naively assumes that there is a self that is reborn. It is thus superseded by the Teaching of the Lesser Vehicle, whose analysis shows that there is no abiding, unchanging entity that can be grasped as a self. Rather, what is erroneously grasped as the self is merely an illusion produced by an ever-changing concatenation of different constitutive elements or dharmas. Tsung-mi's critique in this section points out that the Teaching of Humans and Gods cannot account for how karma works because it cannot explain "who" produces karma and "who" experiences its results.

[708c23] 今詰之曰。既由造業受五道身、未審誰人造業、誰人受報。

[708c23] Now I will assess [this teaching] critically. Granted that we receive a bodily existence in [one of] the five destinies[31] as a result of our having generated karma, it is still not clear who generates karma and who experiences its retribution.

His critique continues, showing that this teaching cannot locate an agent that produces karma, and his analysis anticipates the dharma analysis developed in the Teaching of the Lesser Vehicle. It also calls to mind the passage in the *Chuang-tzu* on the impossibility of ever determining a "genuine ruler" among "the hundred joints, nine openings, [and] six inward organs."[32]

---

consulted, place the punctuation after *ching* 經. Moreover, Kishinami (3.9), Atsuta (p. 66), and Kamata (p. 60) all emend *ching* to read *chiao* 教; I have accordingly translated *fo-ching* 佛經 as "the teachings of the Buddha."

31. The five modes of rebirth mentioned above: those of the denizens of hell, hungry ghosts, animals, humans, and gods. Often a sixth destiny, that of titans (*asura*), is added (as Tsung-mi did earlier in his discussion of Confucianism and Taoism, see above 708b24-25).

32. 4/2/15-17; see Graham's translation in "On Seeing Things as Equal," p. 151.

[708c25]　若此眼耳手足能造業者、初死之人眼耳手足宛
然、何不見聞造作。若言心作、何者是心。若言肉心、肉
心有質繫於身內。如何速入眼耳辨外是非。是非不知、因
何取捨。且心與眼耳手足俱為質閡。豈得內外相通運動應
接同造業緣。若言但是喜怒愛惡發動身口令造業者、喜怒
等情、乍起乍滅、自無其體。將何為主而作業耶。

[708c25] If the eyes, ears, hands, and feet are able to generate
karma, then why, while the eyes, ears, hands, and feet of a
person who has just died are still intact, do they not see,
hear, function, and move? If one says that it is the mind that
generates [karma], what is meant by the mind? If one says
that it is the corporeal mind, then the corporeal mind has
material substance and is embedded within the body. How,
then, does it suddenly enter the eyes and ears and discern
what is and what is not of externals? If what is and what is
not are not known [by the mind], then by means of what
does one discriminate them? Moreover, since the mind is
blocked off from the eyes, ears, hands, and feet by material
substance, how, then, can they pass in and out of one another, function in response to one another, and generate karmic
conditions together? If one were to say that it is just joy,
anger, love, and hate that activate the body and mouth and
cause them to generate karma, then, since the feelings of
joy, anger, and so forth abruptly arise one moment and
abruptly perish the next and are of themselves without substance, what can we take as constituting the controlling
agent and generating karma?

The corporeal mind (*ju-t'uan hsin* 肉團心) that Tsung-mi refers to
in this passage is the lowest of four types of mind that he enumerates in the *Ch'an Preface,* where he identifies it as *ho-li-t'o-ye* (紇
利陀耶; Skt., *hṛdaya*), "the mind of the five internal organs."[33] The
Teaching of Humans and Gods is thus unaware of the other three

33. See T 48.401c17ff.; cf. TS 138b2-6 and TSC 209c1-4. The other
three are the object-receiving mind (*yüan-lü hsin* 緣慮心; i.e., the mind of
the eight consciousnesses), the mind that accumulates and produces (*chi-
ch'i hsin* 集起心; i.e., the ālayavijñāna), and the true mind (*chien-shih hsin*
堅實心; i.e., the mind that is unchanging and untainted by defilements and
that is seen as suchness). For a more detailed discussion of Tsung-mi's
four types of mind, see K 74-76; B133-136; and Mochizuki 1.475c.

higher types of mind that are taught in the succeeding teachings.[34] Tsung-mi goes on to consider a different tack by which a proponent of this teaching might explain the generation of karma.

[709a4] 設言不應如此別別推尋、都是我此身心能造業者、此身已死誰受苦樂之報。若言死後更有身者、豈有今日身心造罪修福。令他後世身心受苦受樂。據此則修福者屈甚、造罪者幸甚。如何神理如此無道。故知但習此教者、雖信業緣不達身本。

[709a4] If one were to say that the investigation should not be pursued in a disconnected fashion like this, but that it is our body-and-mind as a whole that is able to generate karma, then, once this body has died, who experiences the retribution of pain and pleasure? If one says that after death one has another body, then how can the commission of evil or the cultivation of merit in the present body-and-mind cause the experiencing of pain and pleasure in another body-and-mind in a future life? If we base ourselves on this [teaching], then one who cultivates merit should be extremely disheartened and one who commits evil should be extremely joyful. How can the holy principle be so unjust? Therefore we know that those who merely study this teaching, even though they believe in karmic conditioning, have not yet reached the origin of their bodily existence.

Tsung-mi's critique characteristically concludes by pointing out the adverse ethical implications of this teaching—that is, it does not provide a solid foundation for ethical action. His point is that if the body and mind are taken as a single totality, then the body-and-mind in this present existence would be entirely different from the body-and-mind in another existence in the future. If that were so, then there would be no personal continuity, it would be someone else who reaped the merit and demerit of one's actions, and the teaching of karma would lose all moral force.

More broadly, Tsung-mi's critique raises a question that has a long history in Buddhism: who experiences the fruits of karma? In one of the texts contained in the *Kindred Sayings* of the Pāli Canon, for example, the Buddha points out that it is just as mistaken to say that the person who commits an action and the person who

34. As Yüan-chüeh observes (*Chieh* 123a).

experiences its result are the same as it is mistaken to say that the person who commits an action and the person who experiences its result are not the same; whereas the first case represents the error of eternalism, the second represents that of annihilationism. The Buddha goes on to explain that the middle way between these two extremes consists in the teaching of conditioned origination (*pratītyasamutpāda; yüan-ch'i* 緣起), which explains how there can be continuity without any one thing that continues without change.[35]

Like the Buddha's answer in this "Hīnayāna" text, Tsung-mi's explanation of the way in which the Teaching of the Lesser Vehicle supersedes the Teaching of Humans and Gods is implicitly based on conditioned origination; it explains how the illusion of the self is a result of the contingent coming together of the body and mind as a result of "the force of causes and conditions," which "arise and perish from moment to moment, continuing in a series without cease."

## THE HEAVENS OF THE REALMS OF DESIRE, FORM, AND FORMLESSNESS

### Six Heavens in the Realm of Desire
1. the retainers of the four great kings
   (*caturmahārājakāyika*)
2. the thirty-three gods (*trāyastrimśa*)
3. the yāmas (*yāma*)
4. the satisfied (*tusita*)
5. those who delight in their own creations (*nirmāṇarati*)
6. those who delight in the creations of others (*paranirmi-tavaśavartin*)

35. See *Samyutta-nikāya* 2.76 (translated by Rhys Davids in *The Book of the Kindred Sayings* 2.51-52), where *pratītyasamutpāda* is explained in terms the twelvefold chain of ignorance, impulse, consciousness, name and form, six senses, contact, sensation, craving, grasping, becoming, birth, and old age and death.

THE HEAVENS OF THE REALMS OF DESIRE, FORM, AND FORMLESSNESS
(*Continued*)

## Four Main Heavens in the Realm of Form
## and their Subdivisions

1. the retinue of Brahma (*brahmakāyika*)
   Brahma chaplains (*brahmapurohita*)
   great Brahmas (*mahābrahma*)
2. limited splendor (*parīttābha*)
   immeasurable splendor (*apramānābha*)
   radiance (*ābhāsvara*)
3. limited beauty (*parīttaśubha*)
   immeasurable beauty (*apramānāśubha*)
   complete beauty (*śubhakṛtsna*)
4. cloudless (*anabhraka*)
   merit born (*punyaprasava*)
   abundant fruit (*bṛhatphala*)
   effortless (*avṛha*)
   no heat (*atapa*)
   beautiful (*sudṛśa*)
   well-seeing (*sudarśana*)
   sublime (*akaniṣṭha*)

## Four Heavens in the Realm of Formlessness

1. infinite space (*ākāśānantyāyatana*)
2. infinite consciousness (*vijñānānantyāyatana*)
3. nothingness (*ākiṃcanyāyatana*)
4. neither conceptualization nor non-conceptualization
   (*naivasaṃjñānasaṃjñāyatana*)

# The Teaching of the Lesser Vehicle

The second Buddhist teaching that Tsung-mi discusses in the *Inquiry into the Origin of Humanity* is the Teaching of the Lesser Vehicle, commonly referred to by its Sanskrit name "Hīnayāna." Being the product of Mahāyāna polemics, the use of the designation "Hīnayāna" is fraught with difficulties.[1] Although Mahāyāna Buddhists pejoratively dubbed the earlier forms of Buddhism from which they wanted to distinguish themselves as belonging to the "Hīnayāna" or "Lesser Vehicle," members of those earlier traditions never recognized the legitimacy of the new Mahāyāna scriptures on which this designation was based. Mahāyāna began sometime around the end of the first century B.C. or the beginning of the first century A.D. as a fringe movement within Indian Buddhism and, down until at least the seventh century, clearly remained in the minority. Those traditions it branded as "Hīnayāna" constituted what was, in an Indian context, mainstream Buddhism.

The non-Mahāyāna traditions of Buddhism are traditionally reckoned as consisting of some eighteen schools. The only one of these to survive is the Theravāda, which is found today in the south and southeast Asian countries of Sri Lanka, Burma, Thailand, and Cambodia. By contrast, Mahāyāna Buddhism is found today in Tibet, Nepal, Mongolia, China, Korea, Japan, and Vietnam. All of the traditions of Buddhism to take hold in China were Mahāyāna, and outside of texts the Chinese had little if any direct acquaintance with "Hīnayāna" Buddhists. Even though the use of the designation "Hīnayāna" is problematic within the context of Indian Buddhism, it is fully justified within that of Chinese Buddhism, as long as we bear in mind that this designation does not refer to a historic reality within Indian Buddhism but to a disembodied and ahistorical ab-

1. For an excellent discussion of the current scholarship on the place of the Mahāyāna traditions within the overall history of Buddhism, see Paul Williams, *Mahāyāna Buddhism: The Doctrinal Foundations*.

straction in terms of which Chinese Buddhists defined themselves. Chinese Buddhists thus tended to understand Hīnayāna generically as referring to a type of understanding rather than as referring to specific groups of Buddhists.

Hīnayāna teachings are found in the collections of scriptures known as the *Nikāyas* (preserved in the Pāli Canon) and the *Āgamas* (originally composed in Sanskrit and now largely preserved in Chinese translation), as well as the Vinaya and Abhidharma. The scriptures contained in these collections purport to record the original sermons preached by the Buddha (although it is clear that the form in which they exist today is the product of a complex literary and historical development by the subsequent tradition). Since the teachings of the Buddha found in the early scriptures were often inconsistent and ambiguous, and were thus susceptible to varying interpretations, different sects began to coalesce around different doctrinal positions. Thus a whole new category of texts appeared, those of the Abhidharma, which sought to systematize the Buddha's teachings into a coherent body of doctrine. Tsung-mi's Teaching of the Lesser Vehicle thus includes the scriptures contained in the *Āgamas* (corresponding to the Pāli *Nikāyas*) and the treatises contained in the Abhidharma literature, which are also some of the main sources for the Teaching of Humans and Gods. The primary source that Tsung-mi relies on for his account of the Teaching of the Lesser Vehicle is Vasubandhu's *Abhidharmakośabhāṣya* (*A-p'i-ta-mo chü-she lun*) in Hsüan-tsang's Chinese translation (completed in 654). As Tsung-mi notes in the conclusion to his discussion of this teaching in the *Ch'an Preface:*

> The various scriptures of the *Āgamas* in 618 fascicles and the treatises of the [*Mahā*]*vibhāṣa* and the [*Abhidharma*]*kośa*[*bhāṣya*] in 698 fascicles all just propound this [teaching of] the Lesser Vehicle and [that of] the previous [teaching of] the Causes and Effects of Humans and Gods.[2]

Mahāyāna Buddhists criticized Hīnayāna Buddhists on a wide range of counts. In doctrinal terms, the dharma analysis elaborated in the Abhidharma became a primary target of Mahāyāna criticism. Mahāyāna Buddhists willingly granted that the breaking down of the personality into its psycho-physical components (skandhas) or the explaining of personal continuity in terms of the twelve-link chain of conditioned origination (*pratītysamuptāda; yüan-ch'i* 緣起) suc-

2. T 48.403b24-25; K 104; cf. B 163-164.

ceeded in countering the belief in self, but they went on to criticize the terms in which this analysis was conducted, pointing out that it tended to reify (and thus attribute a kind of self to) the categories (dharmas) it used. Mahāyāna Buddhists contended that these dharmas, like the concept of self, were also conceptually constructed—that is, they had no independent reality, they only existed as concepts, and they were therefore "empty." In this way the Mahāyāna critique went beyond the Hīnayāna analysis by positing a twofold nonself: the concepts of self and dharmas were both empty.[3] The cardinal Mahāyāna teaching of emptiness (*śūnyatā; k'ung* 空) can thus be seen as developing out of a critique of the dharma analysis found in the Abhidharma literature; it built on the earlier teaching of no-self by extending it to apply to the dharmas. The Mahāyāna teaching of emptiness was proclaimed in the Perfection of Wisdom (*Prajñāpāramitā*) scriptures and systematized philosophically in Madhyamaka treatises.

Tsung-mi's ordering of the teachings within the *Inquiry* does not reflect the order of their chronological development (as will be treated more fully in the following chapters). Thus, instead of having the Teaching of the Lesser Vehicle be superseded by Madhayamaka (i.e., the Teaching That Refutes Phenomenal Appearances), he has it superseded by Yogācāra (i.e., the Teaching of the Phenomenal Appearance of the Dharmas), and, rather than using the standard Madhyamaka critique of the Hīnayāna dharma theory, he draws on the historically later Yogācāra understanding of mind. Hence he criticizes the Teaching of the Lesser Vehicle for its superficial understanding of mind. Although the dharma theory, in terms of which it analyzes all experience, succeeds in overcoming the attachment to self that had marred the previous Teaching of Humans and Gods, it, in turn, can be faulted for not realizing that the various dharmas that it posits are themselves merely a projection of an underlying consciousness, the ālayavijñāna. The Teaching of the Lesser Vehicle is accordingly superseded by the Teaching of the Phenomenal Appearances of the Dharmas, for which the ālayavijñāna is the central tenet.

3. Such, at least, is the way the situation is often described in Chinese texts, which were generally not concerned with the complexities of the Indian Buddhist context. Paul Williams has pointed out that the historical situation was actually more complex, since the Abhidharma traditions that taught the inherent existence of dharmas were not identical with the non-Mahāyāna traditions as a whole; there were also non-Mahāyāna traditions that taught the absence of self in dharmas (see his *Mahāyāna Buddhism*, pp. 46-47).

Much of the section on the Teaching of the Lesser Vehicle in the *Inquiry* is identical with the corresponding section of the *Ch'an Preface,* the Teaching That Cuts Off Delusion and Extinguishes Suffering (*tuan-huo mieh-k'u chiao* 斷惑滅苦教). The opening passage of the section in the *Ch'an Preface* is not found in the *Inquiry:*

> The Teaching That Cuts off Delusion and Extinguishes Suffering maintains that the three realms [of desire, form, and formlessness] are insecure and are all like the suffering in the burning house;[4] it enables [beings] to cut off their accumulation of karma and delusion, to practice the path, and to realize extinction. Because it accords with the capacities [of inferior beings], the categories of dharmas spoken of [in this teaching] are thoroughly differentiated in order to discriminate the true and false, to discern the unenlightened and enlightened, to distinguish attraction and aversion, and to make clear cause and effect. It holds that the five aggregates in sentient beings are altogether without a self. It is only that bodily form and cognitive mind. . . .[5]

Another major difference between Tsung-mi's account of this teaching in these texts is that the two long notes dealing with cosmogony and the difference between the Buddhist and Taoist explanations of the origin of the world given in the *Inquiry* do not appear in the *Ch'an Preface.* This difference reflects both the cosmogonic emphasis of the *Inquiry* as well as the literati audience to whom it was addressed.

### SYNOPSIS

Tsung-mi's account of the Teaching of the Lesser Vehicle begins with an implicit reference to conditioned origination (*pratītyasamutpāda; yüan-ch'i* 緣起) as the explanation for the origin of the illusion of self.

[709a11]　二小乘教者、説形骸之色、思慮之心、從無始來因緣力故、念念生滅相續無窮、如水涓涓、如燈焰焰。身心假合似一似常。凡愚不覺執之為我。

[709a11] The Teaching of the Lesser Vehicle holds that from [time] without beginning bodily form and cognitive mind,

---

4. A reference to the famous parable in the third chapter of the *Lotus Sūtra.*

5. T 48.403a21-26; cf. B 158-159.

because of the force of causes and conditions, arise and perish from moment to moment, continuing in an endless series, like the trickling of water or the flame of a lamp. The body and mind come together contingently, seeming to be one and seeming to be permanent. Ignorant beings in their unenlightenment cling to them as a self.

Tsung-mi's reference to the flame of a lamp derives from the *Abhidharmakośabhāsya:* "There is no self; there are only the aggregates. Created by defilement (*kleśa; fan-nao* 煩惱) and karma, they enter a womb as a result of their continuity in the intermediate existence. It is like the flame of a lamp."[6] The *Abhidharmakośa-bhāsya* goes on to comment on this verse:

There is action (karma) and its fruit, but there is no agent that can be ascertained. That is to say, [there is no agent that] is able to abandon these aggregates [here in this life] and resume those aggregates [there in another] independent of the contingency of dharmas (*fa-chia* 法假). What is the contingency of dharmas? Depending on the existence of this, that exists; because of the production of this, that is produced, as is fully set forth in [the teaching of] conditioned origination. . . . The aggregates perish from moment to moment and are incapable of transmigration. Because they are created by repeated defilement and karma, the aggregates in the intermediate existence are made to continue in a series and enter a womb. For example, it is like the flame of a lamp: even though it perishes from moment to moment, it is able to continue in a series and evolve to another place.[7]

The aggregates or skandhas (*yün* 蘊) are the five psycho-physical components of which the personality is composed—namely, form (*rūpa; se* 色), here meaning the sense organs and body, sensation (*vedanā; shou* 受), conceptualization (*samjñā; hsiang* 想), impulse (*samskāra; hsing* 行), and consciousness (*vijñāna; shih* 識). The truth of no-self (*anātman; wu-wo* 無我) is established in various early scriptures by showing that none of the aggregates can be grasped as the self because each is impermanent; nor can we exercise control over any of them. As the *Discourse on the Charac-*

6. T 29.47b27-28; cf. La Vallée Poussin 2.56-57 and Pruden 2.399.
7. Ibid., 47c5-7, 9-12.

*teristic of No-Self* explains, when the body is sick, we cannot will it better. Because the body is impermanent, a cause of suffering, and subject to change, it is not fit to be regarded as mine or as my self. The same holds for the other four aggregates as well.[8]

Tsung-mi goes on to state that attachment to this illusory self (*ātmagrāba; wo-chih* 我執) gives rise to the three poisons, which collectively constitute the defilements (*kleśa; fan-nao* 煩惱), which in turn lead to the generation of karma in its three modes (i.e., physical, verbal, and mental).

[709a14] 實此我故即起貪（貪名利以榮我）瞋（瞋違情境恐侵害我）癡（非理計校）等三毒。三毒擊意發動身口造一切業。業成難逃。故受五道苦樂等身（別業所感）三界勝劣等處（共業所感）。於所受身還執為我、還起貪等造業受報。

[709a14] Because they value[9] this self, they give rise to the three poisons of greed (coveting reputation and advantage in order to promote the self), anger (being angry at things that go against one's feelings, fearing that they will trespass against the self), and delusion (conceptualizing erroneously). The three poisons arouse thought, activating body and speech and generating all karma. Once karma has come into being, it is difficult to escape. Thus [beings] receive a bodily existence (determined by individual karma) of pain and pleasure in the five destinies and a position (determined by collective karma) of superior or inferior in the three realms. In regard to the bodily existence that they receive, no sooner do [beings] cling to it as a self then they at once give rise to greed and so forth, generate karma, and experience its retribution.

Tsung-mi concludes his synopsis by drawing a parallel between the four stages of each individual existence and the four phases of each cosmic cycle.

8. See the *Anattalakkhana-sutta* in *Saṃyutta-nikāya* 3.66ff, translated by Woodward in *The Kindred Sayings* 3.59-60. As Steven Collins points out in his discussion of this passage, the argument suggests the interrelation of the three marks of all conditioned things: "what is impermanent is unsatisfactory; what is unsatisfactory is not-self" (*Selfless Persons*, p. 98).

9. In place of the *pao* 實 found in the *Inquiry*, Kamata's version of the *Ch'an Preface* has the homophonous character *pao* 保 (to preserve); the Taishō version of the *Ch'an Preface*, however, agrees with the *Inquiry*.

[709a18]    身則生老病死；死而復生。界則成住壞空；空
而復成。

[709a18] In the case of bodily existence, there is birth, old age, sickness, and death; [beings] die and are born again. In the case of a world, there is formation, continuation, destruction, and emptiness; [worlds] are empty and are formed again.

Formation, continuation, destruction, and emptiness refer to the four phases of one cosmic cycle. Each of these phases or kalpas lasts for one incalculable eon (*asamkhyeyakalpa; a-seng-ch'i-yeh-chieh* 阿僧祇劫 or *wu-shu-chieh* 無數劫) and is made up of twenty intermediate kalpas (*antarakalpa; chung-chieh* 中劫). A great kalpa (*mahākalpa; ta-chieh* 大劫), one complete cosmic cycle, is thus composed of eighty intermediate kalpas.[10]

## COSMOGONY

Tsung-mi's mention of the four phases in each cosmic cycle justifies his extended note on cosmogony, one of the most interesting sections of his discussion of the Teaching of the Lesser Vehicle, in which he draws from the systematic account of the *Abhidharmakośabhāsya* to summarize the well-known cosmogony found with minor variations in numerous Buddhist sources. In his autocommentary, Tsung-mi details how, after the end of one cosmic cycle when the universe has been totally destroyed, the receptacle world (*bhājanaloka; ch'i-chieh* 器界, that is, the physical world that contains sentient beings) is created again at the end of the kalpa of emptiness. The receptacle world is composed of three concentric circles. The first is the circle of wind:

[709a19]    (從空劫初成世界者、頌曰：空界大風起、傍廣數無
量、厚十六洛叉、金剛不能壞。此名持界風。

[709a19] (As for the first formation of the world from the empty kalpa, a verse says that a great wind arises in empty space, its expanse is immeasurable, its thickness is sixteen hundred thousand [leagues], and not even a diamond could harm it.[11] It is called the wind that holds the world together.

10. See *Abhidharmakośabhāsya*, T 29.62b28-c6; cf. La Vallée Poussin 2.181-187 and Pruden 2.475-479.

11. That the phrase translated as "not even a diamond could harm it" (*chin-kang pu-neng-huai* 金剛不能壞) should not be rendered as "as in-

Tsung-mi is here paraphrasing the verse describing the formation of the receptacle world found in the *Abhidharmakośabhāsya:*
"As for the establishment of the receptacle world, at the very bottom there is the circle of wind; its vastness is immeasurable and its
thickness is sixteen hundred thousand leagues (*yojanas*)."[12] The
circle of wind contains the second circle, that of water.

[709a20] 光音金藏雲布及三千界。雨如車軸下、風遏不聽流。

深十一洛叉。

[709a20] In the light-sound [heaven] a golden treasury cloud spreads
throughout the great chiliocosm. Raindrops [as large as] cart hubs
come down, but the wind holds it in check and does not let it flow
out. Its depth is eleven hundred thousand [leagues].

Tsung-mi is here following the *Abhidharmakośabhāsya's* description of the formation of the circle of water: "A great cloud arises,
and its rain pours onto the circle of wind. The raindrops are like
cart hubs; the mounting water forms a circle; . . . its depth is eleven
hundred twenty thousand leagues. Why does the circle of water
not flow over the side? . . . Some say that it is made not to overflow
by being held in by the wind, like a basket holding grain."[13] The
circle of water surrounds the third circle, that of gold.

The light-sound (*ābhāsvara; kuang-yin* 光音) heaven,[14] the
abode of the radiant gods, is the third and highest sphere of the

---

destructible as a diamond" is indicated by the passage from the *Abhidharmakośabhāsya* on which Tsung-mi's account is based: "The substance of the
circle of wind is solid. If a mighty champion were to strike it vigorously
with a diamond wheel, the diamond would shatter and the circle of wind
would remain unscathed" (T 29.57a17-18; cf. La Vallée Poussin 2.139 and
Pruden 2.451).

12. T 29.57a7-8; cf. La Vallée Poussin 2.138 and Pruden 2.451.
13. T 29.57a19-25; cf. La Vallée Poussin 2.139-140 and Pruden 2.451-452.
14. The term that Tsung-mi uses for this heaven, *kuang-yin* 光音, is different from that used by Hsüan-tsang in his translation of the *Abhidharmakośabhāsya, chi-kuang-ching* 極光淨. These two Chinese translations of
*ābhāsvara* reflect divergent theories about its etymology. The first divides the
term into *ābhā*, light, and *svara*, sound, while the second divides it into *ābhās*,
light, and *vara*, supreme. Perhaps the first theory is the basis of (or is based
on) the belief that the *ābhāsvara* gods communicate through the medium of
light. See also Jayawardhanna, "Ābhassara," *Encyclopaedia of Buddhism* 1.13-
16; Kanaoka, "Ābhāsavara," ibid. 1.16-17; and Mochizuki 2.1028a-b.

second meditation heaven in the realm of form. As will be explained more fully below, it is the place where beings are reborn when the universe comes to an end and the place from where they descend to be born as humans when a new universe begins.

Each universe is composed of a central mountain, eight surrounding rings of mountains, nine seas, and four continents. One thousand universes constitute one small chiliocosm; one thousand small chiliocosms constitute one medium chiliocosm; and one thousand medium chiliocosms constitute one great chiliocosm.[15]

[709a20] 始作金剛界、次第金藏雲、注雨満其内、先成梵王
界、乃至夜摩天。風鼓清水成、須彌七金等。滓濁為山地、四
洲及泥犂、鹹海外輪圍、方名器界立。時經一增減。

[709a20] After the diamond world is created, a golden treasury cloud then pours down rain and fills it up, first forming the Brahma [heavens, and then going on to form all the other heavens] down to the Yāma [heaven]. The wind stirs up the pure water, forming Mount Sumeru, the seven gold mountains, and so on. When the sediment forms the mountains, earth, the four continents, and hell, and a salty sea flows around their circumference, then it is called the establishment of the receptacle world. At that time one [period of] increase/decrease has elapsed.

Tsung-mi is here referring to the formation of the circle of gold.[16] Churned by the wind, the upper part of the circle of water turns golden, like milk turning to cream, and congeals to form the circle of gold. Mount Sumeru, the axis mundi, stands on top of the circle of gold. It is surrounded by eight concentric rings of mountains, the first seven being made of gold and the outermost being made of iron. Each ring of mountains is separated from the others by a sea. The ring of iron mountains is surrounded by a salty sea, out of which the four continents arise.[17]

15. Because a great chiliocosm is composed of one thousand universes to the third power (i.e., one billion), it is referred to as a "three-thousands" (i.e., 1,000 x 1,000 x 1,000) great chiliocosm. The Chinese term used here, *san-ch'ien chieh* 三千界, is an abbreviation of *san-ch'ien ta-ch'ien shih-chieh* 三千大千世界 (Skt. *trisāhasramahasāhāsro lokadhātu*) and does not mean three thousand worlds, as it would seem to imply. See Mochizuki 2.1598a-c and Lamotte, *The Teaching of Vimalakīrti*, p. 275.

16. Following Ching-yüan's gloss (*Fa-wei lu* 100a); Tsung-mi has "diamond world" (*chin-kang-chieh* 金剛界).

17. See *Abhidharmakośabhāṣya*, T 29.57b2-c18; cf. La Vallée Poussin 2.141-145 and Pruden 2.452-454.

(A computer enhanced drawing by Jean Deichman based
on the diagram appearing in Mochizuki, *Bukkyō daijiten*
3.2514a)

A period of increase/decrease refers to an intermediate kalpa.
The creation of the receptacle world is accomplished during the first
intermediate kalpa of the kalpa of formation. The beings that inhabit
this world are created during the remaining nineteen intermediate
kalpas. The first intermediate kalpa of the next phase of the cosmic
cycle, the kalpa of continuation, is one in which human life decreases
from eighty thousand to ten years. During each of the next eighteen
intermediate kalpas, human life gradually increases to eighty thousand
years and then decreases to ten years, at a rate of one year per century.
During the last intermediate kalpa of the kalpa of continuation, human
life again increases from ten years back up to eighty thousand years.
It is because the span of human life increases and decreases during
each of these intermediate kalpas that Tsung-mi refers to them as
periods of increase/decrease. During the first nineteen intermediate
kalpas of the next phase in the cosmic cycle, the kalpa of destruction,
the beings that inhabit the receptacle world are destroyed, and during
the last intermediate kalpa the receptable world is destroyed. Then
follows the kalpa of emptiness, which also lasts for twenty intermediate kalpas.[18]

18. See *Abhidharmakośabhāṣya*, T 29.62c-63b; cf. La Vallée Poussin
2.181-187 and Pruden 2.475-479. See also Nattier, *Once Upon a Future Time*,
pp. 15-19.

Tsung-mi then goes on to describe the creation of human beings:

[709a22] 乃至二禪福盡、下生人間。初食地餅林藤；後粳米不
銷、大小便利、男女形別。分田立主求臣佐、種種差別。經十
九增減。兼前總二十增減、名為成劫。

[709a22] Finally, when the merit of [beings in] the second meditation
[heaven] is exhausted, they descend to be born as humans. They
first eat earth cakes and forest creepers; later the coarse rice is undigested and excreted as waste, and the figures of male and female
become differentiated. They divide the fields, set up a ruler, search
for ministers, and make distinctions as to the various classes. [This
phase] lasts nineteen periods of increase/decrease. Combined with
the previous [period during which the receptacle world was formed]
it makes twenty periods of increase/decrease and is called the kalpa
of formation.

Tsung-mi's account condenses that found in the *Abhidharmakośabhāṣya*. At the end of the kalpa of destruction all beings, except
those whose roots of merit are destroyed, are reborn in the *ābhāsvara*
heaven, within the second meditation heaven in the realm of form,
where they reside throughout the duration of the kalpa of emptiness.
Those beings whose roots of merit are destroyed are reborn in the
hells of other universes. When the merit of the beings in the *ābhāsvara*
heaven is exhausted, they descend to be reborn as human beings.
They still have all the characteristics of the radiant gods of the
*ābhāsvara* heaven: they are made of mind, feed on joy, radiate light,
traverse the air, and continue in glory. Gradually, the earth appears
as a kind of foam on the surface of the primeval waters. It is a savory
earth, which tastes as sweet as honey. Smelling its fragrance, one
being eats of it, and other beings follow suit. With the eating of the
savory earth, their bodies become gross and heavy, and their radiance
disappears. Thus are born the sun, moon, and stars. As the savory
earth disappears with beings' attachment to it, earth cakes appear.
As beings become attached to their taste, they too begin to disappear,
and forest creepers appear in their stead. These also disappear with
beings' attachment to them, and rice spontaneously begins to grow.
Being a still grosser form of food, when beings eat this rice, some of
it remains undigested and their bodies produce wastes. It is at this
juncture in the process of materialization that beings first become
differentiated sexually. One being starts to store up rice for future
consumption, and others, fearing that there will not be enough to go
around, follow his example. With this development, the rice begins
to disappear, and cultivation becomes necessary. The people then

divide the land up into fields, but since some steal rice from others' fields, they elect a ruler to protect the fields. Thus the process of social differentiation begins.[19]

This myth is found with slight variations in a wide range of Buddhist sources.[20] Its importance in providing the foundation for Buddhist social thought has been insightfully analyzed by Tambiah,[21] and we need only note some of its main features here. The creation of the world and human beings is described as a process of devolution from an ethereal state of spirituality to one of gross materiality. This devolution into materiality is accompanied by increasing differentiation (of the physical world, between the sexes, etc.) and increasing immorality (greed, lust, etc.). The formation of society is therefore necessary to protect humans from the painful consequences of their unchecked desires. Human society is contractual and is founded on the institution of kingship.

### COMPARATIVE EXPLANATION

Tsung-mi's note goes on to explain how the various elements in this Buddhist cosmogony correspond to the accounts found in the Taoist and Confucian sources that he discussed earlier in part 2 on Confucianism and Taoism.

> [709a23]　議曰。空界劫中、是道教指云虛無之道。然道體寂照靈通、不是虛無。老氏或迷之、或權設務絕人欲。故指空界為道。空界中大風、即彼混沌一氣；故彼云道生一也。金藏雲者、氣形之始、即太極也。雨下不流、陰氣凝也。陰陽相合方能生成矣。梵王界乃至須彌者、彼之天也。滓濁者地、即一生二矣。二禪福盡下生、即人也、即二生三、三才備矣。地餅已下乃至種種、即三生萬物。此當三皇已前穴居野食、未有火化等。

> [709a23] [I will now] elaborate on [the above]. [The period of time] during the kalpa of empty space is what the Taoists designate as the Way

19. See T 29.65b18-19c; cf. La Vallée Poussin 2.204-206 and Pruden 2.487-488; see also La Vallée Poussin, "Cosmogony and Cosmology," p. 190.

20. The oldest version is that found in the *Aggañña-sutta*, translated by Rhys Davids as "A Book of Genesis" in *Dialogues of the Budhha* 3.77-94. This version is repeated in the *Mahāvastu* (Jones, trans., 1.285-293). A parallel account in the Chinese *Āgamas* can be found in T 1.37b28ff. A somewhat different version appears in the *Visuddhimagga* 13 (translated by Ñānamoli in *The Path of Purification*, pp. 458-459).

21. See his *World Conqueror and World Renouncer*, pp. 9-16.

of nothingness. However, since the essence of the Way is tranquilly illuminating and marvellously pervasive, it is not nothingness. Lao-tzu was either deluded about this or he postulated it provisionally to encourage [people] to cut off their human desires. Therefore he designated empty space as the Way. The great wind [that arises] in empty space corresponds to their one pneuma of the primordial chaos; therefore they say that the Way engenders the one. The golden treasury cloud, being the beginning of the pneuma's taking form, is the great ultimate. The rain coming down and not flowing out refers to the congealing of the yin pneuma. As soon as yin and yang blend together, they are able to engender and bring [all things] to completion. From the Brahma Kings' realm down to Mount Sumeru corresponds to their heaven, and the sediment corresponds to the earth, and that is the one engendering the two. The merits [of those in] the second meditation [heaven] being exhausted and their descending to be born refers to human beings, and that is the two engendering the three, and the three powers [of the cosmos] thus being complete. From the earth cakes to the various classes is the three engendering the myriad things. This corresponds to [the time] before the three kings when people lived in caves, ate in the wilderness, did not yet have the transforming power of fire, and so on.

Tsung-mi's reference to the time when people lived in caves is drawn from the *Book of Rites:* "Formerly the ancient kings had no houses. In winter they lived in caves which they had excavated, and in summer in nests which they had framed. They knew not yet the transforming power of fire, but ate the fruits of plants and trees, and the flesh of birds and beasts, drinking their blood, and swallowing (also) the hair and feathers."[22]

The care with which Tsung-mi spells out the correspondences between this Buddhist cosmogony and Taoist theory is noteworthy.[23] Tsung-mi's effort to match specific items in the Buddhist account with specific items in Taoist cosmogony would have been appropriate for the literati audience to whom the essay was addressed, but what is even more remarkable is the presupposition on which Tsung-mi's approach is based: that both accounts must be describing the same process. The possibility that both might reflect fundamentally irreconcilable conceptions never seems to have occurred to

22. See *Li chi* 7.3a-b, as translated by Legge 1.369.
23. Especially in light of the fact that it was precisely the kind of effort that his Hua-yen predecessors Ch'eng-kuan and Hui-yüan had stridently criticized; see my *Tsung-mi and the Sinification of Buddhism,* pp. 256-260.

him. Tsung-mi does not dismiss the Taoist account as false. It is only a less perfect version of what is recorded in Buddhist texts. It must therefore be taken seriously, and Tsung-mi takes pains to account for the discrepancies between the two accounts.

[709a27] 但以其時無文字記載故、後人傳聞不明；展轉錯謬、諸家著作種種異説。佛教又縁通明三千世界、不局大唐、故内外教文不全同也。

[709a27] It is only because there were no written records at the time that the legendary accounts of people of later times were not clear; they became increasingly confused, and different traditions wrote up diverse theories of sundry kinds. Moreover, because Buddhism penetrates and illuminates the great chiliocosm and is not confined to China, the writings of the inner and outer teachings are not entirely uniform.

After this extended excursus on Buddhist and Taoist cosmogonies, Tsung-mi returns to the meaning of the other two kalpas, those of continuation and destruction.

[709b1] 住者住劫；亦經二十增減。壞者壞劫；亦二十增減。前十九增減壞有情；後一增減壞器界。能壞是火水風等三災。空者空劫；亦二十增減中。空無世界及諸有情也。)

[709b1] "Continuation" refers to the kalpa of continuation; it also lasts for twenty [periods of] increase/decrease. "Destruction" refers to the kalpa of destruction; it also lasts for twenty [periods of] increase/decrease. During the first nineteen [periods of] increase/decrease sentient beings are destroyed; during the last [period of] increase/decrease the receptacle world is destroyed. That which destroys them are the three cataclysms of fire, water, and wind. "Empty" refers to the kalpa of emptiness; it also lasts for twenty [periods of] increase/decrease. During [the kalpa of] emptiness there is neither [receptacle] world nor sentient beings).

According to the *Abhidharmakośabhāsya*, the universe is destroyed by fire, water, and wind. When the universe is destroyed by fire, everything below the second meditation heaven is annihilated; when it is destroyed by water, everything below the third meditation heaven is annihilated; when it is destroyed by wind, everything below the fourth meditation heaven in annihilated. After the universe is destroyed by fire seven times, it is then destroyed by water. This cycle is repeated seven times. After the universe is again destroyed by fire seven times, it is then destroyed by wind. There are thus fifty-six destructions by fire, seven by water, and one by wind, after which the cycle of destructions is repeated again ad infinitum.[24]

[709b2] 劫劫生生輪迴不絶 ; 無終無始如汲井輪。 (道教只知今此世界未成時一度空劫。云虛無混沌一氣等、名為元始。不知空界已前早經千千萬萬遍成住壞空終而復始。故知佛教法中小乘淺淺之教、已超外典深深之説。) 都由不了此身本不是我。不是我者、謂此身本因色心和合為相。

[709b2] Kalpa after kalpa, birth after birth, the cycle does not cease; it is without end and without beginning, like a well wheel drawing up [water]. (Taoism merely knows of the single kalpa of emptiness when the present world had not yet been formed. It calls it nothingness, the one pneuma of the primordial chaos, and so forth, and designates it as the primeval beginning. It does not know that before [the kalpa of] empty space there had already passed thousands upon thousands and ten-thousands upon ten-thousands of [kalpas of] formation, continuation, destruction, and emptiness, which, on coming to an end, began again.[25] Therefore we know that within the teaching of Buddhism even the most superficial Teaching of the Lesser Vehicle already surpasses the most profound theories of the outer [i.e., non-Buddhist] canon.)[26] All this comes about from [beings] not understanding that the body is from the very outset not the self. "Is not the self" refers to the fact that the body originally takes on phenomenal appearance because of the coming together of form and mind.

24. See T 29.66a28-67a22; cf. La Vallée Poussin 2.209-217 and Pruden 2.490-495; see also the *Visuddhimagga* 13 (translated by Ñāṇamoli in *The Path of Purification,* pp. 456-463) for a detailed description of the various destructions.

25. The first of the ten differences that Ch'eng-kuan discusses between Buddhism, on the one hand, and Confucianism and Taoism, on the other, is that Confucianism and Taoism posit a primordial beginning while Buddhism does not. See *Yen-i ch'ao* (T 36.106a27-b1): "The Buddhists establish the causes and conditions of birth-and-death without fixing a commencement or beginning. The Confucianists and Taoists have a great commencement and a great beginning."

26. See Ch'eng-kuan's *Hua-yen ching shu* (T 35.521b20-21): "Now, in only having set forth true causality, the various [non-Buddhist] opinions have already been completely refuted. In this way, the most superficial teaching of Buddhism already surpasses the most profound teachings of the non-Buddhists."

## EXTENDED ANALYSIS

Not only can the "self" be seen to be composed of the five aggregates, but the five aggregates can also be further divided. In a manner that recalls his criticism of the Teaching of Humans and Gods, Tsung-mi shows that the analysis of the self into ever smaller elements leads to absurdity. He begins by dividing the aggregates into physical and mental components.

[709b6]　今推尋分析、色有地水火風之四大、心有受（能領納好惡之事）想（能取像者）行（能造作者念念遷流）識（能了別者）之四蘊。若皆是我、即成八我。況地大中復有衆多。謂三百六十段骨、一一各別、皮毛筋肉肝心脾腎、各不相是、諸心數等亦各不同。見不是聞、喜不是怒。展轉乃至八萬四千塵勞、既有此衆多之物。不知定取何者為我。若皆是我。我即百千。一身之中多主紛亂。離此之外復無別法。翻覆推我皆不可得。便悟此身但是衆緣似 [假] 和合相元無我人。

[709b6] If we now push our analysis further, form[27] is comprised of the four great elements of earth, water, fire, and wind, whereas mind is comprised of the four aggregates of sensation (that which receives agreeable and disagreeable things), conceptualization (that which forms images), impulses (that which creates and shifts and flows from moment to moment), and consciousness (that which discriminates).[28] If each of these were a self, then they would amount to eight selves. How much more numerous would [the selves] be among the earthly element! That is to say, each one of the three hundred sixty bones is distinct from the others; skin, hair, muscles, flesh, liver, heart, spleen, and kidneys are each not the other. Each of the various mental functions are also not the same; seeing is not hearing, joy is not anger, and so on and so forth to the eighty-four thousand defilements. Since there are so many things, we do not know

27. Form (*rūpa; se* 色) consists of the four great elements and everything derived from them, including the five senses and the five sense objects; see, for example, *Visudhimagga* 14 (translated by Ñānamoli in *The Path of Purification*, p. 489).

28. Tsung-mi's definitions of the four mental aggregates closely follow the definitions given in the *Abhidharmakośabhāsya*; see T 29.3c28, 4a9, and 4a19; cf. La Vallée Poussin 1.14ff and Pruden 1.63ff.

what to choose as the self. If each of them were a self, then there would be hundreds upon thousands of selves, and there would be the utter confusion of many controlling agents within a single body. Furthermore, there is nothing else outside of these [components]. When one investigates them inside and out, a self cannot be found in any of them. One then realizes that the body is just the phenomenal appearance of the seeming[29] combination of various conditions and that there has never been a self.

Tsung-mi concludes this section by considering the soteriological implications of no-self, showing how the four noble truths correspond to successive stages of sainthood, culminating ultimately in the attainment of nirvāṇa without remainder,[30] the consummation of spiritual life in the Teaching of the Lesser Vehicle, wherein the five aggregates that make up the psycho-physical being are finally extinguished.

[709b16]　為誰貪瞋。為誰殺盜施戒 (知苦諦也)。遂不滯心於三界有漏善惡 (斷集諦也)、但修無我觀智 (道諦)、以斷貪等、止息諸業、證得我空眞如 (滅諦)、乃至得阿羅漢果：灰身滅智方斷諸苦。據此宗中、以色心二法、及貪瞋癡、為根身器界之本也。過去未來更無別法為本。

[709b16] On whose account does one have greed and anger? On whose account does one kill, steal, give [alms], and maintain the precepts (knowing the truth of suffering)? Then, when one does not obstruct the mind in good and bad [deeds] that have outflows[31] in the three realms (the truth of cutting off the

29. I have followed the reading in the Taishō text. It should be noted, however, that both Ching-yüan (101b) and Yüan-chüeh (127d) have *chia* 假 in place of *ssu* 似, a reading that makes sense in light of Tsung-mi's statement at the beginning of this section: "The body and mind come together contingently (*chia*), . . ." The texts of all but one of the Japanese commentaries consulted also give *chia* instead of *ssu*. Whichever reading is followed hardly affects the meaning of the passage.

30. This term (*anupadhiśeṣa-nirvāṇa*) was frequently cited by Mahāyāna Buddhists as betraying the narrow spiritual horizon that justified why Hīnayāna Buddhists deserved their pejorative epithet for being followers of the Lesser Vehicle.

31. "Outflows" (*āsrava; yu-lou* 有漏) is used here to mean any action that generates karma, be it good or bad, and further ensnares the sentient being in the ceaseless round of birth that is saṃsāra. The moral injunctions

accumulation [of suffering])[32] and only cultivates the wisdom of the view of no-self (the truth of the path), one thereby cuts off greed and so forth, puts a stop to all karma, realizes the reality of the emptiness of self (the truth of extinction), until eventually one attains arhatship: as soon as one makes one's body as ashes and extinguishes thought, one cuts off all suffering. According to this teaching, the two dharmas of form and mind, as well as greed, anger, and delusion, constitute the origin of the body of senses and the receptacle world. There has never been nor will ever be anything else that constitutes the origin.

"Arhatship" refers to the attainment of the religious goal in Hīnayāna; an arhat or saint is one who has eliminated the causes of birth-and-death and after death is reborn no more.

### CRITIQUE

Tsung-mi's critique of the Teaching of the Lesser Vehicle raises a question that remained a persistent problem for the Buddhist tradition as a whole: how could personal continuity (from moment to moment as well as from lifetime to lifetime) be explained given the lack of any abiding self? Indeed, the development of much of Buddhist scholastic philosophy can be understood as a series of increasingly sophisticated attempts to answer this question. Although the twelve-link chain of conditioned origination was invariably invoked to explain the continuity from lifetime to lifetime, it could not account for continuity during periods when consciousness was not operative (such as in deep sleep or in the most profound states of meditative absorption). The next level of teaching thus posits a substratum of consciousness to account for such states.

[709b21] 今詰之曰。夫經生累世為身本者、自體須無間斷。今五識闕緣不起（根境等為緣）、意識有時不行（悶絕、睡眠、滅盡定、無想定、無想天）、無色界天無此四大。如何持得此身、世世不絕。是知專此教者亦未原身。

---

of the previous Teaching of Humans and Gods, for example, still involve deeds that have outflows in the three realms. For a detailed discussion of *āsrava,* see Hosaka, "Āsrava," *Encyclopaedia of Buddhism* 2.202-214.

32. "Accumulation" refers to the second of the four noble truths, that of the origin of suffering. As Soothill and Hodous note, "The Chinese *chi* 集, 'accumulation' does not correctly translate Samudaya, which means 'origination'" (*A Dictionary of Chinese Buddhist Terms,* p. 394).

[709b21] Now I will assess [this teaching] critically. That which constitutes the source of bodily existence in the experiencing of repeated births and the accumulation of numerous lifetimes must, in itself, be without interruption. [However], the present five [sense] consciousnesses do not arise in the absence of [the necessary] conditions (the sense organs, sense objects, and so forth constitute the conditions), there are times when consciousness[33] does not operate (during unconsciousness, deep sleep, the attainment of extinction,[34] the attainment of nonconsciousness,[35] and among the nonconscious gods),[36] and the gods in the realm of formlessness are not comprised of the four great elements. How, then, do we hold on to this bodily existence lifetime after lifetime without ceasing? Therefore we know that those who are devoted to this teaching have also not yet reached the origin of bodily existence.

The form of Tsung-mi's critique is based on the fifteenth and sixteenth verses, and the commentary to them, of the *Ch'eng wei-shih lun*,[37] the authoritative text for the Teaching of the Phenomenal Appearances of the Dharmas, and thereby anticipates the teaching discussed in the following chapter. According to the *Ch'eng wei-shih lun*, the five sense-consciousnesses[38] have the ālayavijñāna as their support and are dependent on various conditions for their manifes-

33. This refers to the sixth consciousness, *mano-vijñāna* (*i-shih* 意識), mental discrimination.

34. The attainment of extinction (*nirodha-samāpatti*) is the same as *saṃjñā-vedayite-nirodha-samāpatti*, the highest of the nine levels of attainments. For details see *Abhidharmakośabhāṣya*, T 29.24c27ff.; cf. La Vallée Poussin 1.203ff and Pruden 1.225.

35. The attainment of nonconsciousness (*asaṃjñā-samāpatti*) is a state of meditative absorption wherein all mental functioning has been arrested; it occurs in the fourth stage of meditation. See *Abhidharmakośa-bhāṣya*, T 29.24b13ff; cf. La Vallée Poussin 1.199ff and Pruden 1.221ff.

36. The non-conscious gods dwell in the third of the eight spheres of the fourth meditation heaven, that of the gods of abundant fruit (*brhatphala-deva*).

37. See T 31.37a11-38b6; this text and its significance within the Teaching of the Phenomenal Appearances of the Dharmas will be discussed in the following chapter.

38. The five sense-consciousnesses are visual consciousness (*cakṣur-vijñāna*), auditory consciousness (*śrotra-vijñāna*), olfactory consciousness (*ghrāṇa-vijñāna*), gustatory consciousness (*jihvā-vijñāna*), and tactile consciousness (*kāya-vijñāna*).

tation. Since the conditions necessary for their manifestation are often not present, there are times when the five sense-consciousnesses are not activated. Even though the conditions necessary for the manifestation of the sixth consciousness (*mano-vijñāna; i-shih* 意識, the faculty of mental discrimination) are always present, there are still times when it does not operate, as Tsung-mi points out. The Teaching of the Lesser Vehicle only knows of the first six consciousnesses; since there are times when these do not arise, it cannot explain the uninterrupted continuity of experience during times when these consciousnesses are inoperative. Unlike the first six consciousnesses, which are subject to interruption, the seventh and eighth consciousnesses, the *manas* (*mo-na-shih* 末那識) and ālayavijñāna, operate continuously and thus function as a continuum within sentient beings. In this way Tsung-mi's critique of the Teaching of the Lesser Vehicle serves as a natural transition to the next level of teaching, which takes the ālayavijñāna as the underlying basis of both bodily existence and the receptacle world.

# The Teaching of the Phenomenal Appearances of the Dharmas

Yogācāra was one of the two great Mahāyāna scholastic traditions to develop in India. Its basic tenets were set forth in the *Samdhi-nirmocana-sūtra* (most likely written during the fourth century) and systematized in the treatises of Asaṅga and Vasubandhu (composed during the late fourth or early fifth century). These works focus on the constructive role that consciousness plays in determining sentient beings' experience of the phenomenal world, and their central tenet is thus characterized as "consciousness-only" or "representation-only" (*vijñaptimātratā; wei-shih* 唯識). Yogācāra posits the ālayavijñāna as the underlying basis or support (*āśraya; i* 依) for the operation of consciousness, thus addressing the problem of continuity that Tsung-mi raised in his critique of the Teaching of the Lesser Vehicle. The ālayavijñāna is also the basis on which the world of experience is represented in consciousness. It is thus connected with another central Yogācāra doctrine, the theory of the three natures (*trisvabhāva; san-hsing* 三性), which describes three aspects of reality: the imaginary (*parikalpa; pien-chi* 遍計), the dependent (*paratantra; t'a-ch'i* 他起), and the perfected (*pariniṣpanna; yüan-ch'eng* 圓成). The imaginary and perfected natures refer to two different perspectives from which the dependent nature can be seen. In the case of the imaginary, the world is seen in terms of reified concepts (such as self and dharmas) that are projected onto it. Only when these imaginary projections are removed will the world be seen as it really is, an ever-changing combination of interdependent phenomena, and that is what is meant by the perfected nature. The world in either case is the same, only beings' perception of it changes. The dependent nature is thus only seen for what it is from the perspective of the perfected nature. The imaginary nature thus corresponds to deluded experience, and the perfected nature to enlightened wisdom. The shift from delusion to enlightenment

148

is described as the transformation of the basis (*āśraya-parāvṛtti; chuan-i* 轉依), that is, a radical transformation of the basis (i.e., the ālayavijñāna) in terms of which reality is perceived.[1]

The Yogācāra theories of the ālayavijñāna and three natures only make sense when understood as developing out of and reacting to the doctrines of emptiness and the two truths advanced by the other great tradition of Indian Mahāyāna, the Madhyamaka. The Madhyamaka teaching of emptiness was closely related to conditioned origination (*pratītyasamutpāda; yüan-ch'i* 縁起): because all things (dharmas) exist in dependence on one another, they can therefore be said to be empty of any reality of their own (*svabhāva; tzu-hsing* 自性). It was precisely on this ground that Madhyamaka criticized the Hīnayāna dharma theory elaborated in the Abhidharma. Abhidharma can be seen as an attempt to devise a totally impersonal language of dharmas whereby it would be possible to account for experience without recourse to the notion of self. According to the Madhyamaka critique, however, it fell into the trap of reifying the very categories (dharmas) that it had posited to deconstruct the reified concept of self, for the dharmas as well lack any substantial reality of their own.

Madhyamaka had also posited two truths: the conventional (*saṃvṛti; su* 俗) and the ultimate (*paramārtha; chen* 眞), epistemological categories corresponding to the soteriological categories of delusion and enlightenment. It did not, however, explain how the world of conventional experience was connected to that of ultimate truth, thereby leaving unclear how the transformation from delusion to enlightenment could be effected. If, moreover, enlightenment revealed that the conventional world of deluded experience was itself illusory, Madhyamaka could not account for how such delusion arose in the first place. Just as the ālayavijñāna explained the complex feedback system through which delusion arose and was sustained, the Yogācāra doctrine of the dependent nature mediated between conventional and ultimate truth.

1. A good general account of some of the fundamental Yogācāra ideas can be found in the various essays by Nagao Gadjin edited and translated by Leslie Kawamura in *Mādhyamika and Yogācāra*. The theory of the three natures, like other Yogācāra ideas, is far more complex than indicated here. There was always a spectrum of differing opinion; nor were such ideas static, they continued to change along with other doctrinal developments. For a discussion of some of the ways the three-nature theory was interpreted within the Chinese Fa-hsiang tradition, see Sponberg, "The *Trisvabhāva* Doctrine in India and China."

Madhyamaka could also not account for the basis for enlightenment, and this second horn of the Madhyamaka dilemma was
answered by tathāgatagarbha doctrine. Meaning both the "embryo"
or "womb" of the Tathāgata, the tathāgatagarbha referred to the
potentiality for Buddhahood that existed embryonically within all
sentient beings as well as the pure principle of Buddhahood that
appeared enwombed within defiled sentient existence. Even though
this doctrine seems to have been of relatively minor importance in
Indian Buddhism, it assumed a paramount significance in Chinese
Buddhism that enabled it to stand on its own as a distinct tradition
of Mahāyāna alongside of the two great Indian traditions of Madhyamaka and Yogācāra.[2]

The Teaching of the Phenomenal Appearance of the Dharmas
(*fa-hsiang chiao* 法相教) refers to the new version of the Yogācāra
tradition that was introduced into China by the famous pilgrim and
translator Hsüan-tsang (600-664) and codified by his disciple and
collaborator Tz'u-en (632-682), better known as K'uei-chi. This
brand of Yogācāra was distinct from the earlier transmissions of
Yogācāra thought to China, those represented by the Ti-lun tradition
(based on Bodhiruci's translation of Vasubandhu's commentary on the
*Daśabhūmika-sūtra*)[3] and the She-lun tradition (based on Paramārtha's
translation of Asaṅga's *Mahāyānasaṃgraha* and Vasubandhu's commentary).[4] It was this earlier interpretation of Yogācāra that was
taken as orthodox by the Hua-yen tradition with which Tsung-mi
was affiliated. For Tsung-mi this orthodox tradition was given definitive expression in the *Awakening of Faith*, an apocryphal text
that purports to have been authored by the venerable Aśvaghoṣa
and translated into Chinese by Paramārtha but that was most probably composed in China sometime during the third quarter of the

2. For an excellent discussion of the relationship between the Yogācāra,
Madhyamaka, and tathāgatagarbha traditions and their significance within
medieval Chinese Buddhism, see Gimello, "Chih-yen," pp. 214-337.

3. *Shih-ti ching lun*, T no. 1522, completed in 511. Although the
*Daśabhūmika* originated as an independent scripture, it was later incorporated into the *Hua-yen* (*Avatamsaka*) *Sūtra*. It describes the ten stages
(*bhūmi*) of the bodhisattva's career; Vasubandhu's passing references to
the ālayavijñāna in his commentary served as major points of controversy
among Chinese exegetes about whether the absolute was pure or defiled.

4. *She ta-sheng lun*, T no. 1593, done in 563, and T no. 1595, completed
the following year. For a French translation of the *Mahāyānasaṃgraha*,
see Lamotte, *La Somme du Grand Véhicule d'Asaṅga*.

sixth century. Although the points of difference between the early Chinese Yogācāra tradition and that introduced by Hsüan-tsang are manifold and complex, one of the most salient is that the early tradition bore a heavy admixture of tathāgatagarbha thought not found in Fa-hsiang. Whereas the tathāgatagarbha guaranteed the universal accessibility of Buddhahood, the Fa-hsiang tradition held that there was a class of incorrigible beings (*icchantika; i-ch'an-t'i* 一闡提) forever banned from Buddhahood, and it was primarily for that reason that it was branded by the Hua-yen tradition as being only a quasi-Mahāyāna form of Buddhism.

The designation of this tradition as "Fa-hsiang" seems to have been originally coined by Fa-tsang (643-712),[5] the celebrated systematizer of the Hua-yen tradition. It thus reflects a Hua-yen polemical agenda, which thereby sought to indicate the superiority of its own teachings. The Hua-yen tradition, in fact, can be seen as coalescing around an effort to uphold the old Yogācāra-cum-tathāgatagarbha tradition in the face of the new Yogācāra teachings introduced by Hsüan-tsang.[6] To distinguish itself from those Fa-hsiang teachings, Hua-yen styled itself as the Fa-hsing (法性, dharma nature) tradition. As these two designations suggest, the meaning of *hsiang* 相 derives from its contrast with *hsing* 性. Whereas the Fa-hsiang position merely dealt with the superficial characteristics of the dharmas, their phenomenal appearances, the Fa-hsing (i.e., Hua-yen) position revealed the underlying nature on which they were based. "Nature" for Tsung-mi is another term for the tathāgatagarbha, the content of the ultimate teaching within his classification scheme. The translation of *fa-hsiang* 法相 as "phenomenal appearances" thus reflects the Hua-yen point of view assumed by Tsung-mi and not the way the term would have been understood within a Fa-hsiang doctrinal context. Within the framework of Fa-hsiang thought, *hsiang,* as a translation of the Sanskrit *lakṣaṇa,* is not weighted with the ontological connotation given to it by Hua-yen and should more properly be understood as meaning simply "characteristic" or "mark."

5. It is possible that this designation may have been suggested by the title of the fourth chapter of Hsüan-tsang's translation of the *Samdhinir-mocana-sūtra* (*Chieh shen-mi ching,* T no. 676), "Chapter on the Phenom-enal Appearance of All Dharmas" (*I-ch'ieh fa-hsiang p'in* 一切法相品), wherein the cardinal Yogācāra doctrine of the three natures (*trisvabhāva*) is set forth (see T 16.693a-c; cf. Lamotte, *Samdhinirmocana Sūtra: L'Ex-plication des mystères,* pp. 188-192).

6. This theme is developed by Gimello, "Chih-yen," pp. 338-414.

In his *Ch'an Preface* Tsung-mi characterizes the Fa-hsiang tradition as the Teaching That Refutes Objects by Means of Consciousness (*chiang-shih p'o-ching chiao* 將識破境教). He goes on to explain this characterization in his autocommentary, saying that although the previous Teaching of the Lesser Vehicle had destroyed the belief in a substantially existing self (ātman), it still held on to the belief in the reality of things (dharmas). The present teaching corrects this error by showing that things (dharmas) arise from the evolution of consciousness and, accordingly, have no substantial reality of their own. Tsung-mi continues, saying that according to this teaching the things (dharmas) that arise and perish from moment to moment "are not connected with suchness (*tathatā; chen-ju* 眞如)."[7]

Tsung-mi's last point is based on the *Awakening of Faith*, which describes the ālayavijñāna as being based on the mind as suchness (*hsin chen-ju* 心眞如), which is identified with the tathāgatagarbha. It thus implicitly criticizes the Fa-hsiang tradition for failing to recognize the connection between the tathāgatagarbha and ālayavijñāna. The Fa-hsiang position accordingly regards suchness as static, that is, as not involved in the production of all pure and impure phenomenal appearances (*hsiang* 相). Thus, for Tsung-mi, the Fa-hsiang teaching falls short in only recognizing one aspect of the absolute mind (*i-hsin* 一心): while it acknowledges its "unchanging" (*pu-pien* 不變) character, it wholly ignores its "conditioned" (*sui-yüan* 隨緣) character. In other words, it does not realize that the phenomenal appearances (*hsiang*) that it purports to analyze are the functioning (*yung* 用) of the mind as suchness as it accords with conditions (*sui-yüan* 隨緣). But it is just the conditioned aspect of suchness that is of vital importance for Tsung-mi because it links the tathāgatagarbha with the ālayavijñāna and thereby accounts for how suchness accords with conditions to form all pure and impure states. Elsewhere Tsung-mi refers to this conditioned aspect of suchness as nature origination (*hsing-ch'i* 性起), which provides the theoretical basis on which he develops his account of the process of phenomenal evolution in the concluding section of the *Inquiry*—his answer, that is, to the question of the origin of the human condition.

In Tsung-mi's view, it is because the Fa-hsiang teaching lacks the principle of nature origination that there is nothing to mediate between the ālayavijñāna and suchness, the realm of defiled activity

7. See T 48.403b24-26; K 104; cf. B 164.

and that of unconditioned purity. It is thus guilty of a fundamental dualism. Nature origination, on the other hand, bridges this gap by affirming that all phenomenal appearances (*hsiang* 相) are nothing but a manifestation (*yung* 用) of the nature (*hsing* 性) that is their very essence (*t'i* 體). Nature origination overcomes this dualism by making use of the conceptual paradigm of essence and function (*t'i-yung* 體用). The various polarities that Tsung-mi employs—such as nature and phenomenal appearance(s) or root (*pen* 本) and branch(es) (*mo* 末)—all conform to this paradigm. Essence, nature, and root, on the one hand, and function, phenomenal appearance(s), and branch(es), on the other, are all interchangeable.

In his conclusion to the section on this teaching in the *Ch'an Preface,* Tsung-mi notes that it is based on the *Saṃdhinirmocana-sūtra,* the *Yogācārabhūmi-śāstra,* and the *Ch'eng wei-shih lun.*[8] The *Saṃdhinirmocana* and the *Yogācārabhūmi* were important sources for the Indian Yogācāra tradition. The *Ch'eng wei-shih lun,* however, was a Chinese creation, in which Hsüan-tsang's disciple and collaborator K'uei-chi played a major editorial role, and it is the text on which the sectarian identity of the Fa-hsiang tradition is based. It consists in an abridged synopsis of various Indian commentaries to Vasubandhu's *Thirty Verses* (*Triṃśikā*).[9] It is thus a composite work, for which there is no single corresponding Indian text. K'uei-chi's commentary identifies the various commentarial opinions cited in the text, giving special authority to those of Dharmapāla.[10] Tsung-mi was well acquainted with the *Ch'eng wei-shih lun* and, according to his own testimony, had used it along with K'uei-chi's commentary in the composition of his own two-fascicle commentary to Vasubandhu's *Thirty Verses* written between 819 and 820.[11]

8. T 48.403c11-13; K 104; cf. B 169.

9. A translation of the *Triṃśikā* can be found in Stefan Anacker's *Seven Works of Vasubandhu.*

10. As the availablity of Sthiramati's text has revealed, not all of K'uei-chi's attributions were correct. I would like to thank Dan Lusthaus for sending me his chapter, "The Legend of the Transmission of the *Ch'eng wei-shih lun,*" from his work in progress on Buddhist phenomenology, which provides a refreshing reappraisal of the significance of Dharmapāla.

11. TSC 225d. Since Tsung-mi's commentary is not mentioned in the catalogue compiled by Ŭi-ch'ŏn in 1101, it must have already been lost by that time (see Kamata, *Shūmitsu kyōgaku no shisōshi-teki kenkyū,* p. 95).

Tsung-mi's account of the Teaching of the Phenomenal Appearances of the Dharmas begins with a brief synopsis based on the *Ch'eng wei-shih lun*.

[709b26]　三大乘法相教者、説一切有情無始已來、法爾有八種識。於中第八阿頼耶識、是其根本。頓變根身器界種子、轉生七識。皆能變現自分所縁、都無實法。

**[709b26] The Teaching of the Phenomenal Appearances of the Dharmas within the Great Vehicle holds that all sentient beings from [time] without beginning inherently[12] have eight kinds of consciousness. Of these, the eighth—the ālayavijñāna—is the fundamental basis. It instantaneously evolves into the body of the senses, the receptacle world, and the seeds, and transforms, generating the [other] seven consciousnesses. All [eight consciousnesses] evolve and manifest their own perceiving subject and perceived objects,[13] none of which are substantial entities.**

According to the *Ch'eng wei-shih lun* (a position K'uei-chi attributes to Dharmapāla), consciousness evolves (*pariṇāma; pien* 變) into a subjective and objective part (*darśanabhāga; chien-fen* 見分 and *nimittabhāga; so-fen* 所分). Since these two aspects of consciousness are born from causes and conditions, they are accorded reality as dependently existing (*paratantra; i-t'a* 依他). It is on the basis of this twofold division of consciousness, moreover,

12. *Fa-erh* 法爾, Hsüan-tsang's translation of *dharmatā*.

13. In his *Ch'an Preface* Tsung-mi adds, by way of a note, "the eye [consciousness] takes form as its object, . . . the seventh [consciousness] takes the subjective [aspect of the ālaya] as its object, and the eighth [consciousness] takes the [body of the] senses, the seeds, and the receptacle world as its objects." In stating that the seventh consciousness takes the subjective aspect of the ālaya as its object, Tsung-mi is following the position attributed to Dharmapāla. The *Ch'eng wei-shih lun* also gives three variant opinions on the object of the seventh consciousness: that attributed to Nanda, which holds that it is the ālaya itself and its associated dharmas; that attributed to Citrabhānu, which holds that it is the subjective and objective aspect of the ālaya; and that attributed to Sthiramati, which holds that it is the ālaya and its seeds (see T 31.21c17-22a13; cf. La Vallée Poussin 1.250-252 and Wei Tat, pp. 280-283). The main text of the *Ch'an Preface* continues: "Outside of these eight consciousnesses, there are no substantial things at all" (T 48.403b29-c1; K 104; cf. B 165).

that sentient beings falsely imagine the existence of a self (ātman) and things (dharma) as substantial entities. Self and things, however, do not really exist, being nothing more than what is imagined (*parikalpita; pien-chi-so-chih* 遍計所執) by deluded consciousness.

Sthiramati, a major Yogācāra thinker against whom Dharmapāla is often pitted, interprets *pariṇāma* to mean that consciousness is different from one moment to another. He accordingly only regards consciousness as existing dependently (*paratantra*); its dichotomization into a subjective and objective aspect is wholly imagined (*parikalpita*). Thus, while for Dharmapāla consciousness is always manifested in both its subjective and objective aspects, for Sthiramati the subject/object duality is an illusion to be transcended by insight into things as they are.[14]

Consciousness (*vijñāna; shih* 識) operates in eight modes, which are divided into three categories: 1) *vijñāna* (*shih* 識), referring to the five sense-consciousnesses and the faculty of mental discrimination (*mano-vijñāna; i-shih* 意識), 2) *manas* (*i* 意), referring to the ego consciousness (*mo-na-shih* 末那識), and 3) *citta* (*hsin* 心), referring to the ālayavijñāna. The five sense-consciousnesses are named after the sense organs that serve as their support;[15] likewise, the sixth consciousness, *mano-vijñāna,* is named after its support, the seventh consciousness, *manas.* The sixth consciousness is characterized by discrimination and has all dharmas as its object. *Manas,* the seventh consciousness, has the ālaya as both its support and object. It is characterized by intellection and is always accompanied by the four defilements (*kleśa; fan-nao* 煩惱) of delusion of a self, belief in a self, self-conceit, and self-love. In its untransformed state, it clings to the subjective aspect of the ālaya as a true self (ātman). After it has been radically transformed (*āśraya-parāvṛtta; chuan-i* 轉依) by the wisdom that beholds the essential equality of all things, it has suchness and all other dharmas as its object, in addition to the ālaya.[16]

14. If one can discount the partisan championing of Dharmapāla, Ueda presents a clear discussion of the difference between the position of the *Ch'eng wei-shih lun* and Sthiramati in regard to the meaning of *vijñāna-pariṇāma* in his "Two Main Streams of Thought in Yogācāra Thought." See also Weinstein, "The Concept of the Ālaya-vijñāna in Pre-T'ang Chinese Buddhism."

15. I.e., eye-consciousness, ear-consciousness, etc.

16. For a detailed explanation of the first six consciousnesses, see *Ch'eng wei-shih lun,* T 31.26a12-38c4; cf. La Vallée Poussin 1.289-413 and Wei Tat, pp. 340-497. For the seventh consciousness, *manas,* see *Ch'eng*

It is noteworthy that here and elsewhere throughout the *Inquiry* Tsung-mi uses *a-lai-yeh* 阿賴耶, Hsüan-tsang's transliteration of ālaya, instead of *a-li-yeh* 阿梨耶 used by Paramārtha and the *Awakening of Faith*. According to Hsüan-tsang's rendition, ālaya means "receptacle," "repository," or "store" (*tsang* 藏 in Chinese), to which the *Ch'eng wei-shih lun* gives three meanings: it is said to be actively ālaya (*neng-ts'ang* 能藏) in that it stores the seeds (*bīja; chung-tzu* 種子) out of which the mental and physical elements that comprise the phenomenal world develop; it is passively ālaya (*so-ts'ang* 所藏) in that it is in turn "perfumed" by the other seven consciousnesses; and it is the ālaya that is attached to (*chih-tsang* 執藏) by the seventh consciousness. Because the ālayavijñāna is simultaneously cause and effect, its identity—being determined by the sum total of the seeds that it contains at any given moment—is constantly changing; it is for this reason that it differs from the Brahmanical ātman that it superficially seems to resemble.[17] The ālayavijñāna is often spoken of as the root or fundamental consciousness (*mūla-vijñāna; ken-pen-shih* 根本識) because it holds the seeds out of which the other seven consciousnesses evolve. The other seven consciousnesses are accordingly referred to as transformed consciousnesses (*pravṛtti-vijñāna; chuan-shih* 轉識).

According to the *Ch'eng wei-shih lun*,[18] the ālayavijñāna develops internally into seeds and the body of the senses and externally into the receptacle world. Taken together, these three constitute the object (*ālambana; so-yüan* 所緣) or the objective aspect (*nimitta-bhāga; hsiang-fen* 相分) of the ālaya. The *Ch'eng wei-shih lun* defines the receptacle world (*bhājanaloka; ch'i-shih-chien* 器世界)— what we would call the physical environment—as "the place that serves as the support for all sentient beings."[19] It defines the body of the senses (*sendriyakakāya; ken-shen* 根身) as "the sense organs and the body that serves as their support."[20] Seeds (*bīja; chung-tzu* 種子) are the potentialities from which all things are manifested.

---

*wei-shih lun,* T 31.19a29-26a11; cf. La Vallée Poussin 1.225-288 and Wei Tat, pp. 248-337.

17. For a detailed discussion of the ālayavijñāna, see *Ch'eng wei-shih lun,* T 31.7c13-19a28; cf. La Vallée Poussin 1.94-220 and Wei Tat, pp. 102-245. See also Fukaura, "Ālaya-vijñāna," *Encyclopaedia of Buddhism* 1.383-388.

18. T 31.10a17; cf. La Vallée Poussin 1.125 and Wei Tat, pp. 136-137.

19. T 31.10a13-14.

20. T 31.10a15-16.

According to the position attributed to Dharmapāla, there are both innate and acquired seeds.[21] Those that are innate exist inherently in the nature of things (*dharmatā; fa-erh* 法爾) from time immemorial and are of both pure and impure variety. However, they need to be ripened by further conditioning (*vāsanā; hsi-ch'i* 習氣) in order to mature and be manifested as an effect. Once manifested, the effect, in turn, leaves a trace or impression in the ālaya, which becomes the cause for the creation of new seeds. Seeds and their manifestations thus stand in a reciprocal relationship to one another, being simultaneously cause and effect of each other.[22]

The first seven consciousnesses are spoken of as "transformed consciousnesses" (*pravṛtti-vijñāna; chuan-shih* 轉識) because they are transformations of the ālayavijñāna, which is their support. The expression *chuan-sheng* 轉生, as Yüan-chüeh points out,[23] is used in the famous water/wave metaphor in the *Laṅkāvatāra-sūtra*,[24] an important Yogācāra scripture that compares the generation of the seven consciousnesses from the transformation of the ālayavijñāna to the formation of waves on the surface of water stirred by the wind. The *Ch'eng wei-shih lun* also refers to this passage in discussing the relationship of the seven transformed consciousnesses with the ālaya.[25]

Tsung-mi's exposition continues, quoting from the *Ch'eng wei-shih lun* to explain how the various consciousnesses evolve.[26]

[709c1] 如何變耶。謂我法分別熏習力故、諸識生時變似我法。第六七識無明覆故、緣此執為實我實法。

[709c1] How do they evolve? [The *Ch'eng wei-shih lun*] says: "Because of the influence of the karmically conditioned predispositions of the [false] discrimination of self [ātman]

---

21. The notion of innate seeds also serves as the basis for Dharmapāla's theory of *gotra* (*chung-hsing* 種姓), according to which sentient beings are rigidly categorized into five classes in regard to their ultimate spiritual potential. Beings innately devoid of all pure seeds (i.e., the *icchantika*) can never achieve Buddhahood, no matter how much merit they accumulate.

22. For a detailed discussion of seeds, see *Ch'eng wei-shih lun*, T 31.8a5-10a11; cf. La Vallée Poussin 1.100-123 and Wei Tat, pp. 108-135.

23. 129c-d.

24. See T 16.484b12, 523b22, and 594c14—the wording is the same in all three Chinese translations; cf. the translation by Suzuki, p. 42.

25. See T 31.14c14; cf. La Vallée Poussin 1.175 and Wei Tat, pp. 194-195.

26. See *Ch'eng wei-shih lun*, T 31.1b3; cf. La Vallée Poussin 1.10 and Wei Tat, p. 10.

and things [dharma] [in the ālayavijñāna], when the consciousnesses are engendered [from the ālayavijñāna], they evolve into the semblance of a self and things." The sixth and seventh consciousnesses, because they are obscured by ignorance, "consequently cling to [their subjective and objective manifestations] as a substantial self and substantial things."

"Karmically conditioned predispositions" here translates *vāsanā* (*hsün-hsi* 熏習, also *hsi-ch'i* 習氣). *Vāsanā* is closely related to and often used interchangeably with *bīja* (seed). It refers to the traces or impressions of an act that remain in the ālayavijñāna and that ripen already existing seeds as well as create new ones. D. T. Suzuki, who translates *vāsanā* as "habit-energy," notes: "*Vāsanā* literally means 'performing,' or 'fumigation,' that is, it is a kind of energy that is left behind when an act is accomplished and has the power to rekindle the old and seek out new impressions."[27]

Tsung-mi is again following the opinion attributed to Dharmapāla, which holds that only the sixth and seventh consciousnesses are capable of false imagination. Sthiramati, on the other hand, holds that all eight consciousnesses are capable of false imagination.[28]

### DREAM ANALOGY

Tsung-mi continues his exposition of Fa-hsiang thought by quoting an analogy from the *Ch'eng wei-shih lun*.[29]

[709c3]　如患（重病心惛見異色人物也）夢（夢想所見可
知）者。患夢力故、心似種種外境相現。夢時執為實有外
物、寤來方知唯夢所變。我身亦爾：唯識所變。迷故執有
我及諸境、由此起惑造業、生死無窮（廣如前説）。悟解此
理、方知我身唯識所變、識為身本（不了之義如後所破）。

[709c3] "It is like the case of being ill (in grave illness the mind is befuddled and perceives people and things in altered guise) or

27. *Studies in the Lankavatara Sutra,* p. 99. For details on the use of the term in the *Ch'eng wei-shih lun,* see T 31.43a10-b27; cf. La Vallée Poussin 2.473-481 and Wei Tat, pp. 578-585. I would like to thank Alan Sponberg for his suggestion on how to translate this term.

28. See *Ch'eng wei-shih lun,* T 31.45c246a8; cf. La Vallée Poussin 2.517-520 and Wei Tat, pp. 626-629.

29. See T 31.1b5-6; cf. la Vallée Poussin 1.10 and Wei Tat, pp. 12-13. The notes are Tsung-mi's interpolation.

dreaming[30] (the activity of dreaming and what is seen in the dream may be distinguished). Because of the influence of the illness or dream, the mind manifests itself in the semblance of the phenomenal appearance of a variety of external objects." When one is dreaming, one clings to them as substantially existing external things, but, as soon as one awakens, one realizes that they were merely the transformations of the dream. One's own bodily existence[31] is also like this: it is merely the transformation of consciousness. Because [beings] are deluded, they cling to [these transformations] as existing self and objects, and, as a result of this, generate delusion and create karma, and birth-and-death is without end (as amply explained before [in the previous teaching]). As soon as one realizes this principle, one understands that our bodily existence is merely the transformation of consciousness and that consciousness constitutes the root of bodily existence ([this teaching is of] non-final meaning, as will be refuted later [in the following teaching]).

The concluding part of the corresponding section of the *Ch'an Preface* gives a different description of the culmination of spiritual practice according to the *Ch'eng wei-shih lun:*

> Once one realizes that from the outset there was neither self [ātman] nor things [dharmas], that there is only mental consciousness, he thereupon relies on the wisdom of the twofold emptiness [i.e., of ātman and dharma], cultivates practices such as the discernment of consciousness-only as well as the six perfections and the four articles of attraction, gradually overcomes the two obstructions of the defilements (*kleśāvarana; fan-nao chang* 煩惱障) and of the knowable (*jñeyāvarana; so-chih chang* 所知障), verifies

---

30. As Tsung-mi's note to each term indicates, he reads *huan* 患 and *meng* 夢 as separate terms, as also does K'uei-chi. In his commentary on the passage in the *Ch'eng wei-shih lun* from which Tsung-mi is here quoting, K'uei-chi points out that in the case of impaired vision experienced during a high fever, all colors may be perceived as yellowish (T 43.243a9-10). La Vallée Poussin takes *huan-meng* as a compound, which he translates as "nightmare" (cauchemar) (1.10). Wei Tat leaves *huan* untranslated (see p. 13).

31. The corresponding passage in the *Ch'an Preface* also includes external objects (see T 48.403c6; K 104; cf. B 166).

the suchness revealed by the twofold emptiness, the ten
stages [of the bodhisattva] are fully consummated, the
eighth consciousness is transformed, and one attains the
enlightenment of the four wisdoms. When the obstructions
to suchness are exhausted, one attains the great nirvāṇa of
the dharmakāya.[32]

Since the Teaching of the Phenomenal Appearances of the Dharmas is refuted by the following teaching, there is no critique in the
present section.

32. T 48.403c7-11; K 105; cf. B 166-168. See K 114-116 and B 167-169
for details on the meaning of the various terms mentioned in this passage.
For a discussion of K'uei-chi's five-level discernment of "consciousness
only," see Sponberg, "Meditation in Fa-hsiang Buddhism," pp. 30-34.

# The Teaching That Refutes
# Phenomenal Appearances

The Teaching That Refutes Phenomenal Appearances reflects Tsung-mi's interpretation of the basic import of the Madhyamaka teaching of emptiness (*śūnyatā; k'ung* 空). The Madhyamaka tradition—so called because it takes a Middle Way between what it views as two philosophical extremes—is indelibly linked with Nāgārjuna, the great second- or third-century Indian Buddhist thinker who elaborated the philosophical implications of the teaching of emptiness that had been expounded in the Perfection of Wisdom (*Prajñāpāramitā*) scriptures. The earliest Perfection of Wisdom scriptures, composed sometime between the first century B.C. and the first century A.D., belong to the oldest strata of Mahāyāna literature.[1] Whereas these texts merely proclaim their message, Nāgārjuna was the first to argue for it in a philosophically sustained manner. Nāgārjuna had such an impact on the subsequent development of Buddhism that he is often looked back to as second in importance only to the Buddha.

In China Madhyamaka was identified with the Three Treatises (San-lun) tradition because it was based on three treatises translated by Kumārajīva (344-413)—i.e., the *Treatise on the Middle Way* (*Chung lun*), the *Twelve Topics Treatise* (*Shih-erh men lun*), and

---

1. The most frequently cited theory of the historical development of this literature is that put forward by Edward Conze; see pp. 11-16 of the introduction to his *Selected Sayings from the Perfection of Wisdom;* the selected translations in this work also serve as a good introduction to the Perfection of Wisdom literature as a whole. Conze claims that the earliest phase of *Prajñāpāramitā* literature is represented by the *Aṣṭasāhasrika* (Perfection of Wisdom in Eight Thousand Lines) and the *Ratnaguna-samcayagatha,* its verse summary. See also chapter 2 of Paul Williams' *Mahāyāna Buddhism.*

the *Hundred Treatise (Po lun)*.[2] The most important of these texts was the *Treatise on the Middle Way,* which contained the *Stanzas on the Middle Way (Madhyamakārikā)*, Nāgārjuna's most celebrated work, along with a prose commentary by Piṅgala.[3] The *Twelve Topics Treatise* is an obscure and problematic text that had little influence in China and was unknown in the Indian and the Tibetan traditions.[4] The *Hundred Treatise* consists of a commentary to a series of verses by Āryadeva, Nāgārjuna's principal disciple, refuting various positions put forward by non-Buddhist opponents.[5] These three treatises all belong to the earliest phase of the historical development of the Madhyamaka, before the tradition split into its Prāsaṅgika and Svātantrika branches. The Chinese tradition thus has a cast very different from Indo-Tibetan tradition. The Madhyamaka tradition represented in Sanskrit and Tibetan sources is based on the writings of later Madhyamaka thinkers, whose works were translated after the Chinese tradition had already taken form, and so had little or no influence in China, or whose works were never translated into Chinese at all. None of the works of Candrakīrti, the most influential of all of the later Madhyamaka thinkers for the development of the tradition in India and Tibet, was ever translated into Chinese before modern times.

Another text that bore enormous authority for the Madhyamaka tradition in China, and that was sometimes included as a fourth treatise,[6] was the *Great Perfection of Wisdom Treatise (Ta-chih-tu*

2. For a study of this tradition and its Indian roots, see Richard Robinson, *Early Mādhyamika in India and China.*

3. Or *Chung-kuan lun,* as Tsung-mi later refers to it (709c19-20); T no. 1564, Piṅgala's commentary is never mentioned in Sanskrit or Tibetan sources. For a translation of the Sanskrit text of the *Madhyamakārikā,* see Appendix A of Frederick Streng's *Emptiness: A Study in Religious Meaning.* Streng's book itself presents one of the more influential modern academic interpretations of Madhyamaka. See also Kenneth Inada, *Nāgārjuna: A Translation of his Mūlamadhyamakakārikā with an Introductory Essay.*

4. T no. 1568; although the text is attributed to Nāgārjuna, only the verses are by him (twenty-two of the twenty-six verses can be traced to other works by Nāgārjuna). The prose commentary may have been composed by Piṅgala, who may also have compiled the selection of verses. See Robinson, *Early Mādhyamika,* pp. 32-33, and Lindtner, *Nagarjuniana,* pp. 11-12, n. 13.

5. T no. 1569; see Robinson, *Early Mādhyamika,* pp. 33-34.

6. Hence the Three Treatise tradition was also sometimes referred to as the Four Treatise tradition.

*lun*), a massive commentary to the *Perfection of Wisdom in Twenty Five Thousand Lines* attributed to Nāgārjuna by Kumārajīva.[7] This text is almost certainly not a translation of a work by Nāgārjuna. Since it is entirely unknown outside of the East Asian tradition, it is possible that Kumārajīva, its "translator," may have had a major hand in its composition. It was prized by Chinese Buddhists as an authoritative and encyclopedic reference to Mahāyāna Buddhist doctrine.

Tsung-mi views Madhyamaka from the perspective of the tathāgatagarbha literature, especially the *Awakening of Faith*. As his designation suggests, the role of the Teaching That Refutes Phenomenal Appearances is primarily negative—its function is to destroy deluded attachments, for only when deluded attachments have been eliminated can the true nature be revealed as it is in reality: pure and immutable. The teaching of emptiness is thus said to intimate (*mihsien* 密顯) the true nature, but it is not yet ultimate because it is unable to reveal (*hsien-shih* 顯示) it. It thereby paves the way for the next and final teaching, that which Reveals the Nature.

Tsung-mi's assessment of this teaching is based on the qualification of emptiness in tathāgatagarbha texts, which claim that the tathāgatagarbha was taught as an antidote to the psychological dangers inherent in the teaching of emptiness. The tathāgatagarbha doctrine, which assumed particular prominence in Chinese Buddhism, resonated with some of the perennial preoccupations of indigenous Chinese thought, such as its attempt to define human nature, clarify the sources of ethical action, and uncover the underlying ontological matrix from which the phenomenal world evolves. Chinese Buddhists not only valued the tathāgatagarbha doctrine for providing a basis for faith in the universal accessibility of Buddhahood but also found within it a rationale for qualifying the radical negation of the Madhyamaka teaching of emptiness and thus developing a vision of Buddhism that affirmed life in this world. The Chinese appropriation of this doctrine was elaborated in a number of apocryphal texts, most notably the *Awakening of Faith*.

The most important scriptural formulation of this doctrine was made in the *Śrīmālā Sūtra*, which proclaimed that the tathāgatagarbha represented the true meaning of emptiness. The *Śrīmālā Sūtra*

7. T no. 1509; see Robinson, *Early Mādhyamika*, pp. 34-39. For a copiously annotated French translation of the first third of this text, see Lamotte, *Le Traité de la grande vertu de sagesse*, in 5 vols. For an exposition of the central ideas of this text, see Ramanan, *Nāgārjuna's Philosophy*.

thereby implied that the teaching of emptiness as it had been previously expounded in the Perfection of Wisdom scriptures was only
provisional (neyārtha; pu-liao-i 不了義) because it did not recognize the infinite excellent qualities of the Tathāgata. The former
teaching of emptiness was therefore not so much wrong as it was
incomplete and one-sided. The tathāgatagarbha was the ultimate
(nītārtha; liao-i 了義) teaching because it revealed the full meaning
of emptiness. "The wisdom of the tathāgatagarbha is the Tathāgata's
wisdom of emptiness."[8]

The Tathāgata's wisdom of emptiness, moreover, is twofold.
The tathāgatagarbha can be spoken of as being both empty and
not empty in that it is at once empty of all defilements (kleśa; fan-
nao 煩惱) and, at the same time, not empty of all Buddha-dharmas.[9]
The true understanding of emptiness, therefore, entails the recog-
nition that the other side of the tathāgatagarbha's being empty of
all defiled dharmas is its being replete with infinite Buddha-dharmas.
It is on this basis that the Śrīmālā Sūtra represents its teaching as
being of ultimate meaning, in implicit contradistinction to the purely
negative exposition of emptiness in the Perfection of Wisdom scriptural corpus.

The Awakening of Faith, whose adaptation of the tathāgatagarbha doctrine was authoritative for Tsung-mi, follows the Śrīmālā
Sūtra in distinguishing between the empty and not empty aspects
of the absolute: suchness can be said to be both truly empty, "because it is ultimately able to reveal what is real," and truly not empty,
"because it has its own essence and is fully endowed with excellent
qualities whose nature is undefiled."[10]

Because it is not empty, the tathāgatagarbha is endowed with
positive qualities. Tathāgatagarbha texts even went so far as to attribute what had earlier been condemned as the four inverted views
to the dharmakāya: permanence, bliss, selfhood, and purity.[11] The
Awakening of Faith thus stands solidly in the tathāgatagarbha tradition in attributing positive qualities to the absolute. It says that
since suchness (tathatā; chen-ju 眞如)

> was neither born at the beginning of time nor will perish
> at the end of time, it is utterly permanent and steadfast. In

8. T 12.221c13.
9. T 12.221c16-18; cf. Pu-tseng pu-chien ching, T 16.467a17-21.
10. T 32.576b24; cf. Hirakawa, p. 80 and Hakeda, p. 34.
11. See Wayman, The Lion's Roar of Queen Śrīmālā, p. 102.

its nature it is itself fully endowed with all excellent qualities. That is, its essence itself possesses the radiant light of
great wisdom; [the capacity of] universally illuminating the
dharmadhātu; true cognition; the intrinsically pure mind;
permanence, bliss, selfhood, and purity; and calmness,
eternality, and freedom.

The text then adds, in language redolent of the *Śrīmālā Sūtra,*

Therefore it is fully endowed with inconceivable Buddha-
dharmas that are more numerous than the sands of the
Ganges and that are not free from, not cut off from, and
not different from [the essence of suchness].[12]

Elsewhere the *Awakening of Faith* suggests how the teaching
of the tathāgatagarbha serves to overcome the misunderstanding to
which the negative language of the teaching of emptiness is liable.

[Ordinary beings] hear the scriptures proclaim that all dharmas in the world are ultimately empty of [any] essence, that
even the dharmas of nirvāṇa and suchness are also ultimately empty, and that they are from the very beginning
themselves empty and free from all phenomenal appearances. Since they do not understand that [such statements
were taught] in order to break their attachments, they hold
that the nature of suchness and nirvāṇa is merely empty.
How is [this view] to be counteracted? It must be made
clear that the dharmakāya of suchness is in its own essence
not empty but fully endowed with incalculable excellent
qualities.[13]

## Synopsis

The term that Tsung-mi uses to designate this teaching (*p'o-hsiang*
破相) seems to have been first used by Ching-ying Hui-yüan (523-
592) to refer to the third of his fourfold division of the teachings.
Hui-yüan was well versed in both the Ti-lun and She-lun traditions,
and his writings presented a systematic and mature statement of the
earlier Yogācāra tradition in Chinese Buddhism. A review of Hui-
yüan's use of the term sheds light on Tsung-mi's understanding of
the role and character of emptiness within his classification scheme.

---

12. T 32.579a14-18; cf. Hirakawa, pp. 245-246 and Hakeda, p. 65.
13. T 32.580a8-13; cf. Hirakawa, p. 282 and Hakeda, p. 76-77. This is
the second of five biased views enumerated in the *Awakening of Faith.*

Indeed, the principle by which Hui-yüan ranks the teachings follows a rationale implicit in Tsung-mi's ordering of the teachings in the *Inquiry*—that is, it progresses from a naive affirmation of apparent reality, to a thoroughgoing refutation of the terms in which such a view is conceived, which thus makes possible the revelation of the true nature of reality in the highest teaching. According to Hui-yüan's scheme, the first category of teaching, found in the Abhidharma literature, holds that all dharmas, although produced from conditions, still have a self-nature. The second category, found in the *Ch'eng-shih lun*,[14] while denying that dharmas have a self-nature, still holds that they have phenomenal appearances (*hsiang* 相).[15] The third category, that which teaches the emptiness of all dharmas, holds that the self-nature and phenomenal appearances of dharmas are equally unreal, like a mirage seen in the distance: when one draws closer one realizes that both the nature and phenomenal appearance of the water are nonexistent. The fourth category is the true teaching that reveals reality (*hsien shih* 顯實). Hui-yüan writes that this teaching holds that "all dharmas exist by virtue of deluded thinking. While deluded thinking is without substance, its occurrence must be based on something real," which Hui-yüan identifies as the tathāgatagarbha.[16]

[709c9]    四大乘破相教者、破前大小乘法相之執、密顯
後眞性空寂之理。

[709c9] **The Teaching of the Great Vehicle That Refutes Phenomenal Appearances refutes the attachment to the phenomenal appearances of the dharmas in the previous [teachings of] the Great and Lesser Vehicles and intimates the principle of the emptiness and tranquility of the true nature in the later [Teaching That Reveals the Nature].**

14. T no. 1464; the Chinese translation of an otherwise unattested treatise whose Sanskrit title may have been either *Tattvasiddhi* or *Satyasiddhi*. The treatise was the focus of one of the six exegetical traditions of the fifth and sixth centuries.

15. Although the *hsiang* 相 in Hui-yüan's scheme does not refer to the *hsiang* 相 in the Fa-hsiang school, the designation of the brand of Yogācāra established in China by Hsüan-tsang as the Fa-hsiang school provided Tsung-mi with a convenient pretext for appropriating Hui-yüan's terminology as yet another means of demonstrating the inferiority of the Fa-hsiang teaching to that of the tathāgatagarbha.

16. See *Ta-sheng-i chang*, T 44.483a12-29.

"Emptiness" (*k'ung* 空) and "tranquility" (*chi* 寂) are two terms that Tsung-mi often uses to characterize the tathāgatagarbha, which he refers to as "empty tranquil awareness" (*k'ung chi chih* 空寂知) in his *Ch'an Chart:*

> "Empty" means empty of all phenomenal appearances and is still a negative term. "Tranquil" just indicates the immutability of the true nature and is not the same as nothingness. "Awareness" indicates the revelation of the very essence and is not the same as discrimination. It alone is the intrinsic essence of the true mind.[17]

### THE PLACEMENT OF THIS TEACHING

Tsung-mi's note takes up the question of the placement of this teaching within his classification scheme.

> [709c10] （破相之談、不唯諸部般若、遍在大乘經。前之三教依次先後、此教隨執即破、無定時節。故龍樹立二種般若：一共、二不共。共者、二乘同聞信解、破二乘法執故。不共者、唯菩薩解、密顯佛性故。

> [709c10] (Discussions that refute phenomenal appearances are not limited to the various sections of the Perfection of Wisdom but pervade the scriptures of the Great Vehicle. [Although] the previous three teachings are arranged on the basis of their temporal order, [since] this teaching refutes them in accordance with their attachments, it [was taught] without a fixed time period. Therefore Nāgārjuna posited two types of wisdom: the first is the common, and the second is the distinct. The common refers to [that which the followers of] the two vehicles alike heard, believed, and understood, because it refuted the attachment to dharmas of [the followers of] the two vehicles. The distinct refers to [that which] only the bodhisattvas understood, because it intimated the Buddha-nature.

Tsung-mi here invokes the authority of Nāgārjuna, the putative author of the *Great Perfection of Wisdom Treatise (Ta-chih-tu lun)*, to justify his placement of this teaching after that of the Phenomenal Appearances of the Dharmas. To explain how this teaching was taught "without a fixed time period," Yüan-chüeh's commentary quotes the following passage from the *Great Perfection of Wisdom Treatise:* "From the night that he attained the Way until his nirvāṇa,

---

17. HTC 110.437b16-18; K 333.

the Buddha constantly preached [the perfection of] wisdom."[18] Tsung-mi's point is that whereas the order of his arrangement of the previous three teachings follows the chronological order in which they were expounded by the Buddha, the Buddha expounded the present teaching in various forms during the second and third teaching periods in order to refute the attachment to the belief in a substantial self on the part of followers of the Teaching of Humans and Gods and the attachment to the belief in substantial things on the part of followers of the Teaching of the Lesser Vehicle.

Other passages in the *Great Perfection of Wisdom Treatise* distinguish between the two types of wisdom mentioned by Tsung-mi. For example: "There are two types of wisdom. The first is the exposition in common with the śrāvakas. The second is the exposition only for advanced great bodhisttavas abiding in the ten directions."[19] And: "There are two types of wisdom. The first is the exposition only for the great bodhisattvas. The second is the common exposition of the three vehicles."[20]

The "two vehicles" in the *Inquiry* passage refer to those of the śrāvaka and pratyekabuddha, which collectively designate the Lesser Vehicle. The "three vehicles" comprise the first two plus that of the bodhisattva. The Buddha-nature, of course, is another name for the tathāgatagarbha, the content of the Teaching That Reveals the Nature.[21]

Tsung-mi goes on to discuss the disagreements over the relative ranking of Yogācāra and Madhyamaka teachings between the two Indian scholars Śīlabhadra and Jñānaprabha.

[709c12]　故天竺戒賢智光二論師、各立三時教、指此空教、
或云在唯識法相之前、或云在後。今意取後。)

[709c12] Therefore the two Indian śāstra-masters Śīlabhadra and Jñānaprabha each categorized the teachings according to three time periods, but in their placing of this teaching of emptiness, one [i.e.,

18. *Chieh* 130d; I have been unable to locate the original passage.
19. T 25.754b23-25. Śrāvakas here refers to Hīnayānists, and bodhisattvas, to Mahāyānists.
20. T 25.564a21-22.
21. Buddha-nature (*fo-hsing* 佛性) is used synonymously with tathāgatagarbha in the *Nirvāṇa Sūtra* (T no. 374) and related scriptures, such as the *Mahābherīhāraka-sūtra* (T no. 270). For a detailed discussion of the relationship between Buddha-nature and tathāgatagarbha in the *Nirvāṇa* and related sūtras, see Takasaki, *Nyoraizō shisō no keisei,* pp. 127-273.

Śīlabhadra] said that it was before [the Teaching of] the Phenomenal Appearances of the Dharmas of consciousness-only, while the other [i.e., Jñānaprabha] said that it was after. Now I will take it to be after.)

Fa-tsang's *Record Inquiring into the Profundity of the Hua-yen Sūtra* presents an account of the different rankings of the teachings by Śīlabhadra and Jñānaprabha.[22] He writes that in 684 he met the Indian Tripiṭaka master Divākara, who told him that Śīlabhadra and Jñānaprabha were two of the most illustrious teachers at that time at the great monastic university of Nālandā in India. Whereas Śīlabhadra was a follower of Yogācāra,[23] Jñānaprabha was a follower of Madhyamaka,[24] and their manner of dividing the teachings was accordingly different.

Fa-tsang goes on to report that Śīlabhadra divided the Buddha's teachings into three periods, in accordance with the three turn-

22. See *Hua-yen ching t'an-hsüan chi,* T 35.111c8ff.

23. According to Hsüan-tsang's *Record of the Western Regions,* Śīlabhadra had been born as a member of the brahmin caste into the royal family of Samataṭi. He was fond of learning as a youth and travelled throughout India in search of the wise. At Nālandā he met Dharmapāla, under whom he studied and received ordination. He soon rose to prominence as the foremost of Dharmapāla's disciples. After defeating a brahmin from South India in debate, Śīlabhadra was given a city by the ruler of Magadha as a reward. Unable to refuse the gift, Śīlabhadra had the monastery of Guṇamati built there and used the revenues from the city to maintain it. See T 51.914c5ff.; cf. Thomas Watters, *On Yuan Chwang's Travels in India* 2.109-110. According to tradition, Śīlabhadra is supposed to have been one hundred six years old at the time of his first meeting with Hsüan-tsang in 636; for a description of this encounter, see T 50.236c14ff.; cf. Li Yung-hsi, *The Life of Hsüan-tsang,* p. 102ff.

24. There is some question as to the identity of Jñānaprabha. *The Life of Hsüan-tsang* suggests that Jñānaprabha was a prominent disciple of Śīlabhadra (see T 50.261a28-b1; cf. Li Yung-hsi, p. 234). This account seems to conflict with the *T'an-hsüan chi* account, which depicts him as an adherent of a rival school. Thus in his *Yen-i ch'ao* Ch'eng-kuan raises the question of whether the Jñānaprabha referred to in the two accounts is really the same person. He sensibly concludes that whoever Jñānaprabha was hardly affects their different ways of classifying the teachings (see T 36.52c13ff). Mochizuki tries to resolve the issue by pointing out that Śīlabhadra's followers included some adherents of Madhyamaka, concluding that there is no reason to suppose that the Jñānaprabha in the *T'an-hsüan chi* account could not have been the disciple of Śīlabhadra in *The Life of Hsüan-tsang* (see *Bukkyō daijiten* 4.3571c).

ings of the wheel set forth in the *Samdhinirmocana-sūtra* and *Yogācārabhūmi-śāstra*. The first period, represented by the four *Āgamas*, refers to the teaching of the Lesser Vehicle expounded by the Buddha in Deer Park. Even though it teaches that birth is empty, it still does not teach the emptiness of all things (dharmas) and is therefore not the ultimate teaching. The second period, represented by the Perfection of Wisdom scriptures, is also not the ultimate teaching because, although it uses the concept of false imagination (*parikalpa*) to prove the emptiness of all things, it still does not teach the doctrines of the dependent (*paratantra*) and perfected (*pariniṣpanna*) aspects of reality and consciousness-only. The third period, represented by the *Samdhinirmocana-sūtra,* is the ultimate teaching of the true principle of the Great Vehicle that fully sets forth the three aspects of reality (*trisvabhāva*) and the three absences of own-being.[25]

Jñānaprabha, on the other hand, divided the Buddha's teachings into three categories in accordance with the Perfection of Wisdom scriptures and the Madhyamaka treatises. The first referred to the teachings of the Lesser Vehicle expounded by the Buddha in Deer Park. This teaching was geared to those of inferior capacity and held that both the mind and its objects exist. The second referred to the teaching of consciousness-only, was geared to those of medium capacity, and held that although objects are empty, the mind exists. The third referred to the teaching of the non-existence of phenomenal appearances and represents the true ultimate teaching. It is geared to those of superior capacity and held that both mind and its objects are empty.[26] Tsung-mi's criticism of the Fa-hsiang tradition for not recognizing the emptiness of consciousness recapitulates Jñānaprabha's criticism here.

Although Tsung-mi follows Jñānaprabha in placing the Madhyamaka teaching after that of Yogācāra, it should nevertheless be reiterated that, in terms of historical development, Madhyamaka preceded Yogācāra—in fact, Yogācāra doctrines such as the three natures can only be understood as evolving out of the problematic of Madhyamaka. In reversing history and assigning the Fa-hsiang brand of Yogācāra a position inferior to Madhyamaka, Tsung-mi

25. See T 35.111c17-112a1.

26. See T 35.112a2-22. Virtually identical characterizations of Śīlabhadra's and Jñānaprabha's classification schemes can also be found in Fa-tsang's *Ta-sheng ch'i-hsin lun i-chi* (T 44.242a29ff.), Ch'eng-kuan's *Hua-yen ching shu* (T 35.510b23ff.), and Tsung-mi's TS (112d).

follows the traditional Hua-yen valuation of these two teachings. In its classical formulation in Fa-tsang's fivefold classification scheme, the Fa-hsiang brand of Yogācāra is ranked below Madhyamaka, and both teachings are regarded as rudimentary forms of the teaching of the Great Vehicle. The mature teaching of the Great Vehicle is represented by the tathāgatagarbha thought found in the early Chinese Yogācāra tradition of the Ti-lun and She-lun traditions and exemplified in the *Awakening of Faith*. This rubric of subdividing the teaching of the Great Vehicle into rudimentary and mature phases goes back to Fa-tsang's mentor Chih-yen (602-668).[27]

### CRITIQUE OF PREVIOUS TEACHING

Tsung-mi's critique of the Fa-hsiang teaching begins by turning the dream analogy that had been quoted from the *Ch'eng wei-shih lun* at the end of the last chapter against the very teaching it was cited to illustrate.

[709c13] 將欲破之、先詰之曰。所變之境既妄、能變之識豈眞。若言一有一無者（此下却將彼喻破之）則夢想與所見物應異。異則夢不是物、物不是夢、寤來夢滅、其物應在。又物若非夢、應是眞物、夢若非物、以何為相。故知夢時則夢想夢物、似能見所見之殊。據理則同一虛妄、都無所有。

[709c13] Wishing to refute [the Teaching of the Phenomenal Appearances of the Dharmas], I will first assess [the previous teaching] critically. Granted that the object that has evolved is illusory, how, then, can the consciousness that evolves be real? If one says that one exists and the other does not (from here on their analogy will be used to refute them), then the activity of dreaming and the things seen [in the dream] should be different. If they are different, then the dream not being the things [seen in the dream] and the things [seen in the dream] not being the dream, when one awakens and the dream is over, the things [seen in the dream] should remain.[28] Again,

27. Robert Gimello has shown that Chih-yen's systematization of Hua-yen thought in his later writings was in large measure a reaction against the new Yogācāra thought introduced into China by his illustrious contemporary, Hsüan-tsang (see "Chih-yen," chapter 4).

28. In his comment on this sentence, Yüan-chüeh refers to Chuang-tzu's famous dream that he was a butterfly, noting that in the present case the

the things [seen in the dream], if they are not the dream, must be real things, but how does the dream, if it is not the things [seen in the dream], assume phenomenal appearance? Therefore we know that when one dreams, the activity of dreaming and the things seen in the dream resemble the dichotomy of seeing and seen. Logically, then, they are equally unreal and altogether lack existence.

Tsung-mi gives a somewhat different argument in the corresponding section of the *Ch'an Preface:*

Mind and its objects are interdependent because they are empty but seem to exist. Moreover, the mind does not arise alone but is born only in dependence on objects, and objects are not born of themselves but are manifested because they come from the mind. When the mind is empty, objects disappear; when objects are extinguished, the mind is empty. There has never been a mind that is devoid of objects, nor have there ever been objects without a mind.[29]

Tsung-mi goes on to extend the analogy to the different consciousnesses and to cite canonical proof for the position that both mind and its objects are empty.

[709c19] 諸識亦爾、以皆假託眾緣無自性故。故『中觀論』云：「未曾有一法不從因緣生。是故一切法無不是空者。」又云：「因緣所生法、我説即是空。」『起信論』云：「一切諸法唯依妄念而有差別。若離心念即無一切境界之相。」經云：「凡所有相皆是虛妄。」離一切相即名諸佛。（如此等文遍大乘藏。）是知心境皆空、方是大乘實理。若約此原身、身元是空、空即是本。

[709c19] The various consciousnesses are also like this because they all provisionally rely on sundry causes and conditions and are devoid of a nature of their own. Therefore the *Treatise on the Middle Way* says: "There has never been a single thing that has not been born from causes and conditions. Therefore there is nothing that is not empty."[30] And

---

butterfly should have remained after Chuang-tzu woke up (see *Chieh* 131b). For Chuang-tzu's dream, see HY 7/2/94-96, translated by Watson, p. 49.

29. T 48.404a10-13; K 121; cf. B 177.

30. T 30.33b13-14.

further: "Things born by causes and conditions I declare to be empty."[31] The *Awakening of Faith* says: "It is only on the basis of deluded thinking that all things have differentiations. If one is free from thinking, then there are no phenomenal appearances of any objects."[32] The [*Diamond*] *Sūtra* says: "All phenomenal appearances are illusory."[33] Those who are free from all phenomenal appearances are called Buddhas. (Passages like these pervade the canon of the Great Vehicle.) Thus we know that mind and objects both being empty is precisely the true principle of the Great Vehicle. If we inquire into the origin of bodily existence in terms of this [teaching], then bodily existence is from the beginning empty, and emptiness itself is its basis.

Tsung-mi's criticism of the Fa-hsiang teaching reflects that of Jñānaprabha, which characterized Yogācāra as holding that objects are empty while the mind exists. The basis for this characterization rests on the Fa-hsiang claim that the consciousness that exists in dependence on various causes and conditions (*paratantra*) has real existence whereas the objects that have been transformed from the evolution of consciousness are merely products of false imagination (*parikalpita*) and have no real existence. The Madhyamaka critique, which Tsung-mi is here adopting, holds that both mind and its objects are empty because everything produced by causes and conditions is empty and has no real existence of its own.[34]

### CRITIQUE OF PRESENT TEACHING

Tsung-mi now turns to his critique of the Teaching That Refutes Phenomenal Appearances.

[709c26]　今復詰此教曰。若心境皆無、知無者誰。又若都無實法、依何現諸虛妄。且現見世間虛妄之物、未有不依實法而能起者。

[709c26] Now I will also assess this Teaching [That Refutes Phenomenal Appearances] critically. If the mind and its ob-

31. T 30.33b15.
32. T 32.576a9-10; cf. Hirakawa, pp. 71-72 and Hakeda, pp. 32-33.
33. T 8.749a19.
34. For a discussion of the Madhyamaka/Yogācāra debate on this issue see Hirabayashi and Iida, "Another Look at the Madhyamaka vs. Yogācāra Controversy Concerning Existence and Non-existence."

jects are both non-existent, then who is it that knows they do not exist? Again, if there are no real things whatsoever, then on the basis of what are the illusions made to appear? Moreover, there has never been a case of the illusory things in the world before us[35] being able to arise without being based on something real.

Tsung-mi's criticism here recalls that of Hui-yüan quoted earlier: "Although deluded thinking is without substance, its occurrence must be based on something real."

[709c29] 如無濕性不變之水、何有虛妄假相之波。若無淨明不變之鏡、何有種種虛假之影。又前説夢想夢境同虛妄者、誠如所言、然此虛妄之夢、必依睡眠之人。今既心境皆空、未審依何妄現。故知此教但破執情、亦未明顯眞靈之性。故『法鼓經』云：「一切空經是有餘説。」（有餘者餘義未了也。）『大品經』云：「空是大乘之初門。」

[709c29] If there were no water whose wet nature were unchanging, how could there be the waves of illusory, provisional phenomenal appearances? If there were no mirror whose pure brightness were unchanging, how could there be the reflections of a variety of unreal phenomena? Again, while the earlier statement that the activity of dreaming and the dream object are equally unreal is indeed true, the dream that is illusory must still be based on someone who is sleeping. Now, granted that the mind and its objects are both empty, it is still not clear on what the illusory manifestations are based. Therefore we know that this teaching merely destroys feelings of attachment but does not yet clearly reveal the nature that is true and numinous. Therefore the *Great Dharma Drum Sūtra* says: "All emptiness sūtras are expositions that have a remainder."[36] ("Having a re-

35. I am here translating *hsien-chien* 現見 as an adjective modifying *shih-chien* 世間 (see Nakamura, *Bukkyōgo daijiten* 1.336c, where the fourth meaning of *hsien-chien* is defined as *genzai* 現在; *mae ni aru* 前にある). All of the Japanese commentators, however, take *hsien* 現 as an adverb modifying *chien* 見, which thus becomes a verb having *wu* 物 as its object. Not only does this reading create a syntactical break in the middle of the sentence, but *wei yu* 未有 . . . *che* 者 is clearly a predicate modifying *wu* 物.

36. *Mahābherīhāraka-sūtra*, T 9.296b9. In other words, they are not sūtras of ultimate meaning; they are *neyārtha*.

mainder" means that the remaining meaning has not yet been fully expounded.) The *Great Perfection of Wisdom Sūtra* says:
"Emptiness is the first gate of the Great Vehicle."[37]

For Tsung-mi, the ultimate basis for all phenomenal appearances is, of course, the tathāgatagarbha, on which the *Awakening
of Faith* claims the ālayavijñāna to be based. Tsung-mi's reference
to the unchanging wetness of water derives from the *Awakening
of Faith*, which uses the analogy (that water retains its wet nature
whether its surface is stirred into waves by wind or whether it becomes calm again when the wind ceases) to illustrate that the mind
retains its intrinsically enlightened nature whether it is disturbed by
the winds of ignorance or not.[38] Elsewhere Tsung-mi compares intrinsic enlightenment to the luminous reflectivity of a mirror.[39]

37. Tsung-mi is undoubtedly quoting out of context. Although I have
been unable to locate the original passage of the *Great Perfection of Wisdom Sūtra,* it is safe to assume that in the original context of this passage
the teaching of emptiness was spoken of as the first gate of the Great Vehicle because it was the *primary* or principal teaching of the Great Vehicle.
In the context in which Tsung-mi cites the passage, however, the teaching
of emptiness is spoken of as the first gate of the Great Vehicle because it
is the *initial* teaching of the Great Vehicle. Tsung-mi's position is based on
the tathāgatagarbha doctrine that criticizes the one-sided understanding of
emptiness found in the Perfection of Wisdom scriptures and the Madhyamaka treatises.

38. See T 32.576c11-13; Hirakawa, pp. 119-120; cf. Hakeda, p. 41.

39. See *Ch'an Chart,* HTC 110.437d5-7; K 336.

# Conclusion

Tsung-mi concludes the second part of the *Inquiry into the Origin of Humanity* as follows:

[710a6] 　上之四教展轉相望、前淺後深。若且習之、自知未了、名之為淺。若執為了、即名為偏。故就習人云偏淺也。

[710a6] When the above four teachings are compared with one another in turn, the earlier will be seen to be superficial and the later profound. If someone studies [a teaching] for a time, and oneself realizes that it is not yet ultimate, [that teaching] is said to be superficial. But if one clings to [such a teaching] as ultimate, then one is said to be partial. Therefore it is in terms of the people who study them that [the teachings] are spoken of as partial and superficial.

That is to say, each teaching is profound when compared to the one that precedes it and superficial when compared to the one that supersedes it. According to Yüan-chüeh, "superficial" and "profound" are terms that apply to the teachings, and "partial" and "complete" are terms that apply to the people who study them. Yüan-chüeh goes on to quote Ch'eng-kuan: "When someone of complete capacity receives a teaching, there is no teaching that is not complete; but when someone of partial capacity receives a teaching, the complete is also partial."[1]

---

1. *Chieh* 133a.

# Part 3 Directly Revealing the True Source
## The Teaching That Reveals the Nature

The Teaching That Reveals the Nature is the subject of the third part of Tsung-mi's *Inquiry into the Origin of Humanity,* which he entitles "Directly Revealing the True Source" (*chih-hsien chen-yüan* 直顯眞源) and explains in his accompanying note as: "The true teaching of the ultimate meaning of the Buddha (佛了義實教)." The nature, of course, is the Buddha-nature or, as it is known in more technical nomenclature, the tathāgatagarbha. As we saw earlier, in the *Ch'an Preface* Tsung-mi characterizes this teaching as "the Teaching That Directly Reveals That the True Mind Is the Nature" (*hsien-shih chen-hsin chi hsing chiao* 顯示眞心即性教) because it "explicitly reveals" (*hsien-shih* 顯示) the true nature in contrast to the former teaching of "hidden intent" (*mi-i* 密意), which only "intimates" (*mi-hsien* 密顯) it. Elsewhere Tsung-mi says that the ultimate (*nītārtha; liao* 了) teaching is without hidden intent;[1] the teachings of hidden intent are thus all provisional (*neyārtha; pu-liao* 不了). Tsung-mi goes on to point out in his note on this teaching in the *Ch'an Preface* that, in contrast to the two previous teachings, this teaching directly reveals the nature (*hsing* 性) without either affirming or negating phenomenal appearances (*hsiang* 相). Here it should be recalled that the Hua-yen tradition characterized itself as the Fa-hsing tradition as opposed to the Fa-hsiang tradition.

## SYNOPSIS

[710a11]　五一乘顯性教者、説一切有情皆有本覺眞心。無始以來常住清淨、昭昭不昧了了常知。亦名佛性、亦名如來藏。從無始際、妄想翳之不自覺知、但認凡質故、就著結業受生死苦。大覺愍之説一切皆空。又開示靈覺眞心清淨全同諸佛。

1. LS, T 39.529a9-11.

[710a11] The Teaching of the One Vehicle that Reveals the Nature holds that all sentient beings without exception have the intrinsically enlightened, true mind. From [time] without beginning it is permanently abiding and immaculate. It is shining, unobscured, clear, and bright ever-present awareness. It is called both the Buddha-nature and the tathāgatagarbha. From time without beginning deluded thoughts[2] cover it, and [sentient beings] by themselves are not aware of it. Because they only recognize their inferior qualities, they become indulgently attached, enmeshed in karma, and experience the suffering of birth-and-death. The great enlightened one [i.e., the Buddha] took pity upon them and taught that everything without exception is empty. He further revealed that the purity of the numinous enlightened true mind is wholly identical with all Buddhas.

Tsung-mi begins by identifying the Teaching That Reveals the Nature with the one vehicle. The doctrine of the one vehicle was first propounded in the *Lotus Sūtra,* where it was proclaimed as the universal vehicle that subsumed the former teachings of the three vehicles, which were only taught as expedient means to lead śrāvakas, pratyekabuddhas, and bodhisattvas to the one universal Buddha vehicle of the Tathāgatas. Unlike the teaching of the previous three vehicles, which were all taught as expedients, the one vehicle was presented as the Buddha's ultimate revelation of the truth. The *Lotus'* teaching of universal salvation found a natural resonance in the teaching of the tathāgatagarbha, which also provided an explanation for the universal accessibility of Buddhahood. The *Śrīmālā Sūtra,* the primary canonical formulation of the tathāgatagarbha doctrine, was the first scripture to associate the teaching of the one vehicle explicitly with that of the tathāgatagarbha.[3]

The doctrine of intrinsic enlightenment (*pen-chüeh* 本覺) was first explicitly developed in the *Awakening of Faith,* where it is

2. *Hsiang* 相 should be emended to read *hsiang* 想.

3. For a discussion of the relation between the teachings of the one vehicle and the tathāgatagarbha, see Wayman, *The Lion's Roar of Queen Śrīmālā,* pp. 37-39, and Paul, *The Buddhist Feminine Ideal,* pp. 117-120. The teaching of the one vehicle also figures prominently in such *Mahāparinirvāṇa*-related sūtras as the *Mahābherīharaka* (see Takasaki, *Nyoraizō shisō no keisei,* p. 249).

contrasted with experiential enlightenment (*shih-chüeh* 始覺).[4] Although the term *pen-chüeh* does not seem to have a Sanskrit equivalent, it can, nevertheless, be seen as a logical extension of the teaching of the tathāgatagarbha, an idea that can ultimately be traced back to the early teaching of an innately pure luminous mind that is only adventitiously covered over by defilements (*āgantukakleśa*). The *Awakening of Faith* defines intrinsic enlightenment in the following terms: "'Enlightenment' means that the mind itself is free from thoughts. The characteristic of being free from thoughts is like the realm of empty space in that it pervades everywhere. As the one characteristic of the dharmadhātu, it is no other than the undifferentiated dharmakāya of the Tathāgata. Since it is based on the dharmakāya, it is called 'intrinsic enlightenment'."[5]

In both his *Inquiry into the Origin of Humanity* and *Ch'an Preface* Tsung-mi identifies the content of the highest teaching with awareness (*chih* 知), one of several synonyms for the tathāgatagarbha.[6] Sometimes he uses the term "awareness" by itself, and at other times he uses it in combination with other words, such as "numinous awareness" (*ling-chih* 靈知), "numinous awareness unobscured" (*ling-chih pu-mei* 靈知不昧), "ever-present awareness" (*ch'ang-chih* 常知), and "empty tranquil awareness" (*k'ung chi chih* 空寂知). In the *Ch'an Preface* Tsung-mi glosses what he means by "ever-present awareness" in a later part of the corresponding section.[7] After stating that it is not the awareness of realization (*cheng-chih* 證知), he says that the true nature is nevertheless spoken of as aware to indicate that it is different from insentient nature.[8] However, awareness is neither the mental activity of discrimination (*fen-pieh chih shih* 分別之識) nor wisdom (*chih* 智). For canonical authority he then refers to the "The Bodhisattvas Ask for Clarification" chapter of the *Hua-yen Sūtra*,[9] which he claims differentiates between aware-

---

4. Literally, *pen-chüeh* 本覺 refers to the enlightenment that exists a priori, whereas *shih-chüeh* 始覺 refers to the enlightenment that has an inception in time.

5. T 32.576b11-14; cf. Hakeda, p. 37.

6. The rendering of *chih* 知 as "awareness" was first proposed by Buswell in his *Korean Approach to Zen,* p. 165. For further discussion of this term, see idem, "Chinul's Systematization of Chinese Meditative Techniques in Korean Sŏn Buddhism," pp. 214-215.

7. T 48.404c28-405a12; K 131-132; cf. B 192-194.

8. T 48.404c29-405a1.

9. See T 10.69a.

ness (*chih* 知) and wisdom (*chih* 智), pointing out that "wisdom is not shared by the ordinary person (*fan* 凡)," whereas "awareness is possessed by the sage (*sheng* 聖) and ordinary person alike."[10] In his interlinear comments he glosses the "wisdom" in the question as "the wisdom of consummated enlightenment" (*cheng-wu chih chih* 證悟之智) and the "awareness" in the question as "the intrinsically existent true mind" (*pen-yu chen hsin* 本有眞心). He first quotes Mañjuśrī's answer to the bodhisattvas' question: "What is the wisdom of the realm of Buddhas?"

> "The wisdom of all Buddhas freely [penetrates] the three times without obstruction." (Since there is nothing within the past, present, and future that is not utterly penetrated, [it is said to be] free and unobstructed.)[11]

He then quotes Mañjuśrī's answer to their question: "What is the awareness of the realm of Buddhas?"

> "It is not something that can be known by consciousness" (It cannot be known by consciousness. Consciousness falls within the category of discrimination. "Were it discriminated, it would not be true awareness." "True awareness is only seen in no-thought.") "nor is it an object of the mind." (It cannot be known by wisdom. That is to say, if one were to realize it by means of wisdom, then it would fall within the category of an object that is realized, but since true awareness is not an object, it cannot be realized by wisdom.)[12]

What Tsung-mi thus means by "awareness" is not a specific cognitive faculty but the underlying ground of consciousness that is always present in all sentient life. It is not a special state of mind

10. T 48.405a4-5; Tsung-mi makes the same point elsewhere in the *Ch'an Preface,* T 48.406b8-9; K 163.

11. T 48.405a7-8; the question is quoted from the prose section of the scripture at T 10.69a6-7 and its supposed answer from the verse section at 69a19. It is by no means obvious that this line from the verse section is meant as a specific answer to the question in regard to "the wisdom of the realm of Buddhas" stated in the prose section. Nor is it obvious that the *Hua-yen Sūtra* is here concerned with making a distinction between "wisdom" and "awareness." The portion in small type in parenthesis is Tsung-mi's interlinear gloss.

12. T 48.405a9-13; the question is taken from the prose section at T 10.69a8 and its supposed answer from the verse section at 69a25. The two sentences in quotation marks within Tsung-mi's interlinear gloss are quoted from Ch'eng-kuan's commentary and subcommentary respectively—see T 35.612b27 and T 36.261b22.

or spiritual insight but the ground of both delusion and enlightenment, ignorance and wisdom, or, as he aptly terms it, the mind
ground (*hsin-ti* 心地).[13]

### CANONICAL BASIS

As the canonical basis for this teaching, Tsung-mi goes on to quote
the following passage from the *Hua-yen Sūtra*:[14]

[710a16]　故『華嚴經』云：「佛子、無一衆生而不具有
如來智慧。但以妄想執著而不證得。若離妄想、一切智、
自然智、無礙智、即得現前。」

[710a16] Therefore the *Hua-yen Sūtra* says: "Oh sons of
the Buddha, there is not a single sentient being that is not
fully endowed with the wisdom of the Tathāgata. It is only
on account of their deluded thinking and attachments that
they do not succeed in realizing it. When they become free
from deluded thinking, the all-comprehending wisdom, the
spontaneous wisdom, and the unobstructed wisdom will
then be manifest before them."

According to Takasaki Jikidō's reconstruction of the development of the tathāgatagarbha doctrine, this passage served as a
model for the *Tathāgatagarbha Sūtra* (*Ju-lai-tsang ching*), the first
text to propound the tathāgatagarbha teaching explicitly.[15] It occurs in the chapter of the *Hua-yen Sūtra* that Buddhabhadra had
translated as "*Ju-lai hsing-ch'i* 如來性起"[16] and within the Hua-yen
tradition was connected with the development of the theory of nature origination (*hsing-ch'i* 性起). Its significance for Tsung-mi lay
in the fact that it established that the Buddha's enlightenment consisted in his realization that all sentient beings already fully possess

13. See my "Tsung-mi and the Single Word 'Awareness'" for further
discussion of this term.
14. T 10.272c4-7; cf. Cleary 2.314.
15. See *A Study of the Ratnagotravibhāga*, pp. 35-36.
16. According to Takasaki, this chapter seems to have originally circulated as an independent scripture, whose Sanskrit title he reconstructs as
*Tathāgatatotpattisambhava-nirdeśa*, which was translated into Chinese as
the *Ju-lai hsing-hsien ching* (T no. 291) by Dharmarakṣa in the late third
century (see *A Study of the Ratnagotravibhāga*, p. 35). The importance that
this passage had for tathāgatagarbha thought is indicated by its quotation in
full in the *Ratnagotravibhāga* (see T 31.827a29-c1; Takasaki, pp. 189-192).

the enlightened wisdom of the Buddha and are therefore fundamentally identical with all Buddhas. The defilements that appear to obscure this wisdom are merely adventitious. Buddhist practice should thus be directed toward uncovering the original enlightenment that is the fundamental nature of all beings. Enlightenment is a matter of becoming aware of that which has always been present from the very beginning.

[710a19]　便舉一塵含大千經卷之喻。塵況衆生、經況佛智。

[710a19] [The sūtra] then offers the analogy of a single speck of dust containing a sūtra roll [as vast as] the great chiliocosm. The speck of dust represents sentient beings, and the sūtra represents the wisdom of the Buddha.

The analogy posits a great sūtra roll, whose size equals the great chiliocosm. Everything in the great chiliocosm is represented on this great sūtra roll, each representation being the same size as the thing that it represents. Moreover, not only is this great sūtra roll contained within a single speck of dust, but every speck of dust in the universe similarly contains a great sūtra roll. The Buddha is then likened to a wise person whose penetrating vision is able to see the great sūtra roll contained within each speck of dust and who, realizing that they are of no use thus contained, is able to break them open to make the great sūtra rolls within available to all. The sūtra then continues: "The Tathāgata's wisdom is, after all, also like this. Being without measure and obstruction, it is able to benefit all sentient beings everywhere. Although it is fully present within the bodies of sentient beings, it is only because of the deluded thinking and attachments of ignorant beings that they neither know nor are aware of it and do not realize its benefit."[17]

[710a20]　次後又云：「爾時如來普觀法界一切衆生而作是言：奇哉。奇哉。此諸衆生、云何具有如來智慧迷惑不見。我當教以聖道、令其永離妄想、自於身中得見如來廣大智慧與佛無異。」

[710a20] [The *Hua-yen Sūtra*] then goes on to say: "At that time the Tathāgata with his unobstructed pure eye of wisdom universally beheld all sentient beings throughout the universe and said: 'How amazing! How amazing! How can it be that these sentient beings are fully endowed with the wisdom

17. See T 10.272c7-25; cf. Cleary 2.314-315.

of the Tathāgata and yet, being ignorant and confused, do not see it? I must teach them the noble path enabling them to be forever free from deluded thinking and to achieve for themselves the seeing of the broad and vast wisdom of the Tathāgata within themselves and so be no different from the Buddhas.'"

This passage from the *Hua-yen Sūtra*[18] was especially valued in the Ch'an tradition because it was believed to have contained the first words uttered by the Buddha after his enlightenment.[19] Tsung-mi's account of the Teaching That Reveals the Nature in his *Ch'an Preface* adds that this teaching is exemplifed in those scriptures that expound the tathāgatagarbha, such as the *Hua-yen, Ghana-vyūha, Perfect Enlightenment, Śūraṅgama, Śrīmālā, Tathāgata-garbha, Lotus,* and *Nirvāna,* as well as in treatises such as the *Awakening of Faith, Buddha-nature (Fo-hsing),* and *Ratnagotra-vibhāga (Pao-hsing lun).*[20]

### ELABORATION

[710a24]　評曰。我等多劫未遇眞宗、不解返 [反] 自原身、但執虛妄之相、甘認凡下、或畜或人。今約至教原之、方覺本來是佛。故須行依佛行心契佛心、返本還源斷除凡習、損之又損、以至無為。自然應用恒沙、名之曰佛。當知迷悟同一眞心。大哉妙門。原人至此。

[710a24] [I will now] elaborate on [this teaching]. Because for numerous kalpas we have not encountered the true teaching, we have not known how to turn back[21] and find the [true] origin of our bodily existence but have just clung to illusory

---

18. T 10.272c25-273a1; cf. Cleary 2.315.
19. See Miura and Sasaki, *Zen Dust,* p. 254.
20. T 48.405a24-26; K 132; cf. B 197-198.
21. The Taishō text uses *fan* 返, listing *fan* 反 as a variant reading. Both Ching-yüan (104b) and Yüan-chüeh (135a) use *fan* 反, as do the texts of all the Japanese commentaries consulted. The clause in which the character occurs (*pu chieh fan tzu yüan shen* 不解返自原身) is somewhat awkward, and the precise meaning of *fan* is unclear. One thing that is clear, however, is that *fan* cannot here be functioning as a disjunctive conjunction (i.e., *kaette* 返って) as all of the Japanese translations render it. For *fan* to so function, it would have to precede the main verb of the clause (*pu chieh* 不解). I have rendered *fan* as a verb functioning parallel with *yüan* 原; *tzu* 自, of course, is adverbial, modifying *yüan.*

phenomenal appearances, heedlessly recognizing [only] our unenlightened nature, being born sometimes as an animal and sometimes as a human. When we now seek our origin in terms of the consummate teaching, we will immediately realize that from the very outset we are the Buddha. Therefore, we should base our actions on the Buddha's action and identify our minds with the Buddha's mind, return to the origin and revert to the source, and cut off our residue of ignorance, reducing it and further reducing it until we have reached the [state of being] unconditioned.[22] Then our activity in response [to other beings] will naturally be [as manifold as] the sands of the Gang-es—that is called Buddhahood. You should realize that delusion and enlightenment alike are [manifestations of] the one true mind. How great the marvelous gate! Our inquiry into the origin of humanity has here come to an end.

The realization that we are from the outset identical with the Buddha describes the experience of sudden enlightenment (*tun-wu* 頓悟), while the remainder of the passage describes the process of gradual cultivation (*chien-hsiu* 漸修).[23] Tsung-mi illustrates this process of gradual cultivation with an allusion to chapter 48 of the *Lao-tzu:* "In the pursuit of learning one knows more every day; in the pursuit of the Way one does less every day. One does less and less until one does nothing at all, and when one does nothing at all there is nothing that is undone."[24]

---

22. As all of the commentators indicate, the punctuation of the Taishō text is in error; the break should come after *wu-wei* 無為. *Tzu-jan* 自然, moreover, modifies *ying-yung* 應用, which, in the context of the *Awakening of Faith,* describes the inconceivable activity of the Buddha who, because his wisdom is pure, is able to manifest his unlimited excellent qualities without interruption, "responding naturally according to the capacities of beings" (see T 32.576c16-19; cf. Hirakawa, p. 120 and Hakeda, pp. 41-42). In the diagram at the end of the *Ch'an Preface* (T 48.412a), Tsung-mi abridges another passage from the *Awakening of Faith* that says that when Buddhas "exhaust their ignorance and see the intrinsic dharmakāya, they naturally have the manifold functioning of inconceivable activity" (see T 32.579b15-16; cf. Hirakawa, p. 255 and Hakeda, p. 68).

23. For a discussion of Tsung-mi's theory of Sudden Enlightenment followed by Gradual Cultivation, see my "Sudden Enlightenment Followed by Gradual Cultivation."

24. Lau, p. 109.

### SUDDEN AND GRADUAL

Tsung-mi concludes this section of the *Inquiry* by appending a note explaining how his classificatory categories correspond with two others that had long been an important part of the vocabulary used within Chinese Buddhist classification schemes. Traditionally the sudden teaching (*tun-chiao* 頓教) had been associated with the *Hua-yen Sūtra,* which was said to be "sudden" because it was believed to represent a direct revelation of the content of Buddha's enlightenment without making any concessions to the limited ability of his audience to understand the meaning of his words. Since the overwhelming preponderance of the Buddha's followers were unable to grasp the profundity of his message, he then taught a series of gradual teachings (*chien-chiao* 漸教) that resorted to expedients to bring them gradually to the point where they would finally be ready to understand his ultimate teaching. The gradual teachings thus form a graduated progression moving from the most elementary to the most profound. Because they are expedient, the gradual teachings are not ultimate.

Tsung-mi's omission of the sudden teaching as a category within his system of classifying Buddhist teachings marks a striking break with the scholastic tradition that he was affiliated with, for his Hua-yen predecessors (i.e., Chih-yen, Fa-tsang, and Ch'eng-kuan) had all included the sudden teaching as a distinct category within their classification schemes.[25] The sudden teaching was also closely identified with the Southern Ch'an teaching of Shen-hui, the other tradition with which Tsung-mi was associated, which professed to offer a sudden approach to enlightenment in contrast to the discredited gradual approach of the Northern lineage of Shen-hsiu and his successors. For these reasons it was incumbent on Tsung-mi to account for the absence of the sudden and gradual teachings as categories within the classificatory scheme he uses in the *Inquiry.* He begins by explaining the gradual teachings.

[710a29]　（然佛説前五教、或漸或頓。若有中下之機、則從淺至深、漸漸誘接、先説初教、令離惡住善。次説二三、令離染住淨。後説四五、破相顯性、會權歸實、依實教修乃至成佛。

[710a29] (In the Buddha's preaching of the previous five teachings, some are gradual and some are sudden. In the case of [sentient beings

----

25. This issue is discussed in detail in chapter 6 of my *Tsung-mi and the Sinification of Buddhism.*

of] medium and inferior capacity, [the Buddha] proceeded from the
superficial to the profound, gradually leading them forward. He
would initially expound the first teaching [of Humans and Gods], enabling them to be free from evil and to abide in virtue; he would then
expound the second and third [teachings of the Lesser Vehicle and
the Phenomenal Appearances of the Dharmas], enabling them to be
free from impurity and to abide in purity; he would finally discuss the
fourth and fifth [teachings], those that Refute Phenomenal Appearances and Reveal the Nature, subsuming the provisional into the true,
[enabling them] to cultivate virtue in reliance on the ultimate teaching
until they finally attain Buddhahood.

Tsung-mi goes on to explain the sudden teaching.

[710b2]　若上上根智、則從本至末。謂初便依第五頓指一眞
心體。心體既顯、自覺一切皆是虛妄、本來空寂；但以迷故託
眞而起；須以悟眞之智、斷惡修善、息妄歸眞。妄盡眞圓、是
名法身佛。）

[710b2] In the case of [sentient beings of] wisdom of the highest caliber, [the Buddha] proceeded from the root to the branch. That is to
say, from the start he straightaway relied on the fifth teaching to point
directly to the essence of the one true mind. When the essence of the
mind had been revealed, [these sentient beings] themselves realized that
everything without exception is illusory and fundamentally empty and
tranquil; that it is only because of delusion that [such illusory appear-
ances] arise in dependence upon the true [nature]; and that it is [thus]
necessary to cut off evil and cultivate virtue by means of the insight of
having awakened to the true, and to put an end to the false and return
to the true by cultivating virtue.[26] When the false is completely exhausted
and the true is present in totality, that is called the dharmakāya Buddha.)

As this passage suggests, Tsung-mi regarded the sudden teaching not so much as a teaching with a distinct content as a particular
approach that the Buddha adopted toward his disciples of the
highest caliber. This point comes out more clearly in the *Ch'an
Preface*. In response to the question about which teachings are
sudden and gradual, Tsung-mi replies:

It is only because of variations in the style of the World
Honored One's exposition of the teachings that there are
sudden expositions in accordance with the truth and gradual

26. I have deleted the second *hsiu-shan* 修善 that appears in the
Taishō text; cf. Ching-yüan's commentary (104d14).

expositions in accordance with the capacities [of beings].
Although [these different styles of exposition] are also referred to as the sudden teaching and the gradual teaching,
this does not mean that there is a separate sudden and gradual
[teaching] outside of the three [i.e., five] teachings.[27]

This passage makes clear that Tsung-mi understands the terms
"sudden" and "gradual" to refer to methods by which the Buddha
taught, not to separate teachings.

Tsung-mi's description of the sudden teaching in the *Inquiry*
corresponds to what he refers to as the sudden teaching that was
expounded in response to beings of superior capacity.[28] He says
that this type of sudden teaching corresponds to those cases in
which the Buddha "directly revealed the true dharma" to "unenlightened persons of superior capacity and keen insight" who "on
hearing [the Buddha's words] would be suddenly enlightened." He
adds that only after such people had suddenly awakened to their
true nature can they then gradually begin to eliminate the residual
effects of their past conditioning, a process that he compares to the
ocean that has been stirred up by the wind: even though the wind
ceases suddenly, the movement of its waves only subsides gradually.
Tsung-mi then identifies this type of sudden teaching with those
scriptures that expound the tathāgatagarbha. He concludes his discussion by saying that since this type of teaching was expounded
in response to beings of superior capacity, it was not taught during
a set period in the Buddha's teaching career.[29]

As a method by which the Buddha taught, Tsung-mi was able to
include the sudden teaching within the highest category of teaching
in his classification scheme. But it was not identical with the highest
teaching, which contained a gradual component as well. Tsung-mi
thus envisioned a "two-track" system by which the highest teaching

27. T 48.407b13-17; K 184; cf. B 238.
28. *Chu-chi tun-chiao* 逐機頓教, which he distinguishes from the
sudden teaching as a method of exposition (*hua-i tun-chiao* 化儀頓教).
This second type of sudden teaching refers exclusively to the *Hua-yen
Sūtra*. Whereas the first type of sudden teaching was not taught during a
set period of the Buddha's career, the second was "suddenly taught" by
the Buddha "on one occasion" immediately after he had attained enlightenment. This type of sudden teaching was expounded for the sake of
those followers who possessed superior capacities as a result of the mat-
uration of conditions cultivated in past lives.
29. See T 48.407b21-c2; K 185; cf. B 240-241.

could be approached. It could either be approached gradually, through a series of successive approximations, or suddenly, through a direct revelation of the truth. Whereas the sudden teaching was suited only to those of highest capacity, the gradual teachings were suited to those of average or inferior capacity. The Buddha made use of the gradual teachings as an expedient by which he progressively deepened the capacity of his disciples to understand the truth until they were ready to hear the teaching of ultimate meaning, such as that contained in the *Lotus* and *Nirvāna* sūtras, which represented the gradual method by which the highest teaching was taught.

Elsewhere, Tsung-mi makes it clear that, in contrast to the gradual approach, by which the succession of teaching defined the path by which the Buddhist could reach the highest goal, the sudden teaching revealed the truth directly. It was then necessary, however, to go back to the practices contained in the gradual teachings to remove the defilements that prevented one from fully integrating one's insight into one's intrinsically enlightened Buddha-nature into one's actual behavior. In other words, the realization that one was a Buddha was not sufficient to guarantee that one would act like a Buddha. The gradual practices thus played a necessary role in the postenlightenment actualization of the insight afforded by the sudden teaching to beings of superior capacity.[30]

30. For a more detailed discussion of how Tsung-mi understands sudden and gradual in terms of Buddhist practice, see my "Sudden Enlightenment Followed by Gradual Cultivation."

# Part 4 Reconciling Root and Branch
## The Process of Phenomenal Evolution

The concluding part of Tsung-mi's *Inquiry into the Origin of Humanity,* entitled "Reconciling Root and Branch" (*hui-t'ung pen-mo* 會通本末), integrates Confucianism and Taoism, together with the five teachings that he evaluated within his classification of Buddhist teachings, into his final cosmogonic vision. As he states in his opening note:

[710b4] （會前所斥同歸一源皆為正義。）

[710b4] When [the teachings that] have been refuted previously are subsumed together into the one source, they all become true.

In the previous parts of the *Inquiry,* Tsung-mi demonstrated the partial nature of the provisional teachings (i.e., those of Confucianism, Taoism, and the first four Buddhist teachings) by showing that they all fail to discern the ultimate origin of human existence, which is only accomplished by the fifth and final teaching, that which Reveals the Nature. The arrangement of teachings in the previous parts thus describes a process of the return to the ontological ground of phenomenal existence—what Tsung-mi refers to as the "root" (*pen* 本). Tsung-mi's arrangement of the teachings thus also describes the path of soteriological progress and answers the first side of the question posed by his inquiry by revealing the ontological ground of enlightenment, which is the ultimate origin of humanity. The concluding part of the essay turns to the other side of the question posed by his inquiry, attempting to show how the process of phenomenal evolution, whose end product is the sentient condition marked by suffering and delusion, emerges from the intrinsically pure and enlightened nature. The concluding part thus describes a process that moves from the ontological ground or root to its phenomenal manifestations or branches (*mo* 末) and is at once a cosmogony and an aetiology of delusion.

The cosmogony that Tsung-mi elaborates in the concluding part of his essay is derived from the *Awakening of Faith,* and this part more than anywhere else reveals the importance of the *Awakening of Faith* in providing the fundamental framework for the *Inquiry.* This framework is made even clearer in a more primitive version found in his commentary and subcommentary to the *Scripture of Perfect Enlightenment* and his commentary to the *Awakening of Faith,* in which the cosmogonic process is described as unfolding in five stages. Its main structure can most easily be visualized diagrammatically. The meaning of the various terms will be explained in the comments on the translation.

THE PROCESS OF PHENOMENAL EVOLUTION<br/>ACCORDING TO THE AWAKENING OF FAITH

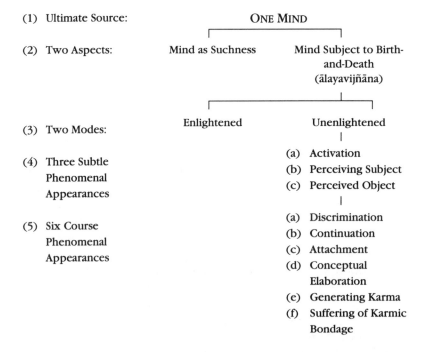

(1)  Ultimate Source:                    ONE MIND

(2)  Two Aspects:          Mind as Suchness          Mind Subject to Birth-and-Death (ālayavijñāna)

(3)  Two Modes:           Enlightened              Unenlightened

(4)  Three Subtle Phenomenal Appearances
 (a)  Activation
 (b)  Perceiving Subject
 (c)  Perceived Object

(5)  Six Course Phenomenal Appearances
 (a)  Discrimination
 (b)  Continuation
 (c)  Attachment
 (d)  Conceptual Elaboration
 (e)  Generating Karma
 (f)  Suffering of Karmic Bondage

Even though the cosmogony in the *Inquiry* is not broken down into numbered stages, it correlates closely with the more clearly articulated cosmogony, in ten demarcated stages, contained in the *Ch'an Preface,* and a comparison with the *Ch'an Preface* version is useful for clarifying structure of cosmogony in the *Inquiry*. Most important for the *Inquiry,* the various cosmogonic stages are linked with different teachings. In fact, this correspondence is the crucial factor that determines Tsung-mi's arrangement of the teachings in the *Inquiry*.

Combining these various schemes together, the correspondence of the different cosmogonic stages in the *Ch'an Preface* with the stages in the *Awakening of Faith* from which they derive together with the different teachings with which they correspond in the *Inquiry* can be represented as follow.

CORRESPONDENCE BETWEEN COSMOGONIC STAGES AND
TEACHINGS IN THE *INQUIRY*

| *AWAKENING OF FAITH* | *CH'AN PREFACE* | TEACHING |
|---|---|---|
| One Mind | | Reveals Nature |
| Ālayvijñāna | | |
| Enlightened Mode | 1. Intrinsic Enlightenment | |
| Unenlightened Mode | 2. Unenlightenment | Refutation |
| Activity of Ignorance | 3. Arising of Thoughts | Phenomenal Appearances |
| Perceiving Subject | 4. Arising of Perceiving Subject | |
| Perceived Objects | 5. Manifestation of Perceived Objects | |
| Discrimination | | |
| Continuity | 6. Attachment to Dharmas | |
| Attachment | | |
| Conceptual Elaboration | 7. Attachment to Self | Lesser Vehicle |
| | 8. Defilements | |
| Generating Karma | 9. Generating Karma | Humans and Gods |
| Suffering of Karmic Bondage | 10. Experiencing the Consequences | |

Tsung-mi's theory of phenomenal evolution explains how the world of delusion and defilement, the world in terms of which unenlightened beings experience themselves, evolves out of a unitary ontological ground that is both intrinsically enlightened and pure. Beings' suffering in delusion is a function of the epistemological dualism out of which the world of their experience is constructed. Religious practice thus entails the recovery of a primordial state of perfection before the bifurcation of consciousness into subject and object. While the terms in which Tsung-mi explains his theory are thoroughly Buddhist, his underlying cosmogonic model is one that has deep resonances with indigenous Chinese models. Such models presume that the world is generated through a process by which an originally undifferentiated whole divides into a primordial polarity, through whose interaction the world of differentiated phenomena is then generated.

### PROCESS OF PHENOMENAL EVOLUTION

The theoretical foundation on which Tsung-mi's theory of phenomenal evolution is based is nature origination, which explains how phenomenal appearances arise from the nature, which is made possible by the *Awakening of Faith's* explanation of how the mind as suchness accords with conditions to give rise to all phenomena.

> [710b5]　眞性雖為身本、生起蓋有因由、不可無端忽成身相。但緣前宗未了、所以節節斥之、今將本末會通、乃至儒道亦是。

> [710b5] Although the true nature constitutes the [ultimate] source of bodily existence, its arising must surely have a causal origin, for the phenomenal appearance of bodily existence cannot be suddenly formed from out of nowhere. It is only because the previous traditions had not yet fully discerned [the matter] that I have refuted them one by one. Now I will reconcile root and branch, including even Confucianism and Taoism.

### The Teaching That Reveals the Nature

Tsung-mi begins with the true nature, which is the ultimate source from which phenomenal evolution proceeds. He goes on to point out in his autocommentary how the successive stages in this process can be correlated with the different teachings, each of which accounts for different phases.

> [710b7]　（初唯第五性教所説。從後段已去、節級方同諸教、各如注説。）謂初唯一眞靈性、不生不滅、不增不減、不變不易。衆生無始迷睡不自覺知、由隱覆故名如來藏、依如來藏故有生滅心相。

> [710b7] (At first there is only that which is set forth in the fifth teach-
> ing of the Nature. From the following section on, [each] stage [in the
> process of phenomenal evolution] will be correlated with the various
> teachings, as will be explained in the notes.) **At first there is only
> the one true numinous nature, which is neither born nor de-
> stroyed, neither increases nor decreases, and neither changes
> nor alters. [Nevertheless], sentient beings are [from time]
> without beginning asleep in delusion and are not themselves
> aware of it. Because it is covered over, it is called the tathā-
> gatagarbha, and the phenomenal appearance of the mind that
> is subject to birth-and-death comes into existence based on
> the tathāgatagarbha.**

Tsung-mi's statement that "because it is covered over, it is
called the tathāgatagarbha" plays on the Chinese translation of
tathāgatagarbha as *ju-lai-tsang* 如來藏, where *tsang* used as verb
(*ts'ang*) means to "conceal."[1] It is also fully consonant with many
of the standard metaphors used in the *Tathāgatagarbha Sūtra*[2] and
other texts to illustrate the meaning of the tathāgatagarbha.

Tsung-mi refers to this stage of the process of phenomenal
evolution as that of intrinsic enlightenment (*pen-chüeh* 本覺) in his
*Ch'an Preface,* where he compares the fact that "all sentient beings
without exception have the true mind of intrinsic enlightenment"
with "a wealthy and respected person, upright and wise, living in
his own home."[3]

### The Teaching That Refutes Phenomenal Appearances

The next phase corresponds to the second stage, that of unenlightenment, enumerated in the *Ch'an Preface.* Tsung-mi's claim that
this stage is accounted for by the fourth teaching is forced, for it

1. The *Fo-hsing lun,* for example, states: "Because the Tathāgata (*ju-
lai* 如來) is itself hidden and not manifest, it is designated as 'concealed'
(*ts'ang* 藏)" (T 31.796a19-20).

2. This text is famous for its enumeration of nine metaphors, according
to which the tathāgatagarbha is compared to: (1) a Buddha hidden within
a lotus, (2) honey surrounded by bees, (3) a grain of rice within its husk,
(4) gold lost in the dirt, (5) treasure hidden under the ground, (6) the seed
from which a great tree grows, (7) a golden image wrapped in a foul gar-
ment, (8) the womb of an outcast woman impregnated by a king, and (9)
a golden image within the earthen mold in which it is cast (see T 16.457a-
460b).

3. T 48.409b6-7; cf. K 217 and B 269.

has nothing to do with emptiness. Rather, it is based entirely on the *Awakening of Faith*. His pairing of this stage with the Teaching That Refutes Phenomenal Appearances represents a procrustean attempt to make this teaching fit into his cosmogonic scheme and reflects the incomplete integration of emptiness into Tsung-mi's schematic structure.

[710b10] （自此方是第四教亦同破此已生滅諸相。）所謂不生滅眞心與生滅妄想和合、非一非異、名為阿頼耶識。此識有覺不覺二義。

[710b10] (From here on corresponds to the fourth teaching, which is the same as [that which] Refuted the Phenomenal Appearances that are subject to birth-and-death.) The interfusion of the true mind that is not subject to birth-and-death and deluded thoughts that are subject to birth-and-death in such a way that they are neither one nor different is referred to as the ālayavijñāna. This consciousness has the aspects both of enlightenment and un-enlightenment.

Tsung-mi here introduces the two aspects of the one mind described in the *Awakening of Faith*. The first is the mind as suchness (*hsin chen-ju* 心眞如), which the text defines as that which neither is born nor dies. The second is the mind subject to birth-and-death (*hsin sheng-mieh* 心生滅), which refers to the ālayavijñāna, in which the tathāgatagarbha and that which is subject to birth-and-death are interfused. In his commentary to the *Awakening of Faith*, Fa-tsang had referred to the first as the unchanging (*pu-pien* 不變) aspect of the one mind and the second as its conditioned (*sui-yüan* 隨緣) aspect. The two together totally comprehend all dharmas.[4]

Elsewhere Tsung-mi explains the mind of suchness by quoting the following passage from the *Awakening of Faith:*

The mind as suchness is the one dharmadhātu. It is characterized as all-embracing and is the essence of the teachings. What is called the nature of the mind neither is born nor dies. It is only on the basis of deluded thinking that all of the dharmas come to be differentiated. If one frees oneself from deluded thoughts, then there are no longer any phenomenal appearances of external objects.[5]

4. T 32.576a6-7; cf. Hirakawa, p. 69 and Hakeda, p. 31.
5. T 32.576a8-10 (cf. Hirakawa, pp. 71-72 and Hakeda, pp. 32-33); quoted in TS 116d6-9 and LSC 125b16-18. Tsung-mi's subcommentary

The second aspect of the one mind, the mind subject to birth-and-death, exists "on the basis of the tathāgatagarbha."[6] The *Awakening of Faith* identifies this aspect of the one mind with the ālayavijñāna, which it defines as: "the interfusion of that which is not subject to birth-and-death [i.e., the mind as suchness] and that which is subject to birth-and-death in such a way that they are neither one nor different."[7]

The relationship between these two aspects of the one mind, which are neither one nor different, traces back to a paradox at the core of the tathāgatagarbha doctrine: the tathāgatagarbha is at once intrinsically pure and identical with the dharmakāya and yet appears to be defiled. The two aspects of the one mind thus seem to be a matter of perspective, and their difference can be seen as corresponding to the point of view of ultimate and conventional truth. The tathāgatagarbha as seen from the enlightened perspective of a Buddha is perfectly pure and undefiled. It is only due to the deluded thinking of unenlightened beings that it appears to be otherwise.[8]

In so identifying the ālayavijñāna with the tathāgatagarbha, the *Awakening of Faith* stands in the tradition of the *Laṅkāvatāra-sūtra*.[9] This identification grounds the process of conditioned origination on an intrinsically pure ontological foundation. This means that the defilements that appear to obscure the intrinsically enlightened mind of suchness are merely the manifestation of that mind as it accords with conditions and have no independent basis of their own. The relationship between the tathāgatagarbha and ālayavijñāna is thus the basis on which the Hua-yen tradition establishes its theory of nature origination and is the central issue in terms of which it distinguishes its type of Yogācāra from that of Fa-hsiang.

---

goes on to quote the rest of this passage, which says that since the nature of the mind is ineffable and inconceivable, "all locutions are provisional designations, lack reality, and are merely used in accordance with deluded thinking" (T 32.576a10-14; quoted in TSC 264b10-13). The text concludes by stating that the term "suchness" does not designate anything at all but is only a device used to put an end to discursive discourse (T 32.576a13-14).

6. T 32.576b8; cf. Hirakawa, p. 95 and Hakeda, p. 36.

7. T 32.576b8-9.

8. For an exploration of the ramifications of this paradox, see my "The Problem of Theodicy in the *Awakening of Faith*."

9. For one of the many instances that could be cited, see T 16.556b29-c1: "The ālayavijñāna is called the tathāgatagarbha."

The ālayavijñāna is characterized by a dynamic ambivalence, as represented by its two modes, which embrace and give rise to all dharmas.[10] The first is enlightened (*chüeh* 覺), and the second is unenlightened (*pu-chüeh* 不覺). The *Awakening of Faith* defines "enlightened" as meaning "that the essence of the mind is free from thoughts. The characteristic of being free from thoughts is like the realm of empty space in that there is nowhere it does not pervade. As the single characteristic of the dharmadhātu, it is the undifferentiated dharmakāya of the Tathāgata. Since it is based on the dharmakāya, when it is spoken of it is referred to as 'intrinsic enlightenment.'"[11]

The *Awakening of Faith* goes on to distinguish intrinsic enlightenment (*pen-chüeh* 本覺) from experiential enlightenment (*shih-chüeh* 始覺). Experiential enlightenment, moreover, is contrasted with unenlightenment (*pu-chüeh* 不覺). In fact, the text states that experiential enlightenment can only be spoken of in the context of unenlightenment. Experiential enlightenment constitutes the process by which one awakens to the ultimate source of the mind. Intrinsic enlightenment is at once the ontological ground that makes experiential enlightenment possible as well as that which experiential enlightenment realizes.[12]

In the *Ch'an Preface* Tsung-mi uses an analogy of a dreaming person to explain the different stages in the process of phenomenal evolution. The analogy of delusion as a state of being asleep is naturally suggested by the term used for enlightenment, *chüeh* 覺, which literally means "to awaken." Tsung-mi thus likens unenlightenment to a wealthy and respected person falling asleep within his home and forgetting who he is.[13] The imagery of awakening/sleep to represent enlightenment/delusion allows Tsung-mi to finesse the problem of the origin of ignorance without having to address it head on. But it is not a real solution, for the problem of ignorance remains. It is inherent in the paradox of the tathāgatagarbha, which is pure and yet appears to be defiled, a paradox that, short of enlightenment, remains a mystery that must be accepted on faith. The problem becomes even more intractable with the recasting of the tathāgatagarbha into a monistic ontology in the *Awakening of Faith,* where it takes on the force of the analogous problem of theodicy in the Western monotheistic religions.[14]

10. T 32.576b10; cf. Hirakawa, p. 95 and Hakeda, p. 36.
11. T 32.567b11-14; cf. Hirakawa, p. 102 and Hakeda, p. 37.
12. T 32.567b11-c4; partially quoted in TSC 265d1-5.
13. T 48.409b7-9; cf. K 217 and B 269.
14. See my "The Problem of Theodicy in the *Awakening of Faith*."

## The Teaching of the Phenomenal Appearances of the Dharmas

The next phase corresponds to the third through sixth stages in Tsung-mi's ten-stage scheme (i.e., arising of thoughts, arising of perceiving subject, manifestation of perceived objects, and attachment to dharmas). It is accounted for by the Teaching of the Phenomenal Appearances of the Dharmas.

> [710b13] （此下方是第三法相教中亦同所説。）依不覺故、最初動念、名為業相。又不覺此念本無故、轉成能見之識及所見境界相現。又不覺此境從自心妄現、執為定有、名為法執。

[710b13] (From here on corresponds to that which was taught in the third teaching of the Phenomenal Appearances of the Dharmas.) When thoughts first begin to stir because of the unenlightened aspect [of the ālayavijñāna], it is referred to as the phenomenal appearance of activity. Because [sentient beings] are also unaware that these thoughts are from the beginning non-existent, [the ālayavijñāna] transforms into the manifestation of the phenomenal appearance of a perceiving subject and its perceived objects. Moreover, being unaware that these objects are deludedly manifested from their own mind, [sentient beings] cling to them as fixed existents, and that is referred to as attachment to things.

The phenomenal appearance of activity (*yeh-hsiang* 業相) corresponds to the first of the three subtle phenomenal appearances in the *Awakening of Faith,* which also refers to it as the activity of ignorance (*wu-ming yeh* 無明業).[15] This stage represents the first subtle movement of thought, which initiates the process of phenomenal evolution by giving rise to bifurcation of consciousness into subject and object. Tsung-mi designates this stage as the arising of thought (*nien-ch'i* 念起) in his *Ch'an Preface,* where he likens it to the dreams that naturally arise in the mind of a sleeping person. It corresponds to the evolution of the ālayavijñāna in the *Ch'eng wei-shih lun.*

The perceiving subject (*neng-chien chih shih* 能見之識) refers to the second subtle phenomenal appearance in the *Awakening of Faith.*[16] Tsung-mi designates this stage as the arising of the perceiving subject (*chien-ch'i* 見起) in his *Ch'an Preface,* where he likens it to the activity of dreaming. It corresponds to the subjective mode

15. See T 32.577a8-10; cf. Hirakawa, p. 142 and Hakeda, p. 44.
16. See T 32.577a10-11.

of the ālayavijñāna (darśanabhāga; chien-fen 見分) in the Ch'eng wei-shih lun.

The perceived objects (so-chien ching-chieh 所見境界) refers to the third subtle phenomenal appearance in the Awakening of Faith.[17] Tsung-mi designates this stage as the arising of the manifestation of perceived objects (ching-hsien 境現) in his Ch'an Preface and identifies it with the manifestation of the body of the senses and receptacle world; he goes on to liken it to a wealthy and respected person who, within his dream, sees himself dwelling in squalor and misery, perceiving things that he likes and dislikes. It corresponds to the objective mode of the ālayavijñāna (nimittabhāga; hsiang-fen 相分) in the Ch'eng wei-shih lun.

Attachment to things (fa-chih 法執; i.e., dharmagrāha) corresponds to the first and second coarse phenomenal appearances enumerated in the Awakening of Faith, those of discrimination (chih 智) and continuation (hsiang-hsü 相續):

> 1. The phenomenal appearance of discrimination: based on perception of objects, the mind thus gives rise to the discrimination of likes and dislikes.
>
> 2. The phenomenal appearance of continuation: based on such discriminations, awareness of pleasure and pain is produced, and the mind thus gives rise to thoughts in association with [such awareness], and [those thoughts continue] without cease.[18]

In his Ch'an Preface Tsung-mi likens this stage to the person clinging to the things that he sees in his dream as real. It is precisely the attachment to dharmas that is overcome by the Teaching of the Phenomenal Appearances of Dharmas.

### The Teaching of the Lesser Vehicle

The following phase is accounted for by the Teaching of the Lesser Vehicle, which enables beings to overcome their attachment to self and defilements (i.e., stages seven and eight in Tsung-mi's tenfold scheme).

[710b16] （此下方是第二小乘教中亦同所説。）執此等故、遂見自他之殊、便成我執。執我相故、貪愛順情諸境、欲以潤我、瞋嫌違情諸境、恐相損惱。愚癡之情展轉增長。

17. See T 32.577a11-12.
18. T 32.577a13-15.

[710b16] (From here on corresponds to that which was taught in the second teaching of the Lesser Vehicle.) Because they cling to these, [sentient beings] then perceive a difference between self and others and immediately form an attachment to the self. Because they cling to the phenomenal appearance of a self, they hanker after things that accord with their feelings, hoping thereby to enhance themselves, and have an aversion to things that go against their feelings, fearing that they will bring harm to themselves. Their foolish feelings thus continue to escalate ever further.

Attachment to self (*wo-chih* 我執; i.e., *ātmagrāha*) corresponds to the third and fourth coarse phenomenal appearances enumerated in the *Awakening of Faith,* those of attachment (*chih-ch'ü* 執取) and conceptual elaboration (*chi-ming-tzu* 計名字):

3. The phenomenal appearance of attachment: based on the continuation [of such thoughts], one objectifies perceptual objects, fixating on their pleasurefulness or painfulness, and the mind thus gives rise to attachment.

4. The phenomenal appearance of conceptual elaboration: based on such deluded attachments, one thus distinguishes among them in terms of provisional concepts.[19]

In his *Ch'an Preface* Tsung-mi likens attachment to self to the dreaming person identifying with the person in the dream.

The elaboration of foolish feelings on the basis of attachment to self corresponds to the stage Tsung-mi refers to as the defilements (*fan-nao* 煩惱; i.e., *kleśa*) in the *Ch'an Preface.* They refer to the three poisons of greed, anger, and delusion. Tsung-mi likens them to the person hankering after those things in the dream that accord with his feelings and forming an aversion to those things in the dream that go against his feelings.

### The Teaching of Humans and Gods

The next phase corresponds to the last two stages (i.e., generating karma and experiencing the consequences) in Tsung-mi's tenfold scheme and is accounted for by the Teaching of Humans and Gods. Note that it is at the point in the process of rebirth when consciousness first enters a womb that Tsung-mi introduces the Confucian and Taoist

19. T 32.577a16-18.

notion of vital force (*ch'i* 氣). Tsung-mi thus clearly accepts this concept as contributing an integral part to the overall understanding of phenomenal evolution. The two teachings are not wrong; they only err in taking their explanation to be the ultimate answer.

[710b19] （此下方是第一人天教中亦同所説。）故殺盜等、心神乘此惡業、生於地獄鬼畜等中。復有怖此苦者、或性善者、行施戒等、心神乘此善業、運於中陰入母胎中（此下方是儒道二教亦同所説。）禀氣受質。（會彼所説以氣為本。）

[710b19] (From here on corresponds to that which was taught in the first teaching of Humans and Gods.) **Therefore, when one commits [evil deeds] such as murder or theft, one's spirit, impelled by this bad karma, is born among the denizens of hell, hungry ghosts, or animals. Again, when one who dreads suffering or is virtuous by nature practices [good deeds] such as bestowing alms or maintaining the precepts, one's spirit, impelled by this good karma, is transported through the intermediate existence into the mother's womb** (from here on corresponds to that which was taught in the two teachings of Confucianism and Taoism) **and receives an endowment of vital force and material substance.** ([This] incorporates their statement that the vital force constitutes the origin.)

This final stage of the process of phenomenal evolution whereby beings come to be born as humans corresponds to the last two of the six coarse phenomenal appearances found in the *Awakening of Faith,* giving rise to karma (*ch'i-yeh* 起業) and the suffering of karmic bondage (*yeh-hsi-ku* 業繫苦):

> 5. The phenomenal appearance of generating karma: based on such conceptual elaboration, one categorizes [one's experience], forming an attachment to it, and thus commits various actions (karma).

> 6. The phenomenal appearance of the suffering of karmic bondage: based on one's actions (karma), one experiences the consequences and is thus not free.[20]

In the *Ch'an Preface* Tsung-mi likens the stage of generating karma (*tsao-yeh* 造業) to the wealthy and respected person dreaming that he steals from and abuses another or that he practices kindness and

20. T 32.577a18-20; cf. Hakeda, p. 45.

spreads virtue. He likens the stage of experiencing the consequences to the wealthy and respected person dreaming that he is arrested, put in a cangue, and punished, or that he is recommended for office.

The term translated as "spirit" in the *Inquiry* passage is *hsin-shen* 心神, a term that was sometimes used by Chinese Buddhists to designate "the transmigrating entity."[21] In the present instance Tsung-mi is using it to designate what in Buddhist technical terminology is usually be referred to as the *gandharva,* which refers to the being in the intermediate existence. The *Abhidharmakośa-bhāṣya* defines the intermediate existence (*antarābhava; chung-yu* 中有; Tsung-mi uses *chung-yin* 中陰) as the five aggregates during the period between death and rebirth, adding that since the being in the intermediate existence has not yet reached the place toward which it is destined it cannot be said to be born.[22] The intermediate existence is one of the four phases of existence in the cycle of birth, the others being conception, the lifetime proper, and death. The *Abhidharmakośabhāṣya* refers to the being in the intermediate existence as a body, although it is a subtle body that can only be seen by those who have attained the superknowledge of the divine eye. It feeds on odors, is able to pass through solid objects, and has the form of the being to which it is destined to be reborn. A being in the intermediate existence destined to be reborn as a human has a fully developed body the size of a five or six year old child. Seeing its future parents making love, the intermediate being feels attraction for the parent of the opposite sex and hostility toward the parent of the same sex, and affixes itself to the place

21. See Liebenthal, "The Immortality of the Soul in Chinese Thought," p. 336. *Shen* 神 is an enormously important term whose rich connotations cannot be done justice in the space of a brief note. Suffice it to say that it has the general connotation of the divine or spiritual and is used to refer to benevolent spiritual beings, whereas *kuei* 鬼, the contrasting term with which *shen* is often coupled, has the general connotation of the demonic and is used to refer to malevolent spiritual beings. In the *Book of Rites,* *shen* refers to the *hun* 魂 soul, which upon death returns to heaven. It is associated with yang and light and is seen to be a positive spiritual force. In contrast, *kuei* refers to the *p'o* 魄 soul, which upon death returns to the earth. It is associated with yin and darkness and is seen to be a negative spiritual force. For a good summary of how these terms are used in the *Book of Rites,* see De Groot, *The Religious System of China* 4.3-8. De Groot also notes that *shen* is often associated with *ling* 靈 (4.12).

22. T 29.44b7-8; cf. La Vallée Poussin 2.31-32 and Pruden 2.383.

where their organs are joined together, imagining that it is he or she with whom they are having intercourse. Thus the being comes to enter its mother's womb, whence its aggregates become dense.[23]

Not only can mind (*hsin* 心) and vital force (*ch'i* 氣) here be seen as corresponding to name (*nāma* 名) and form (*rūpa* 色), but, as will be made clear further on, they also correspond to the subjective and objective aspect of the ālayavijñāna in the scheme of the *Ch'eng wei-shih lun*.

[710b23]　氣則頓具四大漸成諸根；心則頓具四蘊漸成諸識。十月滿足生來名人。即我等今者身心是也。故知身心各有其本、二類和合方成一人。天修羅等大同於此。

[710b23] The moment there is vital force, the four elements are fully present and gradually form the sense organs; the moment there is mind, the four [mental] aggregates are fully present and form consciousness. When ten [lunar] months have come to fruition and one is born, one is called a human being. This refers to our present body-and-mind. Therefore we know that the body and mind each has its origin and that as soon as the two interfuse, they form a single human. It is virtually the same as this in the case of gods, titans, and so forth.

Tsung-mi goes on to show how karma determines the particular circumstances within which one is reborn.

[710b26]　然雖因引業受得此身、復由滿業故貴賤貧富壽夭病健盛衰苦樂。謂前生敬慢為因、今感貴賤之果、乃至仁壽殺夭施富慳貧。種種別報不可具述。是以此身、或有無惡自禍、無善自福、不仁而壽、不殺而夭等者、皆是前生滿業已定。故今世不同所作自然如然。外學者不知前世、但據目覩、唯執自然。（會彼所說自然為本。）

[710b26] While one receives this bodily existence as a result of one's directive karma, one is in addition honored or demeaned, impoverished or wealthy, long or short lived, ill or healthy, prospering or declining, distressed or happy, because of one's particularizing karma. That is to say, when the respect

23. See T 29.45c10-47a16; cf. La Vallée Poussin 2.43-52 and Pruden 2.390-395). See also Kalupahana and Tamura, "Antarābhava," *Encyclopaedia of Buddhism* 1.730-733.

or contempt shown [to others] in a previous existence serves as the cause, it determines the result of one's being honored or demeaned in the present, and so on and so forth to the benevolent being long-lived, the murderous short-lived, the generous wealthy, and the miserly impoverished. The various types of individual retribution [are so diverse that they] could not be fully enumerated. Therefore, in this bodily existence, although there may be cases of those who are without evil and even so suffer disaster, or those who are without virtue and even so enjoy bounty, or who are cruel and yet are long-lived, or who do not kill and yet are short-lived, all have been determined by the particularizing karma of a previous lifetime. Therefore the way things are in the present lifetime does not come about from what is done spontaneously. Scholars of the outer teachings do not know of previous existences but, relying on [only] what is visible, just adhere to their belief in spontaneity. ([This] incorporates their statement that spontaneity constitutes the origin.)

"Directive karma" (*yin-yeh* 引業) is that which draws (*yin* 引) beings toward the destiny (*gati*) in which they are to be reborn; that is, it determines their mode of existence as a god, human, animal, and so forth. "Particularizing karma" (*man-yeh* 滿業) is that which fills out (*man* 滿) the specific details of their existence.[24] Tsung-mi's explanation shows how karma operates as a moral principle to account for the injustices and inequalities experienced in life. Note that Tsung-mi uses his explanation of karma to reject spontaneity (*tzu-jan* 自然), much as he had earlier in the section on Confucianism and Taoism. Moral action can only have meaning and be effective within the causal framework established by the Buddhist theory of karma.

In the next passage Tsung-mi brings in the mandate of heaven, recapitulating the criticism he made earlier at the end of the first part of the *Inquiry*.

---

24. See *Abhidharmakośabhāṣya*, T 29.92b10-11, which compares directive karma to the broad brushstrokes by which a painter delineates the outline of a figure and particularizing karma to his use of various colors to flesh out the image (cf. La Vallée Poussin 3.200 and Pruden 2.678). For a discussion of these two types of karma, see Mochizuki, *Bukkyō daijiten* 1.178b-c and 5.4754a-b.

[710c5]　復有前生少者修善老而造惡、或少惡老善、故
今世少小富貴而樂老大貧賤而苦、或少貧苦老富貴等。故
外學者不知唯執否泰由於時運。（會彼所説皆由天命。）

[710c5] Moreover, there are those who in a previous life cultivated virtue when young and perpetuated evil when old, or
else were evil in their youth and virtuous in their old age; and
who hence in their present lifetime enjoy moderate wealth
and honor when young and suffer great impoverishment and
debasement when old, or else experience the suffering of impoverishment in youth and enjoy wealth and honor in old age.
Thus scholars of the outer teachings just adhere to their belief
that success and failure are due to the sway of fortune. ([This]
incorporates their statement that everything is due to the mandate of
heaven.)

The following passage, more than anywhere else in the *Inquiry*,
is remarkable for showing the extent to which Tsung-mi applies his
synthetic approach. Not only does he assimilate Confucian and Taoist terminology into a Buddhist frame of reference, he also incorporates the Fa-hsiang scheme of the division of the ālayavijñāna
into subjective and objective modes into the process of phenomenal
evolution derived from the *Awakening of Faith*.[25] The evolution of
the mind and objects refers to the subjective and objective evolution
of the ālayavijñāna as set forth in the *Ch'eng wei-shih lun*. The
primal pneuma is thus nothing but the objective evolution of the
ālayavijñāna internally into the body of the senses, and heaven and
earth are its objective evolution externally into the receptacle world.
The various correspondences Tsung-mi establishes prove for him
that the concepts put forward by the two teachings as an explanation
for the ultimate ground of existence, when thoroughly examined,
turn out to refer to epiphenomena in the process of phenomenal
evolution. They are thus clearly subordinated to his own Buddhist
vision, but at the same time they are also shown to make their own
essential, albeit limited, contribution to that vision.

[710c8]　然所禀之氣、展轉推本、即混一之元氣也；所
起之心、展轉窮源、即眞一之靈心也。究實言之、心外的

---

25. Tsung-mi's incorporation of *Ch'eng wei-shih lun* terminology into
his cosmogonic scheme stands in marked contrast to the hostile attitude
toward Fa-hsiang evinced by his Hua-yen predecessors.

無別法。元氣亦從心之所變、屬前轉識所現之境、是阿賴
耶相分所攝。從初一念業相、分為心境之二。心既從細至
麁、展轉妄計乃至造業。（如前敍列。）境亦從微至著、展
轉變起乃至天地（即彼始自太易五重運轉乃至太極。太極生兩
儀。彼説自然大道、如此説眞性、其實但是一念能變見分；彼
云元氣如此一念初動、其實但是境界之相。）業既成熟、即從
父母禀受二氣、與業識和合、成就人身。據此則心識所變
之境、乃成二分、一分即與心識和合成人、一分不與心識
和合、即成天地山河國邑。三才中唯人靈者、由與心神合
也。佛説内四大與外四大不同、正是此也。

[710c8] Nevertheless, the vital force with which we are endowed, when it is traced all the way back to its origin, is the
primal pneuma of the undifferentiated oneness; and the mind
that arises, when it is thoroughly investigated all the way back
to its source, is the numinous mind of the absolute. In ultimate
terms, there is nothing outside of mind. The primal pneuma
also comes from the evolution of mind, belongs to the category
of the objects that were manifested by the previously evolved
consciousness, and is included within the objective aspect of
the ālaya[vijñāna]. From the phenomenal appearance of the
activation of the very first thought, [the ālayavijñāna] divides
into the dichotomy of mind and objects. The mind, having
developed from the subtle to the coarse, continues to evolve
from false speculation to the generation of karma (as previously
set forth). Objects likewise develop from the fine to the crude,
continuing to evolve from the transformation [of the
ālayavijñāna] into heaven and earth. (The beginning for them starts
with the grand interchangeability and evolves in five phases to the great
ultimate. The great ultimate [then] produces the two elementary forms.
Even though they speak of spontaneity and the great Way as we here
speak of the true nature, they are actually nothing but the subjective
aspect of the evolution [of the ālayavijñāna] in a single moment of
thought; even though they talk of the primal pneuma as we here speak
of the initial movement of a single moment of thought, it is actually
nothing but the phenomenal appearance of the objective world.) When
karma has ripened, then one receives one's endowment of
the two vital forces from one's father and mother, and, when
it has interfused with activated consciousness, the human
body is completely formed. According to this, the objects that

are transformed from consciousness immediately form two divisions: one division is that which interfuses with consciousness to form human beings, while the other division does not interfuse with consciousness and is that which forms heaven and earth, mountains and rivers, and states and towns. The fact that only humans among the three powers [of heaven, earth, and humanity] are spiritual is due to their being fused with spirit. This is precisely what the Buddha meant when he said that the internal four elements and the external four elements are not the same.

### CLOSING EXHORTATION

Tsung-mi brings his essay to a close with an exhortation alluding to the realization of the threefold body of the Buddha. The dharmakāya refers to the absolute ground on which Buddhahood is based; the sambhogakāya refers to the body of glory in which Buddhas enjoy the fulfillment of their vows in their pure lands; and the nirmāṇakāya refers to the manifestation of Buddhas in human form among sentient beings.[26]

[710c21]　哀哉寡學異執紛然。寄語道流：欲成佛者、必須洞明麁細本末。方能棄末歸本返 [反] 照心源。麁盡細除、靈性顯現、無法不達。名法報身。應現無窮、名化身佛。

[710c21] How pitiable the confusion of the false attachments of shallow scholars! Followers of the Way, heed my words: If you want to attain Buddhahood, you must thoroughly discern the coarse and the subtle, the root and the branch. Only then will you be able to cast aside the branch, return to the root, and turn your light back upon the mind source. When the coarse has been exhausted and the subtle done away with, the numinous nature is clearly manifest and there is nothing that is not penetrated. That is called the dharmakāya and sambhogakāya. Freely manifesting oneself in response to beings without any bounds is called the nirmāṇakāya Buddha.

26. For a lucid explanation of the meaning of the three bodies of the Buddha, see Nagao, "On the Theory of Buddha Body," in *Mādhyamika and Yogācāra*.

# Glossary of Names, Terms, and Texts

*Ābhāsvara: see* light-sound heaven.

**Abhidharma** (*a-p'i-ta-mo* 阿毘達磨): a genre of scholastic philosophy that emerged within early Indian Buddhist circles and that was later adopted by some Mahāyāna philosophers (most notably, the Yogācārins) and strongly criticized by others (most notably, the Mādhyamikas); its dharma theory sought to give a totally impersonal account of human experience without recourse to the notion of self; abhidharma texts often gloss the term as meaning the "higher" (in the sense of meta) dharma.

*Abhidharmakośabhāṣya* (*A-p'i-ta-mo chü-she lun* 阿毘達磨俱舍論): a systematic compendium of the views of the Vaibhāṣika and Sautrāntika traditions, attributed to Vasubandhu; one of the main sources for Tsung-mi's Teaching of the Lesser Vehicle.

*Āgamas* (*A-han* 阿含): collections of sermons attributed to the Buddha corresponding to the *Nikāyas* contained in the Pāli Canon; originally composed in Sanskrit and now partially preserved in Chinese translation.

**Aggregates**: *see* five aggregates.

**Ālayavijñāna** (*a-li-yeh-shih* 阿梨耶識, *a-lai-yeh-shih* 阿賴耶識; *tsang-shih* 藏識): the key Yogācāra doctrine of the "store consciousness," the eighth consciousness that operates as the underlying continuum in mental life and functions as the underlying projective consciousness on which delusion is ultimately based. The ālayavijñāna stores the seeds out of which the mental and physical elements that comprise the phenomenal world develop; it stores all experiences as karmically-charged seeds, which, under the proper conditions, ripen as actions (whether mental, verbal, or physical), which in turn create new seeds. It is thus karmically conditioned by the other seven consciousnesses. The ālayavijñāna is also that which is grasped at by the seventh consciousness (*manas*) as the self.

*Analects* (*Lun yü* 論語): the collected sayings of Confucius.

**Arhat** (*lo-han* 羅漢): one who has eliminated the causes of rebirth and who, upon death, enters into final nirvāṇa; derogated by Mahāyāna Buddhists as an inferior ideal of sainthood characteristic of "Hīnayāna" Buddhism. The term originally designated one worthy of offerings and was one of ten epithets commonly applied to the Buddha.

**Asaṅga** (Wu-cho 無着, fourth century): the founder of the Yogācāra tradition of Mahāyāna Buddhism in India. One of his most important works was the *Mahāyānasaṃgraha* (*She ta-sheng lun* 攝大乘論), a comprehensive treatise outlining central Yogācāra doctrines and practices; this work, in Paramārtha's Chinese translation, became the basis for the She-lun tradition of early Chinese Yogācāra.

**Aśvaghoṣa** (Ma-ming 馬鳴, second century): author of the great epic biography of the Buddha, the *Buddhacarita;* putative author of the *Awakening of Faith.*

*Avataṃsaka:* see *Hua-yen Sūtra.*

*Awakening of Faith in Mahāyāna* (*Ta-sheng ch'i-hsin lun* 大乘起信論): an influential apocryphal text probably composed in China during the third quarter of the sixth century; falsely attributed to Aśvaghoṣa; especially important for its teaching of intrinsic enlightenment (*pen-chüeh*), which developed the Indian Buddhist doctrine of the tathāgatagarbha into a monistic ontology based on the mind as the ulimate ground of all experience. This text provided the foundation for Tsung-mi's systematic exposition of Buddhism in his *Inquiry.*

**Bodhisattva** (*p'u-sa* 菩薩): although the term originally referred to the spiritual career of the historical Buddha before he had achieved enlightenmnent, it came to designate the Mahāyāna ideal of sainthood (in contrast to the arhat); one who vows to attain supreme enlightenment in order to liberate all beings. Mahāyāna also developed a whole pantheon of celestial bodhisattvas who could intervene on behalf of their devotees.

*Book of Rites* (*Li chi* 禮記): one of the five Confucian classics; served as a major authority on ritual.

*Buddhacarita* (*Fo-so-hsing tsan ching* 佛所行贊經): one of the most famous epic biographies of the Buddha, by Aśvaghoṣa.

**Buddha-nature** (*fo-hsing* 佛性): the nature or potentiality for Buddhahood that, according to tathāgatagarbha theory, exists inherently in all sentient beings; often used synonymously with the tathāgatagarbha by Chinese Buddhists. The content of the highest teaching in Tsung-mi's *Inquiry,* that which Reveals the Nature.

***Buddha-nature Treatise*** (*Fo-hsing lun* 佛性論): an important tathāgatagarbha text, most likely composed in China, based on the *Ratnagotravibhāga.*

**Ch'an** (禪): more popularly known by its Japanese pronunciation as "Zen," Ch'an was one of the main traditions of Chinese Buddhism to develop during the T'ang dynasty (618-907); it claimed to represent a mind-to-mind transmission of the Buddha's enlightened understanding passed down through an unbroken lineage of patriarchs. The designation derives from the Sanskrit *dhyāna,* transliterated as *ch'an-na* 禪那 in Chinese, and is associated with the tradition's emphasis on meditation.

***Ch'an Chart:*** full title, *Chung-hua ch'uan-hsin-ti ch'an-men shih-tzu ch'eng-hsi t'u* 中華傳心地禪門師資承襲圖 (Chart of the Master-Disciple Succession of the Ch'an Gate that Transmits the Mind Ground in China), in one fascicle, written between 830 and 833, in reply to P'ei Hsiu's (787-860) questions about the teachings and lineal filiations of four of the major Ch'an traditions current during the late T'ang; it is in this text that Tsung-mi develops his critique of the Hung-chou Ch'an tradition. Its original title was probably *P'ei Hsiu shih-i wen* 裴休拾遺問.

***Ch'an Preface:*** full title, *Ch'an-yüan chu-ch'üan-chi tu-hsü* 禪源諸詮集都序 (Preface to the Collected Writings on the Source of Ch'an), in two fascicles, written around 833, Tsung-mi's preface to his collection of the writings of the various Ch'an traditions of the late T'ang that he assembled as a special section of the Buddhist Canon; correlates the different Ch'an traditions with the different doctrinal teachings.

***Ch'eng wei-shih lun*** (成唯識論): an abridged synopsis of various Indian commentaries to Vasubandhu's *Thirty Verses* (*Trimśika*), compiled by Hsüan-tsang with the collaboration of K'uei-chi; K'uei-chi's commentary upholds the position of Dharmapāla as orthodox; the text on which the sectarian identity of the Fa-hsiang tradition is based.

**Ch'eng-kuan** (澄觀, 738-839): honored as the fourth patriarch in the Hua-yen tradition; author of a massive commentary and subcommentary to the 80-fascicle translation of the *Hua-yen Sūtra* completed by Śikṣānanda in 699; one of Tsung-mi's teachers.

**Chih-yen** (智儼, 602-668): honored as the second patriarch in the Hua-yen tradition; argued against the new Yogācāra teachings introduced to China by Hsüan-tsang.

**Chiliocosm**: one thousand universes; a great chiliocosm (*trisāhas-ramahābhāsro lokadhātu; san-ch'ien ta-ch'ien shih-chieh* 三千大千世界) equals one billion universes.

**Ching-ying Hui-yüan** (淨影慧遠, 523-596): well-versed in both the She-lun and Ti-lun traditions, his compendium of Buddhist doctrine, the *Ta-sheng i-chang* 大乘義章, represents the culmination of sixth-century Chinese Buddhist scholarship and laid the groundwork for the subsequent development of Hua-yen.

*Chuang-tzu* (莊子): one of the great Taoist classics and masterpieces of Chinese literature; the first seven or "inner" chapters are believed to represent the fourth-century B.C. writings of Chuang-tzu.

*Classic of Change* (*I ching* 易經 or *Chou i* 周易): one of the five Confucian classics; a book of divination, whose commentaries, traditionally ascribed to Confucius, reflect early Chinese cosmological speculations on the principles of the universe.

*Classic of Filiality* (*Hsiao ching* 孝經): an important Confucian text centering on the virtue of filial piety.

*Classic of History* (*Shu ching* 書經 or *Shang shu* 尚書): one of the five Confucian classics; contains documents allegedly dating from the legendary emperor Yao to the early Chou dynasty (1222-256 B.C.).

*Classic of Poetry* (*Shih ching* 詩經 or *Mao shih* 毛詩): one of the five Confucian classics; contains 305 poems traditionally believed to have been selected by Confucius from a body of 3,000 poems.

**Conditioned origination** (*pratīyasamutpāda; yüan-ch'i* 緣起): the doctrine that all things exist in dependence on one another and therefore have no essence of their own. Classically formulated in the twelve-link chain of conditioned origination: old age and death are conditioned by birth, which is conditioned by becoming, which is conditioned by grasping, which is conditioned by craving, which is conditioned by sensation, which is conditioned by contact, which is conditioned by the six modalities, which are conditioned by name and form, which are conditioned by consciousness, which is conditioned by impulses, which are conditioned by ignorance. This doctrine was developed in early Buddhism to explain how there could be continuity in mental life, as well as from one life to another, in the absence of a self. Within Madhyamaka its meaning was extended to explain the emptiness of all dharmas. Its meaning was further expanded within Hua-yen to denote the totalistic vision of the unimpeded interpenetration of each and every phenomenon with each and every other phenomenon.

**Consciousness-only** (*vijñaptimātratā; wei-shih* 唯識): the Yogācāra doctrine that what beings experience as "reality" is really only a mentally constructed projection of the ālayavijñāna.

**Conventional truth** (*saṃvṛti-satya; su-ti* 俗諦): the ordinary or relative truth; that which is provisionally or expediently true, as distinguished from that which is ultimately true.

**Cosmogony**: a theory or myth having to do with the creation (genesis) of the universe (cosmos); as distinguished from a cosmology, which gives a description of the structure of the universe.

**Defilements** (*kleśa; fan-nao* 煩惱): also rendered as "afflictions," "perturbations," and "passions," the term has a broad range of interpretations in Buddhism; in the context of tathāgatagarbha theory, it refers to that which covers over the tathāgatagarbha and thereby conceals it from deluded beings; for Tsung-mi it specifically refers to the three poisons of greed, anger, and delusion.

**Dependent nature** (*paratantra-svabhāva; t'a-ch'i-hsing* 他起性): according to the Yogācāra doctrine of the three natures, the interdependent realm of phenomena that can be seen either through imaginary projections or in its perfected aspect.

**Dharma** (*fa* 法): a term with a wide range of meanings in Buddhism; as one of the three treasures in which Buddhists take refuge (along with the Buddha and the sangha or community), it refers to the Buddha's teaching and, by extension, the truth realized by the Buddha. Within the dharma theory developed within the Abhidharma, it has the technical meaning of the basic categories into which all experience can be analyzed. In other contexts it simply means thing or entity.

**Dharmadhātu** (*fa-chieh* 法界): a term for the absolute, synonymous with the tathāgatagarbha in its true aspect untainted by the defilements that appear to cover it over; literally, the "dharma-element" that inheres in all beings as the "cause" of their enlightenment as well as the "essence of all dharmas" or the "realm of dharma" that is realized in enlightenment.

**Dharmakāya** (*fa-shen* 法身): the Buddha as the eternal body of the truth, as distinguished from the perishable physical body of the Buddha that was subject to birth, old age, and death; ultimate reality; one of the three bodies of the Buddha along with the sambhogakāya and nirmāṇakāya.

**Dharmapāla** (Hu-fa 護法): an Indian Yogācāra scholar whose opinions K'uei-chi upheld as orthodox for what became known as the Fa-hsiang tradition.

**Diamond Sūtra** (*Vajracchedikā-sutra; Chin-kang po-jo ching* 金剛般若經): a short Perfection of Wisdom scripture noted for its bold paradoxes; it became especially popular within Ch'an because of its association with the Sixth Patriarch, Hui-neng.

**Divākara** (Jih-chao 日昭): an Indian Tripiṭaka master and translator whom Fa-tsang met in 684.

**Doctrinal classification** (*p'an-chiao* 判教): a hermeneutical strategy developed by Chinese Buddhists to reconcile the discrepancies in the Buddha's teachings by arranging them hierarchically. Teachings could be ordered according to their content, style, or the chronological sequence in which they were believed to have been delivered. Since the principle of expedient means could be invoked to justify a variety of arrangements, the different scholastic traditions within Chinese Buddhism used doctrinal classification as a means of asserting their sectarian claims to authority. The teachings could also be arranged into a curriculum of study, in which case a particular classification scheme could serve as a map for Buddhist practice.

**Eight attainments** (*pa-ting* 八定): the four stages of meditative absorption and the four formless attainments.

**Emptiness** (*śūnyatā; k'ung* 空): a cardinal Mahāyāna doctrine first proclaimed in the Perfection of Wisdom scriptures and later elaborated philosophically by Nāgārjuna and other Madhyamaka thinkers. Can be understood as an extension of the idea of no-self to all things (dharmas): all dharmas are empty because their existence is contingent on other dharmas—hence they have no perduring essence of their own. Self and dharmas only have reality as conceptual constructs.

**Expedient means** (*upāya; fang-pien* 方便): the basic Buddhist teaching that the Buddha taught different things in different ways at different times in accord with the needs and capacities of his audience. This doctrine was used to justify the production of new

Mahāyāna scriptures, despite their manifest divergence from the texts belonging to the established canon. Mahāyāna scriptures accordingly often claimed that the previous "Hīnayāna" teachings were merely taught as expedients to prepare the way for the subsequent revelation of the Buddha's ultimate message in the Mahāyāna.

**Experiential enlightenment** (*shih-chüeh* 始覺): a key doctrine associated with the *Awakening of Faith;* literally, the enlightenment that has an inception in time, as distinguished from the enlightenment that exists a priori; the initial realization that all beings are intrinsically enlightened and the process of the actualization of enlightenment.

**Fa-hsiang** (法相): a form of Yogācāra Buddhism associated with Hsüan-tsang (600-664) and his disciple K'uei-chi (632-682). Unlike the earlier Yogācāra traditions in China, it rejected the idea of the tathāgatagarbha and so denied the universal accessibility of enlightenment, and for that reason it was regarded as only an elementary form of Mahāyāna by the Hua-yen tradition. The term itself was first applied to this tradition by the Hua-yen thinker Fa-tsang (643-712), who used it to emphasize the inferiority of Fa-hsiang teachings, which only dealt with the "phenomenal appearances of the dharmas," in contrast to Hua-yen, which dealt with the underlying "nature" on which such phenomenal appearances were based.

**Fa-tsang** (法藏, 643-712): honored as the third patriarch in the Hua-yen tradition; he is often said to have systematized Hua-yen teachings in their classical form.

**Five aggregates** (*pañca-skandha; wu-yin* 五蘊): the five psychophysical constituents of which the personality is composed: form (*rūpa; se* 色), sensation (*vedanā; shou* 受), conceptualization (*saṃjñā; hsiang* 想), impulses (*saṃskāra; hsing* 行), and consciousness (*vijñāna; shih* 識).

**Five cardinal virtues** (*wu-te* 五德): the five virtues emphasized in Confucianism: benevolence (*jen* 仁), righteousness (*i* 義), propriety (*li* 禮), wisdom (*chih* 智), and trustworthiness (*hsin* 信).

**Five Classics** (*wu-ching* 五經): the five Confucian classics: the *Classic of Change* (*I ching*), the *Classic of History* (*Shu ching*), the *Spring and Autumn Annals* (*Ch'un-ch'iu*) with the *Tso Commentary* (*Tso chuan*), the *Classic of Poetry* (*Shih ching*), and the *Book of Rites* (*Li chi*).

**Five destinies** (*pañca-gati; wu-tao* 五道, *wu-ch'ü* 五趣): those of gods (*deva; t'ien* 天), humans (*manuṣya; jen-chien* 人間), animals (*tiryagyoni; ch'u-sheng* 畜生), hungry ghosts (*preta; o-kuei* 餓鬼), and denizens of hell (*naraka; ti-yü* 地獄). Sometimes the category of titans (*asura; a-hsiu-lo* 阿修羅) is added to make six destinies. *See* six destinies.

**Five precepts** (*pañca-śīla; wu-chieh* 五戒): not to kill, not to steal, not to lie, not to engage in illicit sexual activity, and not to drink intoxicants; the five precepts form the core of Chinese lay Buddhist practice.

**Four formless attainments** (*catur-ārūpya-samāpatti; ssu-wu-se-ting* 四無色定): the four stages of meditational absorption corresponding to the four heavens in the realm of formlessness: infinite space, infinite consciousness, nothingness, and neither conceptualization nor non-conceptualization.

**Four great elements** (*mahābhūta; ssu-ta* 四大): earth, water, fire, and wind.

**Four noble truths** (*catur-ariyā-satya; ssu-sheng-ti* 四聖諦): the central early Buddhist teaching that all compounded things entail suffering (*duḥkha; k'u* 苦); that there is an origin to suffering (*samudaya; chi* 集); that, because suffering is based on a series of causes and conditions, there is the possibility of an extinction of suffering (*nirodha; mieh* 滅); and that the way to bring about the extinction of suffering is to follow the eightfold noble path prescribed by the Buddha (*mārga; tao* 道).

**Four stages of meditative absorption** (*catur-dhyāna; ssu-ch'an* 四禪): corresponding to the four heavens in the realm of form: dissociated from sense-desires and unwholesome states, the first stage is characterized by five factors—(1) applied thought (*vitarka*), a result of the conquest of torpor and sloth; (2) discursive thought (*vicāra*), a result of the conquest of perplexity; (3) rapture (*prīti*), a result of the conquest of ill-will; (4) joyfulness (*sukha*), a result of the conquest of distraction and regret; and (5) one-pointedness of mind (*ekāgratacitta*), a result of the conquest of sensuous desires. Applied thought and discursive thought are eliminated in the second stage while rapture, joyfulness, and one-pointedness of mind are retained; rapture is eliminated in the third stage while joyfulness and one-pointedness of mind remain; and joyfulness is eliminated in the fourth stage while only one-pointedness of mind remains.

*Great Dharma Drum Sūtra* (*Mahābherīhāraka-sūtra; Fa-ku ching* 法鼓經): an Indian Mahāyāna tathāgatagarbha scripture.

*Great Perfection of Wisdom Treatise* (*Ta-chih-tu lun* 大地度論): a massive commentary to the *Perfection of Wisdom in Twenty Five Thousand Lines*. This text is almost certainly not by Nāgārjuna, as East Asian Buddhists have traditionally maintained; it is possible that Kumārajīva, its "translator," may have had a hand in its composition; it was prized by Chinese Buddhists as an authoritative and encyclopedic reference to Mahāyāna doctrine.

**Great Vehicle:** *see* Mahāyāna.

**Han K'ang-p'o** (韓康伯, 332-380): author of what became the officially-sanctioned commentary to the *Classic of Change*.

**Han Yü** (韓愈, 768-824): a major literary figure in the revival of Confucianism during the late T'ang; author of several influential critiques of Buddhism. Tsung-mi may have taken the title for his *Inquiry* from a series of essays Han wrote; it is possible that Tsung-mi's essay was written as a counter to Han's outspoken criticisms of Buddhism.

**Hermeneutics:** the methodological principles on which the interpretation of a text, or body of texts, is based.

**Hīnayāna** (*hsiao-sheng* 小乘): the pejorative term (meaning Lesser Vehicle) by which Mahāyāna Buddhists designated the earlier traditions of Buddhism from which they wanted to differentiate themselves.

**Hsüan-tsang** (玄奘, 600-664): a celebrated pilgrim and noted translator responsible for introducing a new version of Yogācāra to China, which later became known as the Fa-hsiang tradition.

**Hua-yen** (華嚴): one of the major scholastic traditions of Chinese Buddhism to develop during the T'ang dynasty (618-907). It took its name from the *Hua-yen* (*Avataṃsaka*) *Sūtra,* which it claimed represented the first and most profound teaching of the Buddha, in which the content of his enlightenment was revealed without the recourse to expedients that characterized all other scriptures.

*Hua-yen (Avataṃsaka) Sūtra* (華嚴經): one of the longest Mahāyāna Buddhist scriptures, being a compendium of a number of texts, many of which originally circulated as sūtras in their own right, that were combined together sometime around or before the beginning of the fifth century, when it was first brought to China from Khotan.

First translated in 60 fascicles by Buddhabhadra during 418-422; an expanded version was later translated in 80 fascicles by Śikṣānanda during 695-699; a forty-fascicle translation of the concluding section, the *Gaṇḍhavyūha* (*Ju-fa-chieh p'in* 入法界品), was done by Prajña during 796-798. Chinese Buddhists believed that this scripture was taught immediately after the Buddha's enlightenment, while he was still absorbed in the samādhi of oceanic reflection. It was the main text on which the Hua-yen tradition of Chinese Buddhism based its claim to authority as the most profound teaching of the Buddha.

*Huai-nan-tzu* (淮南子): an important second-century B.C. Taoist compendium of the knowledge a ruler would need to govern effectively.

**Hui-neng** (慧能, 638-713): honored as the Sixth Patriarch in the Southern line of Ch'an; famous for his emphasis on sudden enlightenment; founder of the orthodox Southern line of Ch'an.

**Hung-chou** (洪州): an important Ch'an movement that began in Szechwan during the second half of the eighth century; derived from Ma-tsu Tao-i 馬祖道一 (709-788). Although Tsung-mi was critical of the ethical dangers inherent in its emphasis on spontaneity, the majority of the Ch'an lineages in the Sung dynasty (960-1279) claimed descent from Ma-tsu.

**Imaginary nature** (*parikalpa-svabhāva; pien-chi-hsing* 遍計性): according to the Yogācāra doctrine of the three natures, the deluded way in which the interdependent realm of phenomena is usually seen through the reified concepts of self (ātman) and things (dharmas).

**Intermediate existence** (*antarābhava; chung-yu* 中有, *chung-yin* 中陰): the period between death and rebirth; one of the four phases of existence in the cycle of birth, the others being conception, the lifetime proper, and death.

**Intrinsic enlightenment** (*pen-chüeh* 本覺): a Chinese Buddhist term for which there is no Sanskrit equivalent; an elaboration of the Indian Buddhist idea of the potentiality for enlightenment inherent in all sentient beings; a central doctrine developed in the *Awakening of Faith,* which makes explicit the ontological implications of the tathāgatagarbha theory. For Tsung-mi, intrinsic enlightenment is both the ground that makes enlightenment possible as well as the content of that enlightenment, revealed in the Teaching That Reveals the Nature.

**Jñānaprabha** (Chih-kuang 智光): a renowned seventh-century Indian Madhyamaka master at Nālandā.

**Kalpa** (*chieh* 劫): a cosmic eon, the smallest unit of which is an intermediate kalpa (*antarakalpa; chung-chieh* 中劫), twenty of which comprise one kalpa. There are four kalpas in each cosmic cycle or great kalpa (*mahākalpa; ta-chieh* 大劫): those of formation, continuation, destruction, and emptiness.

**Karma** (*yeh* 業): literally, "action," karma is broadly construed in Buddhism to include physical, verbal, and mental actions. The moral charge associated with various actions entails a necessary result. The doctrine of karma thus offers an explanation for the apparent injustices in the world. It is the central teaching of the Teaching of Humans and Gods, which explains how various good and bad actions in one lifetime lead to pleasurable or woeful rebirth in future lives.

***Kindred Sayings*** (*Saṃyutta-nikāya*): one of the four *Nikāyas* contained in the Pāli canon; corresponds to the *Saṃyukta-āgama*.

*Kleśa: see* defilements.

**K'uei-chi** (窺基, 632-682): sometimes referred to as Tz'u-en 慈恩, Hsüan-tsang's most important disciple and collaborator.

**Kumārajīva** (Chiu-mo-lo-shih 鳩摩羅什, 344-413): an influential Central Asian missionary; many of his translations of some of the most important Mahāyāna texts became standards within East Asian Buddhism; especially important for the introduction Madhyamaka teachings to China.

**K'ung Ying-ta** (孔穎達, 574-648): scholar in charge of the imperial commission to establish the official version of the commentaries and subcommentries to the Five Classics during the T'ang.

***Laṅkāvatāra Sūtra*** (*Leng-ch'ieh ching* 楞伽經): an important Yogācāra scripture associated with the early Ch'an movement in China.

***Lao-tzu*** (老子): one of the central Taoist texts, attributed to the legendary Lao-tzu, revered as the "founder" of Taoism; although traditionally believed to have been composed by Lao-tzu in the sixth century B.C., it was more likely compiled sometime during the third century B.C.

**Lesser Vehicle:** *see* Hīnayāna.

**Li Ao** (李翱, 772-836): an important literatus, student and colleague of Han Yü, and author of the *Fu-hsing shu* 復性書 (Essay on Returning to One's True Nature).

***Lieh-tzu*** (列子): an important Taoist text, often grouped with the *Lao-tzu* and *Chuang-tzu* as the third major Taoist classic; it was compiled sometime during the very beginning of the fourth century A.D. but includes earlier material.

**Light-sound heaven** (*ābhāsvara; kuang-yin* 光音): the abode of radiant gods, the third and highest heaven within the second meditation heaven in the realm of form; the place where beings are born when the universe comes to an end and from which they descend to be born as humans when a new universe begins.

**Liu Ch'iu** (劉虬, 438-495): a Buddhist lay recluse who classified the Buddha's teachings into two broad categories, the sudden and the gradual, the latter being subdivided into five categories.

**Liu Yü-hsi** (劉禹錫, 772-842): an important scholar-official who was associated with Han Yü and later became acquainted with Tsung-mi.

*Lotus Sūtra* (*Saddharmapuṇḍarika-sūtra; Miao-fa lien-hua ching* 妙法蓮華經): an important early Mahāyāna scripture especially noted for its parables, its teaching of expedient means, its revelation of the incalculable life span of the Buddha, and its doctrine of the one vehicle. In Dharmarakṣa's translation (290), and subsequently in that of Kumārajīva (406), it became one of the most influential texts in all of Chinese Buddhism.

*Lun-heng* (論衡): a treatise written by Wang Ch'ung 王充 during the first century A.D.; critiques many of the ideas held at the time.

**Madhyamaka** (Chung-tao 中道): one of the major scholastic traditions of Mahāyāna Buddhism to develop in India. It claims to represent the Middle Way between the philosophical extremes of assertion and denial. The Madhyamaka tradition is indelibly associated with Nāgārjuna, who elaborated the philosophical implications of the doctrine of emptiness proclaimed in the Perfection of Wisdom scriptures.

*Madhyamakakārikā: see Stanzas on the Middle Way.*

**Mahāyāna** (*ta-sheng* 大乘): the Great Vehicle, a movement that began to take form within Indian Buddhism sometime toward the end of the first century B.C. or the beginning of the first century A.D. Distinguishing itself from the earlier traditions, which it pejoratively dubbed "Hīnayāna," it sought to make the highest goal of Buddhahood available to all.

**Manas** (*i* 意): ego consciousness (*mo-na-shih* 末那識), the seventh consciousness, which has the ālayavijñāna as both its support and its object. It is characterized by intellection and is always accompanied by the four defilements of delusion of a self, belief in a self, self-conceit, and self-love.

**Mencius** (Meng-tzu 孟子, ca. 371-289 B.C.): the Confucian most noted for his theory that moral virtues are inherent in human nature.

**Mount Sumeru** (*hsü-mi-san* 須彌山): the axial cosmic mountain around which Buddhist cosmology is organized.

**Nature origination** (*hsing-ch'i* 性起): the doctrine, particularly associated with the Hua-yen tradition, that all phenomena originate from the nature (i.e., the tathāgatagarbha) as the ultimate ground, as distinguished from conditioned origination, which has to do with the interrelation among phenomena.

*Nikāyas:* collections of sermons attributed to the Buddha contained in the Pāli Canon; correspond to the *Āgamas* in Chinese.

**Nirmāṇakāya** (*hua-shen* 化身): one of the three bodies of the Buddha; the manifestion of Buddhas in human form among sentient beings.

**Nirvāṇa** (*nieh-p'an* 涅槃): escape from saṃsāra, the extinction of the flame of craving that leads to rebirth.

*Nirvāṇa Sūtra* (*Nieh-p'an ching* 涅槃經): a Mahāyāna scripture noted for its assertion that all sentient beings have the Buddha-nature.

**Non-ultimate meaning** (*neyārtha; pu-liao-i* 不了義): a provisional or expedient teaching; the Sanskrit term literally means "the meaning that is to be led to"; roughly synonymous with conventional truth.

**No-self** (*anātman; wu-wo* 無我): the central Buddhist teaching that there is no perduring entity that can be grasped as the self; the "self" is merely a conceptual construct for which there is no non-linguistic referent.

**One Vehicle** (*ekayāna; i-sheng* 一乘): a Mahāyāna teaching, especially associated with the *Lotus Sūtra,* that there is ultimately only one universal vehicle to salvation that subsumes all of the other expedient vehicles; the one vehicle was often associated with the tathāgatagarbha in other Mahāyāna texts.

**Pao-t'ang** (保唐): a radical Ch'an tradition that developed in Szechwan during the second half of the eighth century; it interpreted Shen-hui's teaching of no-thought to entail the rejection of all forms of traditional Buddhist practice.

Paramārtha (Chen-ti 眞諦, 499-569): an important translator who played a major role in introducing Yogācāra thought to China.

*Paramārtha: see* ultimate truth.

*Paratantra: see* dependent nature.

*Parikalpa: see* imaginary nature.

*Pariniṣpanna: see* perfected nature.

Perfected nature (*pariniṣpanna-svabhāva; yüan-ch'eng-hsing* 圓成性): according to the Yogācāra doctrine of the three natures, the way in which the interdependent realm of phenomenon is seen in its true aspect, as empty of any substantial reality.

Perfection of Wisdom (*prajñāpāramitā; po-jo po-lo-mi-to* 般若波羅蜜多): refers both to the sixth and highest of the six perfections cultivated by the bodhisattva and to a body of Mahāyāna scriptures that has the doctrine of emptiness as its central revelation.

Period of increase/decrease (*tseng-mieh* 增減): an intermediate kalpa, so called because the kalpa of continuation consists of twenty intermediate kalpas in the course of which human life decreases from 80,000 to ten years during the first intermediate kalpa, and both increases from ten to 80,000 years and decreases from 80,000 to ten years during each of the next eighteen intermediate kalpas, and then increases from ten to 80,000 years during the last intermediate kalpa.

Po Chü-i (白居易, 772-846): a noted poet, literatus, and friend of Tsung-mi's.

*Prajñāpāramitā: see* Perfection of Wisdom.

Pratyekabuddha (*p'i-chih-fo* 辟支佛; *yüan-chüeh* 緣覺, *tu-chüeh* 獨覺): originally referred to those who attain Buddhahood on their own and enter into final extinction without teaching others, hence the term is often translated as "solitary Buddha" (*tu-chüeh* 獨覺); at some point *pratyeka* became confused with the *pratyaya,* and pratyekabuddhas came to be understood to mean those disciples of the Buddha who attain liberation through insight into conditioned origination (*pratītyasamutpāda; yüan-ch'i* 緣起)—hence the Chinese translation as *yüan-chüeh* 緣覺 (condition enlightened). Pratyekabuddhas came to be paired with śrāvakas (those disciples of the Buddha who attain liberation through insight into the four noble truths) as one of the two vehicles of Hīnayāna.

*Ratnagotravibhāga* (*Pao-hsing lun* 寶性論): an Indian Mahāyāna treatise important for systematically formulating tathāgatagarbha theory in its classical form.

**Realm of desire** (*kāmadhātu; yü-chieh* 欲界): the lowest of the three realms in Buddhist cosmology; it includes all five or six modes of existence; so called because beings' rebirth in this realm is governed by desire.

**Realm of form** (*rūpadhātu; se-chieh* 色界): the middle of the three realms in Buddhist cosmology; it consists of four main heavens, which are accessible through the mastery of the four stages of meditative absorption.

**Realm of formlessness** (*arūpadhātu; wu-se-chieh* 無色界): the highest of the three realms in Buddhist cosmology; it is entirely noncorporeal and only accessible through the mastery of the four formless attainments.

**Receptacle world** (*bhājanaloka; ch'i-shih-chien* 器世界): the physical world that contains living things.

**Sambhogakāya** (*pao-shen* 報身): one of the three bodies of the Buddha; the body of glory in which Buddhas enjoy the fulfillment of their vows in their pure lands.

*Saṃdhinirmocana-sūtra* (*Chieh shen-mi ching* 解深密經): a fourth-century Indian Mahāyāna scripture that provided canonical authority for some of the major ideas developed in the Yogācāra tradition; it claimed to supersede the teaching of emptiness as the third turning of the wheel of the dharma.

**Saṃsāra** (*sheng-ssu* 生死): the round of rebirth in which beings are bound; it includes the five or six modes of existence in the three realms.

*Scripture of Perfect Enlightenment* (*Yüan-chüeh ching* 圓覺經): an apocryphal text written in China sometime around the end of the seventh or beginning of the eighth century; it addresses some of the questions raised by the *Awakening of Faith's* teaching of intrinsic enlightenment having to do with the nature and necessity of religious practice. This text precipitated Tsung-mi's first enlightenment experience and was the subject of his major exegetical activity. Tsung-mi found in it justification for his theory of sudden enlightenment followed by gradual cultivation.

**She-lun tradition** (攝論宗): one of the major traditions of the early Chinese Yogācāra, based on Paramārtha's translation of Asaṅga's *Mahāyānasaṃgraha* (*She ta-sheng lun* 攝大乘論) and Vasubandhu's commentary.

**Shen-hui** (神會, 684-758): responsible for championing the cause of Hui-neng as the true Sixth Patriarch and launching an attack on the Northern line of Ch'an for its gradualist teaching; Tsung-mi claimed descent through his Ho-tse 荷澤 lineage.

**Śīlabhadra** (Chieh-hsien 戒賢): a renowned seventh-century Indian Yogācāra master at Nālandā.

**Six destinies** (*ṣaḍ-gati; liu-tao* 六道, *liu-ch'ü* 六趣): the five destinies plus that of titans (*asura; a-hsiu-lo* 阿修羅), the anti-gods of Vedic mythology. *See* five destinies.

**Six perfections** (*ṣaṭ-pāramitā; liu-po-lo-mi-to* 六波羅蜜多; *liu-tu* 六度): giving (*dāna; pu-shih* 布施), morality (*śīla; ch'ih-chieh* 持戒), patience (*kṣānti; jen-ju* 忍辱), vigor (*vīrya; ching-chin* 精進), concentration (*dhyāna; ch'an-ting* 禪定), and wisdom (*prajñā; chih-hui* 智慧)—main practices cultivated by the bodhisattva in Mahāyāna Buddhism.

**Skandha:** *see* five aggregates.

**Soteriology:** the theory and methods of salvation.

**Śrāvaka** (*sheng-wen;* 聲聞): those disciples of the Buddha who attained liberation through hearing and following the instruction of the Buddha; later the term became paired with pratyekabuddha as one of the two vehicles of Hīnayāna Buddhism, in which case it came to be understood to mean those disciples who attain liberation through their insight into the four noble truths.

**Śrīmālā Sūtra** (*Sheng-man ching* 勝鬘經): one of the most important scriptural authorities for the tathāgatagarbha theory; associates the tathāgatagarbha with the one vehicle; claims that the tathāgatagarbha, in its true form, is empty of all defilements and at the same time not empty of all the excellent qualities of Buddhahood.

***Stanzas on the Middle Way*** (*Madhyamakakārikā; Chung-lun* 中論): Nāgārjuna's most celebrated work and major source of Madhyamaka philosophy.

**Sthiramati** (An-hui 安慧): an important Indian Yogācāra thinker, who wrote a commentary to Vasubandhu's *Thirty Verses* (*Triṃśika*);

in East Asian Buddhism his opinions are often pitted against those of Dharmapāla.

**Suchness** (*tathatā; chen-ju* 眞如): a term for true reality; because the way things really are is beyond verbalization and conceptualization, they are said to be "such."

**Tao-yüan** (道圓): the ninth-century Ch'an teacher in Szechwan under whom Tsung-mi became a novice; was affiliated with the Hotse lineage of Southern Ch'an descended from Shen-hui.

**Tathāgata** (*ju-lai* 如來): an epithet for the Buddha; whereas both Sanskrit and Tibetan can meaning either "thus come" or "thus gone," the Chinese translation, *ju-lai,* means "thus come." It designates someone who has gone to or come to the other shore of liberation in the manner of previous Tathāgatas.

**Tathāgatagarbha** (*ju-lai-tsang* 如來藏): literally, the womb or embryo of the Tathāgata; the Buddhadood that exists "embryonically" as an inherent potential within all sentient beings and the Tathāgata that is "enwombed" within the sentient condition. This Indian Buddhist doctrine assumed paramount importance in Chinese Buddhism and was the basis for the development of the idea of intrinsic enlightenment (*pen-chüeh*) in the *Awakening of Faith;* often used synonymously with Buddha-nature. The content of the highest teaching, according to Tsung-mi.

*Tathāgatagarbha Sūtra* (*Ju-lai-tsang ching* 如來藏經): an important early tathāgatagarbha scripture noted for its nine metaphors for the tathāgatagarbha.

**Ten evil deeds** (*daśākuśala; shih-o* 十惡): killing, stealing, adultery, lying, slander, harsh speech, frivolous chatter, covetousness, malice, and false views.

**Ten good deeds** (*daśakuśala; shih-shan* 十善): not to commit the ten evil deeds.

*Thirty Verses* (*Trimśikā; San-shih sung* 三十頌): a work by Vasubandhu that served as the basis around which Hsüan-tsang presented an array of Indian Buddhist commentarial opinion in the *Ch'eng wei-shih lun.*

**Three natures** (*trisvabhāva; san-hsing* 三性): the key Yogācāra doctrine that describes the three aspects in terms of which reality is perceived: the imagined (*parikalpa; pien-chi* 遍計), the dependent (*paratantra; t'a-i* 他依), and the perfected (*pariniṣpanna;*

*yüan-ch'eng* 圓成). The imagined and perfected natures refer to two different perspectives from which the dependent nature can be seen. Whereas the imagined nature views the world in terms of reified concepts of self and objects, the perfected nature sees it as it truly is, as empty of any substantial reality.

**Three Treatises** (San-lun 三論): the early Madhyamaka tradition in China, named after three treatises translated by Kumārajīva: the *Treatise on the Middle Way* (*Chung lun* 中論), the *Twelve Topics Treatise* (*Shih-erh men lun* 十二門論), and the *Hundred Treatise* (*Po lun* 百論).

**Three vehicles** (*triyāna; san-sheng* 三乘): those of the śrāvakas, pratyekabuddhas, and bodhisattvas, as distinguished from the one vehicle.

**Ti-lun tradition** (地論宗): one of the major traditions of the early Chinese Yogācāra, based on Bodhiruci's translation of Vasubandhu's commentary to the *Daśabhūmika-sūtra*, the *Shih-ti ching lun* 十地經論.

*T'i-wei Po-li ching* (提謂波利經): an apocryphal text composed in northern China around 460 by T'an-ching 曇靖. It purports to have been taught on the seventh day after the Buddha's enlightenment to a group of 500 merchants led by Trapuṣa (Ti-wei 提謂) and Bhallika (Po-li 波利); it phrases Buddhist moral injunctions within the framework of Chinese cosmological ideas; it played an important role in the development of lay Buddhist practice in China and is the basis for the Teaching of Humans and Gods.

**Transformation of the basis** (*āśraya-parāvṛtti; chuan-i* 轉依): according to Yogācāra, the radical transformation of the basis (i.e., the ālayavijñāna) in terms of which reality is perceived.

*Treatise on the Middle Way* (*Chung lun* 中論): Kumārajīva's translation of Nāgārjuna's *Stanzas on the Middle Way* (*Madhyamakakārikā*) with a prose commentary by Piṅgala.

**Two truths** (*satya-dvaya; erh-ti* 二諦): those of conventional and ultimate truth.

**Two vehicles** (*erh-sheng* 二乘): those of the śrāvakas and pratyekabuddhas, a term used to refer to Hīnayāna.

**Tz'u-en:** *see* K'uei-chi.

**Ultimate meaning** (*nītārtha; liao-i* 了義): roughly synonymous with ultimate truth; the Sanskrit term literally means "the meaning that has been led to."

**Ultimate truth** (*paramārtha; chen-ti* 眞諦): as distinguished from conventional or provisional truth; because it is beyond words and concepts (which belong to the realm of convention), it is often held to be ineffable. Within the tathāgatagarbha tradition, however, it is given positive expression as the various excellent qualities associated with the absolute.

**Vasubandhu** (Shih-ch'in 世親, fourth or fifth century): reputedly the younger brother of Asaṅga; supposedly wrote the *Abhidharma-kośabhāṣya* in his youth; later converted to the Yogācāra teachings of his brother; author of a number of important Yogācāra treatises and commentaries, including the *Twenty Verses* (*Viṃśatika*) and the *Thirty Verses* (*Triṃśika*), the latter of which forms the core of the *Ch'eng wei-shih lun*.

*Yen-i ch'ao* (演義鈔): full title, *Ta-fang-kuang fo hua-yen ching sui-shu yen-i ch'ao* 大方廣佛華嚴經隨疏演義鈔, Ch'eng-kuan's sub-commentary to his commentary to the *Hua-yen Sūtra*.

**Yogācāra** (*Yü-ch'ieh-hsing-p'ai* 瑜伽行派): one of the major scholastic traditions of Mahāyāna Buddhism, Yogācāra emphasizes the constructive role of consciousness in beings' experience of the phenomenal world, and its central tenet is thus often characterized as "consciousness-only" (*vijñaptimātratā; wei-shih* 唯識). It posits the ālayavijñāna as the underlying support on which this process of mental construction is based. It is also noted for its doctrine of the three natures.

# A Guide to Supplemental Readings

For a good introduction to the general background for the T'ang dynasty, see Denis Twitchett and Arthur F. Wright's Introduction to their jointly edited book, *Perspectives on the T'ang*. For a discussion of the intellectual background for the Confucian revival during the later T'ang, see Edwin Pulleyblank, "Neo-Confucianism and Neo-Legalism in T'ang Intellectual Life, 755-805," in Arthur F. Wright, ed., *The Confucian Persuasion*, pp. 77-114. For a lively and readable discussion of the intellectual climate during the period in which Tsung-mi lived, see Arthur Waley, *The Life and Times of Po Chü-i, 772-846 A.D.* For more recent treatments of the life and thought of some of the major intellectual figures during this period, see Timothy H. Barrett, *Li Ao: Buddhist, Taoist, or Neo-Confucian?*; Jo-shui Chen, *Liu Tsung-yüan and Intellectual Change in T'ang China, 773-819*; and Charles Hartman, *Han Yü and the T'ang Search for Unity*. See also David McMullen, *State and Scholars in T'ang China*, for the institutional context of Confucianism. Unfortunately, there is no comparable treatment of Taoism during the T'ang, although Timothy Barrett's chapter on "Taoism under the T'ang" for the second volume on the T'ang for *The Cambridge History of China* should go a long way toward filling this gap whenever it is eventually published.

## BUDDHIST BACKGROUND

Luis O. Gómez's entry on "Buddhism in India" in the *Encyclopedia of Religion* presents the best, and most well-balanced, brief introduction to Indian Buddhism; it also contains an extensive annotated bibliography. Paul Williams' *Mahāyāna Buddhism: The Doctrinal Foundations* provides an excellent discussion of the Mahāyāna traditions and their place within the history of Indian Buddhism. Arthur Wright's *Buddhism in Chinese History* still offers the most readable general overview of the historical context in which Buddhism developed in China. A good brief introduction to Chinese Buddhism can be found in Erik Zürher's "Beyond the Jade Gate" in *The World of Buddhism,* edited by Heinz Bechert and Richard Gombrich. For background on T'ang Buddhism, see Stanley Weinstein's classic article, "Imperial Patronage in the Formation of T'ang Buddhism," which illustrates the ways in which T'ang Buddhism differed from the style of Chinese Buddhism characteristic of the fifth and sixth centuries by discussing the systems of doctrinal classification (*p'an-chiao*) developed within some of the major T'ang traditions. The best study of Chinese Buddhism during the sixth and seventh centuries remains Robert Gimello's 1976 dissertation, "Chih-yen (602-668) and the Foundations of Hua-yen Buddhism." For a useful, if somewhat polemical, introduction to the hermeneutical problem to which doctrinal classification can be seen as a response, see Robert Thurman, "Buddhist Hermeneutics," *Journal of the American Academy of Religion,* and my response in a later issue of the same journal, "Chinese Buddhist Hermeneutics: The Case of Hua-yen." For a sympathetic and accessible introduction to the Hua-yen thought of Fa-tsang, see Frank Cook's *Hua-yen Buddhism: The Jewel Net of Indra.* My own book on Tsung-mi tries to use an examination of his life and thought as a means for providing an intellectual history of Buddhism during the T'ang, see *Tsung-mi and the Sinfication of Buddhism.* For a briefer discussion of Tsung-mi's life and his understanding of Ch'an (Zen), see Jan Yün-hua's "Tsung-mi: His Analysis of Ch'an Buddhism." For a discussion of how Tsung-mi's system of doctrinal classification is related to his critique of the different Ch'an traditions in the late T'ang, see chapter 9 of my *Tsung-mi and the Sinification of Buddhism.*

## CONFUCIANISM AND TAOISM

Two excellent, but very different, general treatments of Confucianism and Taoism within the context of early Chinese thought can be found in Benjamin Schwartz's *The World of Thought in Ancient China* and A. C. Graham's *Disputers of the Tao.*

Lau's translations of, and introductions to, the *Analects* and the *Mencius* provide a good introduction to the basic Confucian teachings. An excellent discussion of the mandate of heaven appears in chapter 5 of Herrlee Creel's *The Origins of Statecraft in China,* vol. 1, *The Western Chou.* A. C. Graham's "The Background of the Mencian Theory of Human Nature" is especially valuable for laying the ground for understanding the problematic in terms of which the Indian Buddhist notion of tathāgatagarbha later became adapted within Chinese Buddhism.

One of the best general introductions to Taoism can be found in the three entries on Taoism, its history, and its literature by Anna Seidel and Michel Strickmann in the 15th edition of the *Encyclopedia Britannica* (1973). There are far too many translations of the *Lao-tzu* (or *Tao te ching*) in English, and there will probably never be one that wins general acceptance, but my own preference is D. C. Lau's, available in paperback from Penguin books, which also contains a good introduction that brings out the political dimension of the work. Even if not always accurate in detail, Burton Watson's translation of the *Chuang-tzu* generally succeeds in capturing the spirit of the text in lively, colloquial prose (his translation of selected chapters is available in paperback as *Chuang Tzu: Basic Writings* and his translation of the entire text is available in hardcover as *The Complete Works of Chuang Tzu*). For a more accurate and nuanced, but less fluid, translation, see A. C. Graham's *Chuang-tzu: The Inner Chapters.*

For an excellent discussion of Chinese cosmogonic thought during the T'ang, see chapter 3 of Edward H. Schafer's *Pacing the Void: T'ang Approaches to the Stars.* For an interesting but somewhat controversial discussion of the Taoist background, see Norman J. Girardot, *Myth and Meaning in Early Taoism,* especially chapter 2; see also Norman J. Girardot, "The Problem of Creation Mythology in the Study of Chinese Religion," in *History of Religion* 15 (1976): 289-318.

### THE TEACHING OF HUMANS AND GODS

Discussions of karma can be found in almost every introductory book on Buddhism. For an excellent, concise summary, see James P. McDermott, "Karma and Rebirth in Early Buddhism," in Wendy Doniger O'Flaherty, ed., *Karma and Rebirth in Classical Indian Traditions.* For discussions of karma theory as a resolution to the problem of theodicy, see Max Weber, "Theodicy, Salvation, and Rebirth," in *The Sociology of Religion;* and Gananath Obeyesekere, "Theodicy, Sin and Salvation in a Sociology of Buddhism," in Edmund Leach, ed., *Dialectic in Practical Religion.*

For more on the Teaching of Humans and Gods, see my "The Teaching of Men and Gods: The Doctrinal and Social Basis of Lay Buddhist Practice in the Hua-yen Tradition," in Robert M. Gimello and Peter N. Gregory, eds., *Studies in Ch'an and Hua-yen*. For an interesting discussion of the *T'i-wei Po-li ching*, the text on which the Teaching of Humans and Gods is based, see Whalen Lai, "The Earliest Folk Buddhist Religion in China: *T'i-wei Po-li ching* and Its Historical Significance," in David W. Chappell, ed., *Buddhist and Taoist Practice in Medieval Chinese Society*. The most thorough study of the *T'i-wei Po-li ching* can be found in Kyoko Tokuno's dissertation, "Byways in Chinese Buddhism: The *Book of Trapuṣa* and Indigenous Scriptures."

There are scores of academic and popular books on Buddhist meditation. For an excellent, but technical, presentation of traditional meditation theory and practice according to the Pāli Canon and the Theravāda tradition, see Paravahera Vajrañāṇa Mahāthera, *Buddhist Meditation in Theory and Practice;* for a more accessible treatment of the same material, see Winston L. King, *Theravāda Meditation: The Buddhist Transformation of Yoga*. The classical manual of meditation theory and practice for the Theravāda tradition is the *Visuddhimagga,* which is available in English translation by Bhikkhu Ñāṇamoli as *The Path of Purification*. For a general treatment that raises some interesting interpretative problems, see Robert Gimello, "Mysticism and Meditation," in Steven T. Katz, ed., *Mysticism and Philosophical Analysis*. For a discussion of the two poles of Buddhist meditation, see Paul Griffiths, "Concentration or Insight: The Problematic of Theravāda Buddhist Meditation-Theory," in the *Journal of the American Academy of Religion*. For an insightful discussion of the meaning of Buddhist meditation terms, see Alan Sponberg, "Meditation in Fa-hsiang Buddism," in Peter N. Gregory, ed., *Traditions of Meditation in Chinese Buddhism*.

A dated, but still useful, summary of Buddhist cosmology can be found in Louis de la Vallée Poussin's article, "Cosmogony and Cosmology (Buddhist)," in James Hastings, ed., *Encyclopedia of Religion and Ethics*.

## THE TEACHING OF THE LESSER VEHICLE

André Bareau's entry on "Hīnayāna Buddhism" in *The Encyclopedia of Religion* contains a useful survey of the development of the different sectarian traditions and their points of difference. For a basic introduction to Theravāda Buddhism, see the first four chapters of Peter Harvey's *An Introduction to Buddhism: Teachings, History and Practices*. For a more detailed discussion of the Abhidharma disputes, see part 2 of Edward Conze's *Buddhist Thought in India*.

The *Abhidharmakośabhāṣya,* the text on which Tsung-mi bases his account of the Teaching of the Lesser Vehicle, is available in the French translation by La Vallée Poussin; Leo Pruden's English translation of La Vallée Poussin's French translation contains so many errors that it should only be used with extreme caution.

### THE TEACHING OF THE PHENOMENAL APPEARANCES OF THE DHARMAS

Gimello's dissertation provides an illuminating discussion of the relationship among the Madhyamaka, Yogācāra, and tathāgatagarbha legacy of Indian Buddhism and the early Chinese appropriation of tathāgatagarbha theory, and it thus affords the most helpful background for understanding the next three teachings in Tsung-mi's essay: those of the Phenemonal Appearances of the Dharmas, the Refutation of Phenomenal Appearances, and the Revelation of the Nature (see "Chih-yen," pp. 212-337).

For a good general account of some fundamental Yogācāra ideas, see the articles by Nagao Gadjin collected and edited by Leslie Kawamura in *Mādhyamika and Yogācāra,* especially "The Buddhist World View as Elucidated in the Three-nature Theory and its Similes," "Connotations of the Word *Āśraya* (Basis) in the *Mahāyāna-Sūtralaṃkāra,*" "Usages and Meanings of *Pariṇāmanā,*" and "Logic of Convertibility." See also Alan Sponberg, "The *Trisvabhāva* Doctrine in India and China;" Ueda Yoshifumi, "Two Main Streams of Thought in Yogācāra Thought;" Stanley Weinstein, "The Concept of Ālaya-vijñāna in Pre-T'ang Buddhism;" chapter 4 of Paul Williams' *Mahāyāna Buddhism,* and Hattori Masaaki, "Realism and the Philosophy of Consciousness-Only." For a study of the origins and early development of the ālayavijñāna, see Lambert Schmithausen, *Ālayavijñāna: On the Origin and the Early Development of a Central Concept of Yogācāra Philosophy.* Weinstein's "Imperial Patronage" article contains a good, brief account of Hsüan-tsang and the Fa-hsiang School (pp. 291-297). The *Ch'eng wei-shih lun,* the authoritative text for the Fa-hsiang tradition, is available in English translation by Wei Tat (which is based on La Vallée Poussin's French translation). See also the entries on Asaṅga and Yogācāra by Hattori Masaaki, on Vasubandhu by Nagao Gadjin, and on Hsüan-tsang by Alan Sponberg in *The Encyclopedia of Religion,* and the entries on Ālaya-vijñāna by Seibun Fukaura and Asaṅga by Walpola Rahula in *Encyclopaedia of Buddhism.*

## THE TEACHING THAT REFUTES
## PHENOMENAL APPEARANCES

For a discussion of the development of the Prajñāpāramitā literature and an anthology of its teachings, see the introduction and
translations in Edward Conze's *Selected Sayings from the Perfection
of Wisdom*. Chapters 2 and 3 of Paul Williams' *Mahāyana Buddhism* contain excellent discussions of the Perfection of Wisdom
literature within the context of the development of Mahāyāna and
the more philosophical critique articulated within Madhyamaka.
Frederick Streng's *Emptiness: A Study in Religious Meaning* offers a
standard discussion of emptiness and contains, as an appendix, a
translation of Nāgārjuna's *Madhyamakārikā;* see also Kenneth Inada, *Nāgārjuna: A Translation of his Mūlamadhyamakakārikā
with an Introductory Essay*. For a provocative recent interpretation
of early Indian Madhyamaka, see C. W. Huntington, Jr.'s *The Emptiness of Emptiness,* the review by José Cabezón in the *Journal of
the International Association of Buddhist Studies* (1990), and the
subsequent exchange with the author in a later issue of that journal
(1992). For a discussion of the question of how the Indian tradition
was adapted in Chinese Buddhism, see Richard Robinson, *Early
Mādhyamika in India and China*. Douglas Daye's chapter, "Major
Schools of the Mahāyāna: Madhyamaka," in *Buddhism: A Modern
Perspective,* edited by Charles Prebish, can serve as a brief summary of Madhyamaka teachings. See also the entry on "Mādhyamika"
by Kajiyama and the entries on "Nāgārjuna" and "Śūnyam and
Śūnyatā" by Streng in *The Encyclopedia of Religion*. For more on
the tathāgatagarbha qualification of the teaching of emptiness, see
chapter 8 of my *Tsung-mi and the Sinification of Buddhism*.

## THE TEACHING THAT REVEALS THE NATURE

The major scriptural source for the tathāgatagarbha doctrine is the
*Śrīmālā Sūtra,* which is available in English translation by Alex and
Hideko Wayman, *The Lion's Roar of Queen Śrīmālā*. Takasaki
Jikidō discusses the development of the tathāgatagarbha theory in
his introduction to his translation of the *Ratnagotravibhāga,* the
treatise in which the tathāgatagarbha theory was formulated in its
definitive form. For a study of the doctrine in its Indo-Tibetan context, see David Seyfort Ruegg's monumental study, *La Théorie du
Tathāgatagarbha et du Gotra*. An important source for the tradition
in China was the *Fo-hsing lun* (Treatise on Buddha-nature), which

was closely modeled after the *Ratnagotravibhāga;* for a discussion of this text, see Sallie King, *Buddha Nature.* For Tsung-mi, the definitive exposition of tathāgatagarbha theory was found in the *Awakening of Faith in Mahāyāna,* which is available in English translation of Yoshito Hakeda. See also Paul Williams, *Mahāyāna Buddhism,* chapter 5.

For a more detailed discussion of the sudden and the gradual teachings, which Tsung-mi raises at the end of his discussion of this teaching, see chapter 5 of my *Tsung-mi and the Sinification of Buddhism.* For a broader discussion of the meaning of sudden and gradual and their importance in Chinese Buddhism and intellectual history, see the various papers collected in *Sudden and Gradual: Approaches to Enlightenment in Chinese Thought,* edited by Peter N. Gregory.

### RECONCILING ROOT AND BRANCH

Jan Yün-hua discusses Tsung-mi's final reincorporation of the various Buddhist teachings that he had critiqued in the earlier parts of his *Inquiry into the Origin of Humanity* in his "Conflict and Harmony in Ch'an and Buddhism." For a discussion of the problem of theodicy latent in Tsung-mi's system, see my "The Problem of Theodicy in the *Awakening of Faith.*"

# Bibliography of Works Cited

## Primary Sources

*A-p'i-ta-mo chü-she lun* (*Abhidharmakośabhāsya*) 阿毘達磨俱舍論, by Vasubandhu. Translated by Hsüan-tsang 玄奘. T vol. 29, no.1558.

*Ch'an-yüan chu-ch'üan-chi tu-hsü* 禪源諸詮集都序, by Tsung-mi 宗密. T vol. 48, no. 2015.

*Ch'eng wei-shih lun* 成唯識論. Translated by Hsüan-tsang 玄奘. T vol. 31, no. 1585.

*Ch'eng wei-shih lun shu-chi* 成唯識論述記, by K'uei-chi 窺基. T vol. 43, no. 1830.

*Chih-kuan fu-hsing chuan hung-chüeh* 止觀輔行傳弘決, by Chan-jan 湛然. T vol. 46, no. 1912.

*Chin shu* 晉書. 5 vols. Peking: Chung-hua shu-chü, 1974.

*Chiu-ching i-sheng pao-hsing lun* (*Ratnagotravibhāga*) 究竟一乘寶性論. Translated by Ratnamati. T vol. 31, no. 1611.

*Chou-i chu-shu* 周易注書. *Ssu-pu pei-yao,* revised edition, vol. 54.

*Chuang-tzu* 莊子. Harvard-Yenching Sinological Index Series, Supplement no. 20. Cambridge: Harvard University Press, 1956.

*Fo-hsing lun* 佛性論. T vol. 31, no. 1610.

*Han shu* 漢書. *Ssu-pu pei-yao,* revised edition, vols. 209-216.

*Hsiao ching* 孝經. Harvard-Yenching Sinological Index Series, Supplement no. 23. Taipei: Ch'eng-wen Publishing Co., 1966.

*Hsü kao-seng chuan* 續高僧傳, by Tao-hsüan 道宣. T vol. 50, no. 2060.

*Huai-nan-tzu* 淮南子. *Ssu-pu ts'ung-k'an,* vol. 85.

*Hua-yen ching hsing-yüan p'in shu ch'ao* 華嚴經行願品疏鈔, by Tsung-mi 宗密. HTC vol. 7.

*Hua-yen ching t'an-hsüan chi* 華嚴經探玄記 by Fa-tsang 法藏. T vol. 35, no. 1733.

*Hua-yen fa-chieh hsüan-ching* 華嚴法界玄鏡 by Ch'eng-kuan 澄觀. T vol. 45, no. 1883.

*Hua-yen i-sheng chiao-i fen-ch'i chang* 華嚴一乘教義分齊章, by Fa-tsang 法藏. T vol. 45, no. 1866.

*Hua-yen yüan jen lun chieh* 華嚴原人論解, by Yüan-chüeh 圓覺. HTC vol. 104.

*Hua-yen yüan jen lun fa-wei lu* 華嚴原人論發微錄, by Ching-yüan 淨源. HTC vol. 104.

*Hung-ming chi* 弘明集, compiled by Seng-yu 僧祐. T vol. 52, no. 2102.

*Kao-seng chuan* 高僧傳, by Hui-chiao 慧皎. T vol. 50, no. 2059.

*Lao-tzu* 老子. Taipei: Chung Hwa Book Co., 1973.

*Li chi* 禮記. *Ssu-pu pei-yao,* revised edition, vols. 29-30.

*Lieh-tzu* 列子. Taipei: I-wen yin-shu-kuan, 1971.

*Lun heng* 論衡, by Wang Ch'un 王充. *Ssu-pu pei-yao,* revised edition, vols. 389-390.

*Meng-ch'iu* 蒙求, by Li Han 李瀚. I-ts'un ts'ung-shu, vols. 16-17.

*Miao-fa lien-hua ching* 妙法蓮華經. Translated by Kumārajīva. T vol. 9, no. 261.

*Pei-shan lu* 北山錄, by Shen-ch'ing 神清. T vol. 52, no. 2113.

*Pien-cheng lun* 辯正論, by Fa-lin 法琳. T vol. 52, no. 2110.

*Pŏpchip pyŏrhaeng nok chŏryo pyŏngip sagi* 法集別行錄節要並入私記, by Chinul 知訥. Edited by An Chinŏmnyun-sa, 1976.

*Pu-tseng pu-chien ching* 不增不減經, T vol. 16, no. 668.

*San-kuo chih* 三國記. 3 vols. Peking: Chung-hua shu-chü, 1973.

*She ta-sheng lun (Mahāyānasaṃgraha)* 攝大乘論. Translated by Paramārtha. T vol. 31, no. 1595.

*Sheng-man shih-tzu-hou i-sheng ta-fang-pien fang-kuang ching* 勝鬘師子吼一乘大方便方廣經. Translated by Guṇabhadra. T vol. 12, no. 353.

*Shih chi* 史記, by Ssu-ma Ch'ien 司馬遷. *Ssu-pu pei-yao,* revised edition, vols. 201-208.

*Shih-ti ching lun (Daśabhūmikabhāṣya)* 十地經論, by Vasubandhu. Translated by Bodhiruci. T vol. 26, no. 1522.

*Ta chih-tu lun* 大智度論. Translated by Kumārajīva. T vol. 25, no. 1509.

*Ta-fang-kuang fo hua-yen ching* 大方廣佛華嚴經. Translated by Buddhabhadra. T vol. 9, no. 278.

*Ta-fang-kuang fo hua-yen ching* 大方廣佛華嚴經. Translated by Śikṣānanda. T vol. 10, no. 279.

*Ta-fang-kuang fo hua-yen ching shu* 大方廣佛華嚴經疏, by Ch'eng-kuan 澄觀. T vol. 35, no. 1735.

*Ta-fang-kuang fo hua-yen ching sui-shu yen-i ch'ao* 大方廣佛華嚴經隨疏演義鈔, by Ch'eng-kuan 澄觀. T vol. 36, no. 1736.

*Ta-fang-kuang yüan-chüeh hsiu-to-lo liao-i ching* 大方廣圓覺修多羅了義經, T vol. 17, no. 842.

*Ta-fang-kuang yüan-chüeh hsiu-to-lo liao-i ching lüeh-shu* 大方廣圓覺修
多羅了義經略疏, by Tsung-mi 宗密. T vol. 39, no. 1759.

*Ta-sheng ch'i-hsin lun* 大乘起信論. T vol. 32, no. 1666.

*Ta-sheng ch'i-hsin lun i-chi* 大乘起信論義記, by Fa-tsang 法藏. T vol. 44,
no. 1846.

*Ta-sheng ch'i-hsin lun shu* 大乘起信論疏, by Tsung-mi 宗密. *Dainippon
kōtei daizōkyō*, case 31, vol. 8, div. 5, part 2.

*Ta-sheng-i chang* 大乘義障, by Ching-ying Hui-yüan 淨影慧遠, T vol. 44,
no. 1851.

*Yüan jen lun* 原人論, by Tsung-mi 宗密. T vol. 45, no. 1887.

*Yüan-chüeh ching lüeh-shu ch'ao* 圓覺經略疏鈔, by Tsung-mi 宗密. HTC
vol. 15.

*Yüan-chüeh ching ta-shu* 圓覺經大疏, by Tsung-mi 宗密. HTC vol. 14.

*Yüan-chüeh ching ta-shu ch'ao* 圓覺經大疏鈔, by Tsung-mi 宗密. HTC
vols. 14-15.

*Yüan-chüeh ching tao-ch'ang hsiu-cheng i* 圓覺經道場修證儀, by Tsung-
mi 宗密. HTC vol. 128.

*Yü-lan p'en ching shu* 盂蘭盆經, by Tsung-mi 宗密. T vol. 39, no. 1792.

## SECONDARY SOURCES

Anacker, Stefan. *Seven Works of Vasubhandhu: The Buddhist Psychological Doctor.* Delhi: Motilal Banarsidass, 1984.

Atsuta, Ryōchi 熱田霊知. *Genninron* 原人論. Kyoto: Dendōkai, 1896; originally published in 1894.

Barrett, Timothy Hugh. *Li Ao: Buddhist, Taoist, or NeoConfucian?* Oxford:
Oxford University Press, 1992.

Bechert, Heinz and Richard Gombrich, eds. *The World of Buddhism.* New
York: Facts on File, 1984.

Berger, Peter. *The Sacred Canopy.* Garden City: Doubleday, 1969.

Birch, Cyril, ed. *Anthology of Chinese Literature.* New York: Grove Press,
1965.

Broughton, Jeffrey L. "Kuei-feng Tsung-mi: The Convergence of Ch'an and
the Teachings." Ph.D. dissertation, Columbia University, 1975.

Buswell, Robert E., Jr., ed. *Chinese Buddhist Apocrypha.* Honolulu: University of Hawai'i Press, 1990.

———. "Chinul's Systematization of Chinese Meditative Techniques in
Korean Sŏn Buddhism." In *Traditions of Meditation in Chinese Bud-
dhism.* Edited by Peter N. Gregory. Studies in East Asian Buddhism,
No. 4. Honolulu: University of Hawai'i Press, 1987.

———. *The Korean Approach to Zen: The Collected Works of Chinul.* Honolulu: University of Hawai'i Press, 1983.

Buswell, Robert E., Jr., and Robert M. Gimello, eds. *Paths to Liberation: The Mārga and Its Transformations in Buddhist Thought*. Studies in East Asian Buddhism, no. 7. Honolulu: University of Hawai'i Press, 1992.

Cabezón, José. "On Returning to Method and Other Postmodern Turns: A Response to C. W. Huntington, Jr." *Journal of the International Association of Buddhist Studies* 15.1 (1992): 134-143.

————. Review of *The Emptiness of Emptiness. Journal of the International Association of Buddhist Studies* 13.2 (1990): 152-161.

Chan, Wing-tsit. *A Source Book of Chinese Philosophy*. Princeton: Princeton University Press, 1963.

Chappell, David, ed. *T'ien-t'ai Buddhism: An Outline of the Fourfold Teachings*. Tokyo: Daiichi shobō, 1983.

Chen, Jo-shui. *Liu Tsung-yüan and Intellectual Change in T'ang China, 773-819*. Cambridge: Cambridge University Press, 1992.

Ch'en, Kenneth K. S. *Buddhism in China: A Historical Survey*. Princeton: Princeton University Press, 1964.

————. *The Chinese Transformation of Buddhism*. Princeton: Princeton University Press, 1973.

Cleary, Thomas, trans. *The Flower Ornament Scripture*. 3 vols. Boulder: Shambala, 1984-1987.

Collins, Steven. *Selfless Persons: Imagery and Thought in Theravāda Buddhism*. Cambridge: Cambridge University Press, 1982.

Conze, Edward. *Buddhist Meditation*. New York: Harper and Row, 1969.

————. *Buddhist Thought in India*. Ann Arbor: University of Michigan Press, 1967.

————. *The Perfection of Wisdom in Eight Thousand Lines and Its Verse Summary*. Bolinas: Four Seasons Foundation, 1973.

————. *Selected Sayings from the Perfection of Wisdom*. Boulder: Prajñā Press, 1978.

Cook, Francis H. "Fa-tsang's Treatise on the Five Doctrines: An Annotated Translation." Ph.D. dissertation, University of Wisconsin, 1970.

————. *Hua-yen Buddhism: The Jewel Net of Indra*. University Park: Pennsylvania State University Press, 1977.

Cowell, E. B., trans. *The Buddha-karita of Asvaghosha*. In *Buddhist Mahāyāna Texts*. New York: Dover Publications, Inc., 1969.

Creel, Herrlee G. *The Origins of Statecraft in China*, vol. 1. *The Western Chou Empire*. Chicago: University of Chicago Press, 1970.

Daye, Douglas. "Major Schools of the Mahāyāna: Mādhyamika." In *Buddhism: A Modern Perspective*. Edited by Charles S. Prebish. University Park: Pennsylvania State University Press, 1975.

De Groot, J. J. M. *The Religious System of China.* 6 vols. Taipei: Ch'eng Wen Publishing Co., 1976.

Dubs, Homer H. "Han Yü and the Buddha Relic: An Episode in Medieval Chinese Religion." *The Review of Religion* 11:1 (1946): 5-17.

Dumoulin, Heinrich, "*Genninron:* Tsung-mi's Traktat vom Ursprung des Menschen." *Monumenta Nipponica* 1.1 (1938): 178-221.

Edgerton, Franklin. *Buddhist Hybrid Sanskrit Grammar and Dictionary.* 2 vols. New Haven: Yale University Press, 1953.

Forke, Alfred. *Lun-Heng: Philosophical Essays of Wang Ch'ung.* 2 vols. Second edition. New York: Paragon Book Gallery, 1962.

Fujita, Kōtastu. "One Vehicle or Three?" Translated by Leon Hurvitz. *Journal of Indian Philosophy* 3 (1975): 79-166.

Gimello, Robert M. "Chih-yen (602-668) and the Foundations of Hua-yen Buddhism." Ph.D. dissertation, Columbia University, 1976.

———. "Mysticism and Meditation." In *Mysticism and Philosophical Analysis.* Edited by Steven T. Katz. New York: Oxford University Press, 1978.

Gimello, Robert M. and Peter N. Gregory, eds. *Studies in Ch'an and Hua-yen.* Studies in East Asian Buddhism, No. 1. Honolulu: University of Hawai'i Press, 1983.

Girardot, Norman J. *Myth and Meaning in Early Taoism.* Berkeley: University of California Press, 1983

———. "The Problem of Creation Mythology in the Study of Chinese Religion." *History of Religion* 15 (1976): 289-318.

Graham, Angus C. "The Background of the Mencian Theory of Human Nature." *Tsing Hua Journal of Chinese Studies,* n.s., 6 (1967): 215-271. Reprinted in *Studies in Chinese Philosophy and Philosophical Literature.* State University of New York Press, 1990.

———, trans. *The Book of Lieh Tzu.* London: John Murray, 1960.

———, trans. *Chuang-tzu: The Inner Chapters.* London: George Allen & Unwin, 1981.

———. *Disputers of the Tao: Philosophical Argumentation in Ancient China.* LaSalle, IL: Open Court, 1989.

———. *Two Chinese Philosophers: Ch'eng Ming-tao and Ch'eng Yi-ch'uan.* London: Lund Humphries, 1958.

Gregory, Peter N. "The Problem of Theodicy in the *Awakening of Faith.*" *Religious Studies* 22.1 (1986): 63-78.

———. "Sudden Enlightenment Followed by Gradual Cultivation: Tsung-mi's Analysis of Mind." In *Sudden and Gradual: Approaches to Enlightenment in Chinese Thought.* Edited by Peter N. Gregory. Studies in East Asian Buddhism, No. 5. Honolulu: University of Hawai'i Press, 1983.

————, ed. *Sudden and Gradual: Approaches to Enlightenment in Chinese Thought.* Studies in East Asian Buddhism, no. 5. Honolulu: University of Hawai'i Press, 1983.

————. "The Teaching of Men and Gods: The Doctrinal and Social Basis of Lay Buddhist Practice in the Hua-yen Tradition." In *Studies in Ch'an and Hua-yen.* Edited by Robert M. Gimello and Peter N. Gregory. Studies in East Asian Buddhism, no. 1. Honolulu: University of Hawai'i Press, 1983.

————, ed. *Traditions of Meditation in Chinese Buddhism.* Studies in East Asian Buddhism, no. 4. Honolulu: University of Hawai'i Press, 1986.

————. "Tsung-mi and the Single Word 'Awareness' (*chih*)." *Philosophy East and West* 35.3 (1985): 249-269.

————. *Tsung-mi and the Sinification of Buddhism.* Princeton: Princeton University Press, 1991.

Griffiths, Paul J. "Concentration or Insight: The Problematic of Theravāda Buddhist Meditation-Theory." *Journal of the American Academy of Religion* 49 (1981): 606-624.

————. *On Being Mindless: Buddhist Meditation and the Mind Body Problem.* LaSalle, IL: Open Court, 1986.

Haas, Hans. "Tsung-mi's *Yuen-zan-lun,* eine Abhandlung über den Ursprung des Menschen aus dem Kanon des chinesischen Buddhismus." *Archiv für Religionswissenscaft* 12 (1909): 491-532.

Hakeda, Yoshito S. *The Awakening of Faith Attributed to Aśvaghosha.* New York: Columbia University Press, 1967.

————, trans. "On the Original Nature of Man." In *The Buddhist Tradition in India, China and Japan.* Edited by William T. deBary. New York: Random House, 1969.

Hare, E. M. and F. L. Woodward, trans. *The Book of Gradual Sayings (Anguttara-Nikāya) or More-Numbered Suttas.* 5 vols. London: Luzac & Co., 1960-65.

Hartman, Charles. *Han Yü and the T'ang Search for Unity.* Princeton: Princeton University Press, 1986.

Harvey, Peter. *An Introduction to Buddhism: Teachings, History and Practices.* Cambridge: Cambridge University Press, 1990.

Hattori, Masaaki. "Realism and the Philosophy of Consciousness-Only." Translated by William Powell. *The Eastern Buddhist* 21.1 (1988): 23-60.

Herman, Arthur. *The Problem of Evil and Indian Thought.* Delhi, Varanasi, Patna: Motilal Banarsidass, 1976.

Hirabashi, Jay and Shotaro Iida. "Another Look at the Mādhyamika vs. Yogācāra Controversy Concerning Existence and Non-existence." In *Prajñāpāramitā and Related Systems: Studies in honor of Edward*

*Conze.* Edited by Lewis Lancaster. Berkeley: Berkeley Buddhist Studies Series, 1977.

Hirakawa, Akira 平川彰. *Daijō kishin ron* 大乗起信論. Butten kōza 22. Tokyo: Daizō shuppan, 1973.

Horner, Isaline B., trans. *The Book of the Discipline (Vinaya-Piṭaka).* 6 vols. Sacred Books of the Buddhists, vols. 10, 11, 13, 14, 20, 25. London: Luzac & Co., 1949-66.

————, trans. *The Collection of The Middle Length Sayings (Majjhima-Nikāya).* 3 vols. London: Luzac & Co., 1975-77.

Huntington, C. W., Jr. *The Emptiness of Emptiness.* Honolulu: University of Hawai'i Press, 1989.

————. "The Theatre of Objectivity: Comments on José Cabezón's Interpretations of mKhas grub rje's and C. W. Huntington, Jr.'s Interpretations of the Tibetan Translation of a Seventh Century Indian Buddhist Text." *Journal of the International Association of Buddhist Studies* 15.1 (1992): 118-133.

Hurvitz, Leon, trans. *Scripture of the Lotus Blossom of the Fine Dharma (The Lotus Sūtra), Translated from the Chinese of Kumārajīva.* New York: Columbia University Press, 1976.

Inada, Kenneth K. *Nāgārjuna: A Translation of his Mūlamadhyamakakārikā with an Introductory Essay.* Tokyo: Hokuseido Press, 1970.

Jan, Yün-hua. "Conflict and Harmony in Ch'an and Buddhism." *Journal of Chinese Philosophy* 4.3 (1977): 360-381.

————. "Tsung-mi: His Analysis of Ch'an Buddhism." *T'oung Pao* 58 (1972): 1-54.

————. "Tsung-mi's Questions Regarding the Confucian Absolute." *Philosophy East and West* 30.4 (1980): 495-504.

Jay, Jennifer W. "The Li Hsün Faction and the Sweet Dew Incident of 835." *T'ang Studies* 7 (1989).

Johansson, Rune E. A. *The Dynamic Psychology of Early Buddhism.* London: Curzon Press, 1979.

Johnston, E. H. *The Buddhacarita, or Acts of the Buddha.* Calcutta: Baptist Mission Press, 1936; repr. New Delhi: Oriental Books Reprint Corporation, 1972.

Jones, J. J., trans. *The Mahāvastu.* 3 vols. London: The Pali Text Society, 1952-1973.

Kamata, Shigeo 鎌田茂雄. *Chūgoku kegon shisōshi no kenkyū* 中国華厳思想史の研究. Tokyo: Tōkyō daigaku shuppankai, 1965.

————, trans. *Genninron* 原人論. Tokyo: Meitoku shuppansha, 1973.

————. *Shūmitsu kyōgaku no shisōshi-teki kenkyū* 宗密教学の思想史的研究. Tokyo: Tōkyō daigaku shuppansha, 1975.

————, trans. *Zengen shosenshū tojo* 禅源諸詮集都序. Zen no goroku, vol. 9. Tokyo: Chikuma shobō, 1971.

Karlgren, Bernhard. *Analytic Dictionary of Chinese and Sino-Japanese.* Paris: Librairie Orientaliste Paul Geuthner, 1923.

Katō Kumaichirō 加藤熊一郎. *Genninron kōwa* 原人論講話. Tokyo: Heigo shuppansha, 1908.

Kimura Yoshiyuki 木村善之. *Genninron shinkō* 原人論新講. Tokyo: Kōshisha shobō, 1931.

King, Winston L. *Theravāda Meditation: The Buddhist Transformation of Yoga.* University Park: Pennsylvania State University Press, 1980.

King, Sallie B. *Buddha Nature.* Albany: State University of New York Press, 1991.

Kishigami Kairyō 岸上恢料嶺. *Kachū genninron kōgi* 科註原人論講義. Osaka: Sekizenkwan Co., 1901; originally published in 1891.

Lai, Whalen. "The Earliest Folk Buddhist Religion in China: *T'i-wei Po-li Ching* and Its Historical Significance." In *Buddhist and Taoist Practice in Medieval Chinese Society.* Edited by David W. Chappell. Honolulu: University of Hawai'i Press, 1987.

Lamotte, Étienne, *History of Indian Buddhism: From the Origins to the Saka Era.* Translated by Sara Webb-Boin. Louvain: Institut Orientaliste de l'Université de Louvain, 1988.

————, trans. *Saṃdhinirmocana-sūtra: L'Explication des mystères.* Louvain: Université de Louvain, 1935.

————. *La Somme du Grand Véhicule d'Asaṅga (Mahāyānasaṃgraha),* vol. 2, *Traduction et Commentaire.* Louvain: Institut Orientaliste de l'Université de Louvain, 1973.

————. *The Teaching of Vimalakīrti (Vimalakīrtinirdeśa).* Translated by Sara Boin. London: Pali Text Society, 1976.

————. *La Traité de la Grande Vertu de Sagesse de Nāgārjuna (Mahāprajñāpāramitāśāstra).* 5 vols. Louvain: Institut Orientaliste de l'Université de Louvain, 1944, 1949, 1966, 1967, and 1980.

Lau, D. C., trans. *Confucius: The Analects.* Harmondsworth: Penguin Books, 1979.

————, trans. *Lao Tzu, Tao Te Ching.* Harmondsworth: Penguin Books, 1963.

————, trans. *Mencius.* Harmondsworth: Penguin Books, 1970.

La Vallée Poussin, Louis de, trans. *L'Abhidharmakośa de Vasubandhu.* 6 vols. Edited by Étienne Lamotte. *Mélanges chinois et bouddhiques,* vol. 16. Brussels: Institut Belge des Hautes Études Chinoises, 1971.

————. "Cosmogony and Cosmology (Buddhist)." In *Encyclopedia of Religion and Ethics,* vol. 4. 13 vols. Edited by James Hastings. Edinburgh: T. and T. Clark, 1912.

————, trans. *Vijñaptimātrāsiddhi: La Siddhi de Hiuan-tsang.* 2 vols. Paris: Librairie Orientaliste Paul Geuthner, 1928-1929.

Legge, James, trans. *The Chinese Classics.* 5 vols. Oxford: Clarendon Press, 1893.

————. *Li Chi: The Book of Rites.* 2 vols. Edited by Ch'u and Winberg Chai. Reprint ed., New York: University Books, 1967.

————, trans. *The Sacred Books of China: The Texts of Confucianism,* vol. 1. *The Sacred Books of the East,* vol. 5. New York: Charles Scribner's Sons, 1899.

Li, Yung-hsi. *The Life of Hsüan-tsang.* Peking: Chinese Buddhist Association, 1959.

Liebenthal, Walter. "The Immortality of the Soul in Chinese Thought." *Monumenta Nipponica* 8 (1952): 169-196.

Link, Arthur and Tim Lee. "Sun Ch'o's *Yü-tao-lun: A Clarification of the Way.*" *Monumenta Serica* 25 (1966): 169-196.

Lindtner, Chr. *Nagarjuniana: Studies in the Writings and Philosophy of Nāgārjuna.* Delhi: Motilal Banarsidass, 1982.

Liu, Ming-wood. "The *P'an-chiao* System of the Hua-yen School in Chinese Buddhism." *T'oung Pao* 67.1-2 (1981): 10-47.

————. "The Teaching of Fa-tsang: An Examination of Buddhist Metaphysics." Ph.D. dissertation, University of California, Los Angeles, 1979.

Long, Charles. "Cosmogony." In *The Encyclopedia of Religion.* Edited by Mircea Eliade. New York: MacMillan Publishing Co., 1987.

Lopez, Donald S., Jr., ed. *Buddhist Hermeneutics.* Studies in East Asian Buddhism, no. 6. Honolulu: University of Hawai'i Press, 1988.

Makita, Tairyō 牧田諦亮. "Tonkōbon *Daiikyō* no kenkyū 敦煌本題謂経の研究." *Bukkyō daigaku daigakuin kenkyū kiyō* (1968): 137-185 and (1971): 165-197.

Malalasekera, G. P., ed. *Encyclopaedia of Buddhism.* Colombo: Government of Ceylon, 1961.

Masson-Oursel, Paul. "Le *Yuan Jen Louen.*" *Journal Asiatique* (Mars-Avril, 1915): 219-253.

McDermott, James P. "Karma and Rebirth in Early Buddhism." In *Karma and Rebirth in Classical Indian Traditions.* Edited by Wendy Doniger O'Flaherty. Berkeley: University of California Press, 1980.

McMullen, David. *State and Scholars in T'ang China.* Cambridge: Cambridge University Press, 1988.

McRae, John R. "Shen-hui and the Teaching of Sudden Enlightenment in Early Ch'an Buddhism." In *Sudden and Gradual: Approaches to Enlightenment in Chinese Thought.* Edited by Peter N. Gregory. Studies in East Asian Buddhism, no. 5. Honolulu: University of Hawai'i Press, 1987.

Miura, Isshū, and Ruth Fuller Sasaki. *Zen Dust: The History of the Koan and Koan Study in Rinzai (Lin-chi) Zen*. New York: Harcourt, Brace & World, 1966.

Mochizuki, Shinkō 望月信亭. *Bukkyō daijiten* 仏教大辞典. 10 vols. Tokyo: Sekai seiten kankō kyōkai, 1958-1963.

Monier-Williams, Monier. *A Sanskrit-English Dictionary*. Oxford: Clarendon Press, 1899.

Morohashi, Tetsuji 諸橋轍次. *Dai kanwa jiten* 大漢和辞典. 13 vols. Tokyo: Taishūkan shoten, 1957-60.

Murti, T. R. V. *The Central Philosophy of Buddhism*. London: George Allen and Unwin, 1960.

Nagao, Gadjin M. *Mādhyamika and Yogācāra: A Study of Mahāyāna Philosophies*. Edited and translated by Leslie S. Kawamura. Albany: State University of New York Press, 1991.

Nakamura, Hajime 中村元. *Bukkyōgo daijiten* 仏教語大辞典. 3 vols. Tokyo: Tōkyō shoseki, 1975.

Ñāṇamoli, Bhikkhu, trans. *The Path of Purification (Visuddhimagga)*. Kandy: Buddhist Publication Society, 1979.

Nattier, Jan. *Once Upon a Future Time: Studies in a Buddhist Prophecy of Decline*. Berkeley: Asian Humanities Press, 1991.

Nukariya, Kaiten. *The Religion of the Samurai: A Study of Zen Philosophy and Disciple in China and Japan*. London: Luzac and Co., Ltd., 1973; originally published in 1913.

Obeyesekere, Gananath. "Theodicy, Sin and Salvation in a Sociology of Buddhism." In *Dialectic in Practical Religion*. Edited by Edmund Leach. Cambridge: Cambridge University Press, 1968.

Oh, Kang Nam. "A Study of Chinese Hua-yen Buddhism with Special Reference to the Dharmadhātu (*fa-chieh*) Doctrine." Ph.D. dissertation, McMaster University, 1976.

———. "*Dharmadhātu*: An Introduction to Hua-yen Buddhism." *The Eastern Buddhist* 12:2 (1979): 72-91.

Ōtomo Tōtsu 大友洞達. *Genninron shōkai* 原人論詳解. Tokyo: Nihon zensho kankōkai, 1921.

Ōuchi Seiran 大内青巒. *Genninron kōgi* 原人論講義. Tokyo: Kōyūkan, 1904.

Paul, Diana Mary. *The Buddhist Feminine Ideal: Queen Śrīmālā and the Tathāgatagarbha*. Missoula, Montana: Scholars Press, 1980.

Pruden, Leo, trans. *Abhidharmakośabhāsyam by Louis de La Vallée Poussin*. 5 vols. Berkeley: Asian Humanities Press, 1988.

Pulleyblank, Edwin G. "Neo-Confucianism and Neo-Legalism in T'ang Intellectual Life, 755-805." In *The Confucian Persuasion*. Edited by Arthur F. Wright. Stanford: Stanford University Press, 1969.

Pye, Michael. *Skilful Means: A Concept in Mahayana Buddhism*. London: Duckworth, 1978.

Ramanan, K. Venkata. *Nāgārjuna's Philosophy: As Presented in The Mahā-Prajñāpāramitā Śāstra*. Delhi: Motilal Banarsidass, 1979.

Reynolds, Frank E. "Multiple Cosmogonies: The Case of Theravāda Buddhism." In *Cosmogony and the Ethical Order: New Studies in Comparative Ethics*. Edited by Robin W. Lovin and Frank E. Reynolds. Chicago: University of Chicago Press, 1985.

Rhys Davids, Caroline A. F., and F. L. Woodward, trans. *The Book of Kindred Sayings (Sanyutta-Nikāya) or Grouped Suttas*. 5 vols. London: Luzac & Co., 1950-65.

Rhys Davids, T. W., trans. *Dialogues of the Buddha (Dīgha-Nikāya)*. 3 vols. Sacred Books of the Buddhists, vols. 2-4. London: The Pali Text Society, 1977.

Rhys Davids, T. W., and William Stede, *Pāli-English Dictionary*. London: Pali Text Society, 1977.

Robinson, Richard H. *Early Mādhyamika in India and China*. Delhi: Motilal Banarsidass, 1976.

Roth, H., Review of *Myth and Meaning in Early Taoism*. *Journal of the Royal Asiatic Society* 2 (1985).

Ruegg, David Seyfort. *La Théorie du Tathāgatagarbha et du Gotra: Étude sur la sotériologie et la gnoséologie du Bouddhisme*. Paris: École Française d'Extrême-Orient, 1969.

Schafer, Edward H. *Pacing the Void: T'ang Approaches to the Stars*. Berkeley: University of California Press, 1977.

Schmithausen, Lambert. *Ālayavijñāna: On the Origin and the Early Development of a Central Concept of Yogācāra Philosophy*, 2 vols. Studia Philologica Buddhica Monograph Series IV. Tokyo: International Institute for Buddhist Studies, 1977.

———. "On Some Aspects of Descriptions or Theories of 'Liberating Insight' and 'Enlightenment' in Early Buddhism." *Alt- und Neu-Indische Studien* 12 (1981): 199-250.

Schwartz, Benjamin I. *The World of Thought in Ancient China*. Cambridge: Belknap Press of Harvard University Press, 1985.

Sponberg, Alan. "Meditation in the Fa-hsiang Buddhism." In *Traditions of Meditation in Chinese Buddhism*. Edited by Peter N. Gregory. Studies in East Asian Buddhism, no. 4. Honolulu: University of Hawai'i Press, 1986.

———. "The *Trisvabhava* Doctrine in India and China: A Study of Three Exegetical Models." *Bukkyō bunka kenkyū kiyō* 21 (1982): 97-119.

Streng, Frederick J. *Emptiness: A Study in Religious Meaning*. Nashville: Abingdon Press, 1967.

Sung, Z. D. *The Text of the Yi King*. Repr. Taipei: Ch'eng Wen Publishing Co., 1971.

Suzuki, D. T., trans. *The Laṅkāvatāra Sūtra*. London: Routledge Kegan & Paul, Ltd., 1973.

Takakusu, Junjirō. *The Essentials of Buddhist Philosophy*. Honolulu: University of Hawai'i Press, 1949.

Takasaki, Jistudō 高崎直道. *Nyoraizō shisō no keisei* 如来蔵思想の形成. Tokyo: Shunjūsha, 1974.

————. *A Study on the Ratnagotravibhāga (Utttaratantra): Being a Treatise on the Tathāgatagarbha Theory of Mahāyāna Buddhism*. Serie Orientale Roma 33 (1966).

Tambiah, Stanley J. *World Conqueror and World Renouncer*. Cambridge: Cambridge University Press, 1976.

Thurman, Robert. "Buddhist Hermeneutics." *Journal of the American Academy of Religion* 46 (1978): 19-39.

Tokuno, Kyoko. "Byways in Chinese Buddhism: The *Book of Trapuṣa* and Indigenous Scriptures." Ph.D. dissertation: University of California, Berkeley, 1994.

————. "The Evaluation of Indigenous Scriptures in Chinese Buddhist Bibliographical Catalogues." In *Chinese Buddhist Apocrypha*. Edited by Robert E. Buswell, Jr. Honolulu: University of Hawai'i Press, 1990.

Tsukamoto, Zenryū 塚本善隆. *Shina bukkyōshi kenkyū, Hokugi hen* 支那仏教史研究、北魏篇. Tokyo, 1942. Reprinted in *Tsukamoto Zenryū chosakushū* 塚本善隆著作集, vol. 2. Tokyo: Daitō shuppansha, 1974.

Vajirañāṇa, Paravahera. *Buddhist Meditation in Theory and Practice: A General Exposition According to the Pāli Canon of The Theravāda School*. Kuala Lumpur: Buddhist Missionary Society, 1975.

Wada Ryūzō 和田龍造. *Genninron kōroku* 原人論講録. Kyoto: Ōtani daigaku, 1934.

Waley, Arthur. *The Life and Times of Po Chü-i, 772-846 A.D.* London: George Allen and Unwin, 1955.

Warder, A. K. *Indian Buddhism*. Second revised edition. Delhi: Motilal Banarsidass, 1980.

Watson, Burton, trans. *Chuang-tzu: Basic Writings*. New York: Columbia University Press, 1964.

————, trans. *The Complete Works of Chuang Tzu*. New York: Columbia University Press, 1968.

————, trans. *Records of the Grand Historian of China Translated from the Shih Chi of Ssu-ma Ch'ien*. 2 vols. New York: Columbia University Press, 1961.

————, trans. *Records of the Historian: Chapters from the Shih Chi of Ssu-ma Ch'ien*. New York: Columbia University Press, 1969.

Watters, Thomas. *On Yuan Chwang's Travels in India*. New Delhi: Munshiram Manohariai Publishers, 1973.

Wayman, Alex and Hideko, trans. *The Lion's Roar of Queen Śrīmālā: A Buddhist Scripture on the Tathāgatagarbha Theory*. New York: Columbia University Press, 1974.

Weber, Max. "Theodicy, Salvation, and Rebirth." In *The Sociology of Religion*. Boston: Beacon Press, 1964.

Wei Tat, trans. *Ch'eng Wei-Shih Lun: Doctrine of Mere-Consciousness*. Hong Kong: The Ch'eng Wei-Shih Lun Publication Committee, 1973.

Weinstein, Stanley, *Buddhism under the T'ang*. Cambridge: Cambridge University Press, 1987.

———. "The Concept of the Ālaya-vijñāna in Pre-T'ang Chinese Buddhism." In *Bukkyō shisō ronshū*. Tokyo: Daizō shuppan, 1964.

———. "Imperial Patronage in the Formation of T'ang Buddhism." In *Perspectives on the T'ang*. Edited by Arthur Wright and Denis Twitchett. New Haven: Yale University Press, 1973.

Williams, Paul. *Mahāyāna Buddhism: The Doctrinal Foundations*. London: Routledge, 1989.

Yampolsky, Philip B. *The Platform Sutra of the Sixth Patriarch*. New York: Columbia University Press, 1967.

Yusugi Ryōei 湯次了栄. *Kanwa taishō genninron shinshaku* 漢和対照原人論新釈. Kyoto: Bukkyō daigaku shuppan, 1935.

Zürcher, Erik. *The Buddhist Conquest of China: The Spread and Adoptation of Buddhism in Early Medieval China*. 2 vols. Leiden: E. J. Brill, 1959.

# Index

# About the Author

Peter N. Gregory received his Ph.D. from Harvard University in 1981 and has been on the faculty of the University of Illinois since 1984, where he is currently a professor in the Program for the Study of Religion and the Department of East Asian Languages and Cultures. He also serves as executive director and vice-president of the Kuroda Institute for the Study of Buddhism and Human Values. He has published widely in the field of medieval Chinese Buddhism, especially Hua-yen and Ch'an. In addition to his *Tsung-mi and the Sinification of Buddhism,* he has also edited four volumes, including most recently *Religion and Society in T'ang and Sung China,* co-edited with Patricia B. Ebrey.

# KURODA INSTITUTE
## Classics in East Asian Buddhism

The Record of Tung-shan
Translated by William F. Powell

Tracing Back the Radiance:
Chinul's *Way of Zen*
Translated with an Introduction by Robert E. Buswell, Jr.

The Great Calming and Contemplation
A Study and Annotated Translated of the First Chapter of
Chihi's *Mo-Ho Chih-Kuan*
Translated by Neal Donner and Daniel B. Stevenson

The Origin of Humanity
An Annotated Translation of Tsung-mi's
*Yüan jen lun*
with a Modern Commentary
Peter N. Gregory

# KURODA INSTITUTE
## Studies in East Asian Buddhism